Advance Praise for *The What, the So What, and the Now What of Social Justice Education*

"Dr. Blumenfeld's new book is borne of his passion for social justice and multicultural understanding of today's society. Blumenfeld brings the topic into the realm of the familiar by sharing his own personal journey. It almost feels as if the reader is sitting with Dr. Blumenfeld, a friend, and yet this is a powerful educational text. Blumenfeld uses a unique presentation method and grounding of information through the concept of What, So What, and Now What in each section as he investigates and addresses complex and multidimensional questions. This process offers a consistency in Dr. Blumenfeld's presentation. The book is an excellent teaching tool for every level of social justice education from high school to doctoral work."

Ronni Sanlo, Director of and Professor in UCLA Master of Education in Student Affairs Program and Director Emerita, UCLA Lesbian, Gay, Bisexual, and Transgender Center

The What, the So What, and the Now What of Social Justice Education

Virginia Stead, H.B.A., B.Ed., M.Ed., Ed.D.
GENERAL EDITOR

VOL. 12

The Equity in Higher Education Theory, Policy, & Praxis series
is part of the Peter Lang Education list.
Every volume is peer reviewed and meets
the highest quality standards for content and production.

PETER LANG
New York • Bern • Berlin
Brussels • Vienna • Oxford • Warsaw

Warren J. Blumenfeld

The What, the So What, and the Now What of Social Justice Education

PETER LANG
New York • Bern • Berlin
Brussels • Vienna • Oxford • Warsaw

Library of Congress Cataloging-in-Publication Data
Names: Blumenfeld, Warren J., author.
Title: The what, the so what, and the now what
of social justice education / Warren J. Blumenfeld.
Description: New York: Peter Lang, 2019.
Series: Equity in higher education theory, policy, & praxis; vol. 12
ISSN 2330-4502 (print) | ISSN 2330-4510 (online)
Includes bibliographical references and index.
Identifiers: LCCN 2018044638 | ISBN 978-1-4331-6099-8 (hardback: alk. paper)
ISBN 978-1-4331-6098-1 (paperback: alk. paper) | ISBN 978-1-4331-6062-2 (ebook pdf)
ISBN 978-1-4331-6063-9 (epub) | ISBN 978-1-4331-6064-6 (mobi)
Subjects: LCSH: Social justice—Study and teaching.
Classification: LCC LC192.2.B58 2018 | DDC 370.11/5—dc23
LC record available at https://lccn.loc.gov/2018044638
DOI 10.3726/b14632

Bibliographic information published by **Die Deutsche Nationalbibliothek**.
Die Deutsche Nationalbibliothek lists this publication in the "Deutsche
Nationalbibliografie"; detailed bibliographic data are available
on the Internet at http://dnb.d-nb.de/.

The paper in this book meets the guidelines for permanence and durability
of the Committee on Production Guidelines for Book Longevity
of the Council of Library Resources.

© 2019 Peter Lang Publishing, Inc., New York
29 Broadway, 18th floor, New York, NY 10006
www.peterlang.com

All rights reserved.
Reprint or reproduction, even partially, in all forms such as microfilm,
xerography, microfiche, microcard, and offset strictly prohibited.

Printed in the United States of America

This book is dedicated to my good friends Debra Fowler and Miriam Morgenstern and their History UnErased project, for their commitment to social justice education when they opened the K–12 classroom doors to LGBTQ history.

This book is also dedicated to my good friend Katarzyna (Kasia) Krepulec-Nowak of Muzeum Podkarpackie w Krosnie for her compassionate dedication to keeping alive the memories of my dear family and the entire Jewish community who were taken from this world too soon in Krosno, Poland.

TABLE OF CONTENTS

	Figures and Tables	xi
	Acknowledgments	xiii
Part I.	**Terminology**	1
Chapter 1.	Introduction to Social Justice	3
	A Personal Journey	4
	Social Justice	8
	Book Format	9
Chapter 2.	Culture and Identity	11
	Equitable v. Equal	12
	Culture	14
	Identity	15
	Intersectionality	16
	Border Identities	19
Chapter 3.	Social Construction of Identities and Other Forms of "Difference"	21
	Left-Handedness: A Case Study of the *What*, the *So What*, and the *Now What*	21
	"Racialized" Social Constructions	24
	Jews and Jewishness	31

	Disabilities	34
	Sexual Identities	35
Chapter 4.	Socialization	39
	Urie Bronfenbrenner's Bioecological Model of Human Development	41
	The Family as Early Socializing Institution	42
	Bobbie Harro's "Cycle of Socialization"	44
	Indoctrination and Surveillance	46
Chapter 5.	Binaries	49
	Binaries Defined	49
	Binaries: Polytheism and Monotheism	51
	Stigma	53
	Terrorism and Violence	54
	Bullying and Cyberbullying	55
	The Psychology and Sociology of Cyberspace	56
	Scapegoating	61
Chapter 6.	Oppression	63
	Oppression Defined	63
	Hegemony	64
	Colonization	64
	Prejudice and Discrimination and a Case Study	65
	Levels of Oppression	69
	Dominant Group Privilege and the Myth of Meritocracy	76
Chapter 7.	What Causes Prejudice and Discrimination?	81
	Social Learning Theory	82
	Social Modeling Theory: Albert Bandura	82
	Social Rank Theory	85
	Psychodynamic Theories	85
Chapter 8.	Elements, Characteristics, and "Faces" of Oppression	89
	Lee Anne Bell's "Defining Features of Oppression"	89
	Suzanne Pharr's "Elements of Oppression"	90
	Internalized Oppression and Domination	96
	Iris Marion Young's "Five Faces of Oppression"	101
	A Case Study of Cultural Imperialism	103
Chapter 9.	The Many Spokes on the Wheel of Oppression	107
	Ableism	108
	Adultism	111

	Ageism	113
	Cissexism/Transgender Oppression	114
	Class and Classism	115
	Environmental Oppression/"Ecoism"	118
	Ethnocentrism	120
	Heterosexism	124
	Jingoism, Chauvinism, Nativism, Patriotism, and Nationalism	126
	Linguicism	127
	Lookism	129
	Racism and White Supremacy	130
	Religious Oppression	134
	Sexism, Misogyny, Patriarchy	139
	Oppression Affects Everyone	144
Chapter 10.	Backlash	147
	Backlash: A Case in Point	147
	Sherry Watt's "Privilege Identity Exploration Model"	149
Chapter 11.	The Social Production of "Knowledge(s)"	153
Part II.	**Social Justice Education**	**159**
Chapter 12.	Connections between Social Justice Education and Multicultural Education	161
	Robert Kegan	163
	Emily Style	163
Chapter 13.	Dimensions and Characteristics of Multicultural Education	167
	Types of Multicultural Education	169
	James A. Banks' "Approaches to Multicultural Curriculum Reform"	173
	G. D. Borich and M. L. Tombari's "Educator Leadership and Power" Taxonomy	174
Part III.	**Liberatory Praxis**	**179**
Chapter 14.	Liberation	181
Chapter 15.	#NeverAgain Youth-Led Firearms Safety Movement: A Study in Activism	185
	Civil Disobedience	187
	Tinker v. Des Moines Independent Community School District	189

Chapter 16.	Visioning Social Justice and Liberation	191
	Ally (Upstander) and a Conceptual Model	193
	Nancy J. Evans and Jamie Washington's	
	"Steps Toward Becoming an Ally"	193
	Empathy and "Empathic Listening"	194
	Bobbie Harro's "Cycle of Liberation"	197
	Barbara Love's "Liberatory Consciousness"	201
	Suzanne Pharr's "Liberation Politics"	203
	Pat Griffin and Bobbie Harro's "Action Continuum"	204
	Some Additional Social Justice Action Strategies	205
	Rheua Stakely's "Action Strategy Planning Sheet"	207
	"Dialogues on Diversity" and a Conceptual Model	209
	Bullying, Cyberbullying, and Social Norms Theory	211
	Empowering the Bystander to Act as an Upstander	213
	Not on Our Campus! "Principles of Community"	214

Liberatory Praxis Appendices — 217

Appendix A.	Multiple Identities Essay	219
Appendix B.	Critical Consciousness: Reflecting, Thinking, Observing, Reading, Researching, and Writing Through a Critical Lens	223
Appendix C.	Meritocracy Activities	227
Appendix D.	Raising Issues of Religious Pluralism in Schools	231
Appendix E.	Making Universities Welcoming for Students, Staff, Faculty, and Administrators of All Sexual Identities and Gender Identities and Expressions	235
Appendix F.	Immigration as Official U.S. "Racial" Policy: A Brief History	243
Appendix G.	Religious Imperialism: A Case in Point	257
Appendix H.	Investigating Gender Roles Classroom Exercise	261
Appendix I.	A Civics Course on the Second Amendment	263
	Bibliography	267
	Index	285

FIGURES AND TABLES

Figures

Figure 1.1.	Wolf, Simon, and Bascha Mahler.	5
Figure 4.1.	Cycle of Socialization.	43
Figure 5.1.	The Androgynous Form of Shiva and Parvati (Ardhanarishvara).	52
Figure 16.1.	Cycle of Liberation.	198

Tables

Table 3.1.	Lenses of Perception in Understanding the Social Construction of Disability and Issues of Ableism.	35
Table 16.1.	Action Strategy Planning Sheet.	208

ACKNOWLEDGMENTS

I wish to thank the administrators, faculty, students, and staff—past and present—of the Social Justice Education Program at the University of Massachusetts, Amherst for their pioneering and continuing efforts in helping to craft the field of Social Justice Education and for taking actions daily to ensure a more peaceful, just, and equitable world community.

I wish also to thank my brilliant series editor, Dr. Virginia Stead, for her remarkable talents and for her perennial support and encouragement.

PART I

TERMINOLOGY

· 1 ·

INTRODUCTION TO SOCIAL JUSTICE

> [W]hen you think about how a *Challeh* is made, you've the three braids, the three ropes, and that you fold them over in a certain way that at one point in the loaf, one of the [ropes] is most prominent, is higher; and at the next piece of the *Challeh*, … that rope is hidden; it's under the other rope that came out over it. And then there's a third rope that interplays with the first two, … but it's not the same rope that began because it's mixed with the dough of the others. … In terms of what has happened … to each of these ropes … and where they each came from, and how they've interwoven …, once you have a *Challeh* [and] you bake it, you can't take it apart.
>
> —in Blumenfeld, 2001

This statement offered by a participant in my doctoral dissertation who used the metaphor of the *Challeh*—a traditional Jewish braided bread—captures the connections and intertwining of the three strands of the braid motivating a holistic approach that recognizes the interconnections of my life's work. One braid represents my quest for lifelong learning as a student; another embodies my engagement as a community social justice activist and organizer; and another symbolizes my passion and service as an educator. These three strands intertwine to accomplish a synergized agenda that outreaches the sum of the individual parts.

A Personal Journey

One day, when I was very young, I sat upon my maternal grandfather Simon (Shimon) Mahler's knee. Looking down urgently, but with deep affection, he said to me, "Varn" (he always called me "Varn" through his distinctive Polish accent), "you are named after my father, Wolf Mahler. I lived in Krosno, Poland with my father, Wolf, and my mother, Bascha, and 13 brothers and sisters, and aunts, uncles, and cousins."

Simon talked about our family with pride, but as he told me this, he seemed rather sad. I asked him if our relatives still lived in Poland, and he responded that his mother had died of a heart attack in 1934, and his father and most of the remainder of his family were no longer alive. When I asked him how they had died, he told me that they had all been killed by people called "Nazis." I questioned him why the Nazis killed our family, and he responded, "Because they were Jews."

Those words have reverberated in my mind, haunting me ever since.

According to Ashkenazi (European heritage) Jewish tradition, a newborn infant is given a name in honor of a deceased relative. The name is formed by taking the entire name or just the initial letter of the name of the ancestor being honored and forming a new name. I had the good fortune to being named after my great-grandfather Wolf. As it has turned out over the years, he not only gave me my name, but he and my great-grandmother Bascha also gave me a sense of history and a sense of my identity.

Simon left Krosno with three sisters in 1912 bound for New York City, leaving his remaining family members. Already in this country was one older brother. As he left, a series of pogroms targeting Jews had spread throughout the area. He often explained to me that he could only travel by night with darkness as his shield to avoid being attacked and beaten by people who hated Jews. He arrived in the United States on New Years' Eve in a city filled with gleaming lights and frenetic activity, and with his own heart filled with hope for a new life.

Simon returned to Krosno with my grandmother, Eva, in 1932 to a joyous homecoming. This was the first time he had seen his family since he left Poland. He took with him an early home movie camera to record his family on film. While in Poland, he promised that once back in the United States, he would try to earn enough money to send for his remaining family members who wished to come to the United States, but history was to thwart his plans. During that happy reunion, he had no way of knowing that this was to be

Figure 1.1. Wolf, Simon, and Bascha Mahler. Krosno, Poland, 1932.

the last time he would ever see these family members. Just 7 years later, on 1 September 1939, the Nazis invaded Poland.

Simon heard the news sitting in the kitchen of his home in Brooklyn, New York. He was so infuriated, so frightened, and so incensed that he took the large radio from the table, lifted it above his head, and violently hurled it against a wall. He knew what this invasion meant. He knew it signaled the end of the Jewish population in Europe as he had known it. He knew it meant certain death for people he had grown up with, people he had loved, and people who had loved him.

Simon's fears soon became real. He eventually learned from a brother who had eventually escaped into the woods with his wife and young son that Nazi soldiers murdered many members of his family either on the streets of Krosno or up a small hill near the Jewish cemetery. We later learned that the Nazis murdered his father, Wolf, in the Krosno ghetto. The Nazis eventually loaded other friends and relatives onto cattle cars and transported them to Auschwitz and Balzec concentration camps.

Simon never fully recovered from those days in 1939. Though he kept the faces and voices from his homeland within him throughout his life, the Nazis also invaded my grandfather's heart, killing a part of him forever. My mother, Blanche, told me that Simon became increasingly introspective, less spontaneous, and less optimistic of what the future would hold. After the war and continuing today, virtually no Jews reside in Krosno or in all of southwestern Poland.

In this country, my own father suffered the effects of anti-Jewish prejudice. One of only a handful of Jews in his school in Los Angeles in the 1920s and 1930s, many afternoons he returned home injured from a fight. To get a decent job, his father, Abraham, was forced to anglicize the family name, changing it unofficially from "Blumenfeld" to "Fields."

My parents did what they could to protect my sister and myself from the effects of anti-Jewish prejudice, but still I grew up with a constant and gnawing feeling that I somehow did not belong. The time was the early 1950s, the so-called "McCarthy Era"—a conservative time, a time when difference of any sort was held suspect. On the floor of the U.S. Senate, a brash young Senator from Wisconsin, Joseph McCarthy, sternly warned that Communists (often thought of as Jews in public perceptions) corrupt the minds and homosexuals corrupt the bodies of good upstanding Americans, and he proceeded to have them officially banned from government service. In terms of what today would be referred to as LGBTQ people, during this era, there were frequent police raids on their bars, which were usually Mafia owned; the U.S. Postal Service raided their organizations and even published the names of their mailing lists in local newspapers, and people lost their jobs. They were often involuntarily committed to mental institutions. Some underwent electro-shock treatments; some were lobotomized.

Not knowing what else to do at this time, my parents sent me, beginning at age four and lasting for the next eight years, to a child psychologist because they feared that I might be gay (or to use the terminology of the day, "homosexual"). And as it turned out, their perceptions were indeed correct.

My journey of "coming out" as "gay" and then as "agender queer" over successive years was often difficult and painful, but looking back, I conclude that it was certainly rewarding, for it has been the prime motivator for my work as a writer and social justice educator. I am committed to this work, on one level, to ensure a better future for the young people growing up today. To be completely honest, though, a major motivation stems from the fact that, essentially, I haven't felt safe in the world, and, therefore, I have a deep personal stake in the work I am doing. Often, when I leave my little university enclave, I tend to feel like an outsider in my own country. Maybe that feeling will never completely leave me; I don't really know. I can take solace, at least, that the fear has diminished somewhat over the years.

More recently, on a snowy February morning in 2002, while in my university office organizing materials for that day's classes, I received an email message that would forever poignantly and profoundly change my life. A man named Charles Mahler had been looking for descendants of the Mahler family of Poland, and he had come across an essay I had written focusing on Wolf and Bascha Mahler.

Charles informed me that he had survived the German Holocaust along with his sister, parents, and maternal grandparents and uncle, but the Nazis murdered his father's parents (Jacques and Anja Mahler), sister, and her two children, and other relatives following Hitler's invasion and occupation of Belgium, their adopted home country.

My cousin Charles related their story in hiding from August 1942 until the final armistice in Europe. His father, Georg, altered the family's identity papers from Jewish to Christian, and they abandoned Antwerp for what they considered the relative safety of the Belgium countryside. During their plight, members of the Belgium resistance movement and other righteous Christians shepherded them throughout the remainder of the war to three separate locations as the German Gestapo followed closely at their heels. On several occasions, they successfully "passed" as Christian directly under the watchful gaze of unsuspecting Nazis.

Though most of the Jewish inhabitants of Antwerp ultimately perished, many survived. However, at the United States Holocaust Memorial Museum in Washington, D.C. and Yad Vashem (The Holocaust Martyrs' and Heroes' Remembrance Authority in Israel) one will observe "Krosno" chiseled into the glass and stone walls, listing towns and villages where Nazis and their sympathizers decimated entire Jewish communities.

One piece of my family puzzle met a tragic end, another partial segment survived. In both instances, the bystanders determined the balance of power: in Krosno, the overwhelming majority conspired with the oppressors, while in Antwerp, significant numbers dug deeply within themselves transitioning from bystanders into courageous, compassionate, and empathetic upstanders in the face of seemingly insurmountable odds.

Each day we all are called on to make small and larger choices and to take actions. Which side are we on? Today as in the past, no question seems more urgent, for in the spectrum from occasional microaggressions to full-blown genocide, there is no such thing as an "innocent bystander."

For a free download to my manual, "Imagining Poland as a Country with Open Doors to Jewish People," which has application to countries throughout Eastern Europe, follow the link to the webpage below:

https://www.academia.edu/34446442/Imagining_Poland_as_a_Country_with_Open_Doors_to_Jewish_People

Social Justice

What: Though the concept of "social justice" has been defined several ways. According to Lee Anne Bell (2007), social justice includes both a process and a goal: "The goal of social justice is full and equal participation of all groups in a society that is mutually shaped to meet their needs" (p. 1).

I have constructed my definition of social justice as: "The concept that local, national, and global communities function where everyone has equal access to and equitable distribution of the rights, benefits, privileges, and resources, and where everyone can live freely unencumbered by social constructions of hierarchical positions of domination and subordination based on social identities and backgrounds."

We can date the term "social justice" back to the 1840s when it was coined by a Jesuit priest named Luigi Taparelli—b. Prospero Taparelli d'Azeglio, 1793–1862 (Burke, 2010). It became often-used during the revolutions of 1848 and expressed by progressive activists and scholars thereafter. We find the terms in numerous documents, for example, the preamble of the International Labour Organization, an agency of the United Nations, stating that "universal and lasting peace can be established only if it is based upon social justice." In addition, the Vienna Declaration and Programme of Action, a human rights declaration passed by consensus on 25 June 1993 by the World Congress on Human Rights, included "social justice" as the purpose and goal of human rights education.

So What: Universities have established entire programs dedicated to the study of social justice. On a personal note, I earned my doctorate degree from the Social Justice Education Program within the College of Education at the University of Massachusetts at Amherst. Our university and an increasing number of others are offering courses in this field of study to undergraduates and graduates alike, and in continuing education programs.

I consider myself a social justice educator who studies, researches, writes, teaches, and lives projected through a *lens* of social justice. I come into social justice education work with several assumptions: Issues of power, privilege, and domination within U.S. and other societies center around inequitable social divisions related to race, ethnicity, socioeconomic class, the sex we are assigned at birth, gender identity and expression, sexual identity, religion, nationality, linguistic background, physical and mental abilities and appearance, age, and others. Issues around social identities impact generally on our life outcomes, and specifically our educational outcomes, for very often, the social inequities stemming from the larger society are reproduced in schools.

I also believe it imperative to have a grounding in history to help us answer some of the questions regarding how these inequities developed and persisted up to the present time, as well as to help us to correct and balance these inequities.

For me, I experience no separation between my engagement as a student, educator, and community organizer. None of these I consider "part-time activities" nor mere intellectual exercises. Looking back now, I perceive a seamless trajectory between the three ropes in my baked *Challah* of life. These ropes set the parameters for my life and for my very being because long before I joined the AIDS Coalition to Unleash Power (ACT UP) to this very day, "Silence [Still] = Death."

So, if social justice is truly about ensuring a better, more peaceful, and equitable society and world dedicated to the concept of fairness and justice in the relationship between the individual and the state and between states, and devoted to obliterating the barriers of social mobility by working actively for equality of opportunity and economic justice, then why is there such resistance or opposition to the concept by many individuals and organizations in many nations?

Now What: This book is dedicated to investigating and addressing this complex and multidimensional question.

Book Format

I structure the book around a three-part format (Borton, 1970; Rolfe, Freshwater, & Jasper, 2001) that many of us involved in social justice work employ in our classrooms, interactive workshops, presentations, and community organizing.

- Part I: Terminology—the *What* and the *So What* of social justice regarding the terms and definitions involved, and what occurred,
- Part II: Education—the *What* and the *So What* specifically of social justice education regarding types, methods, and pedagogical perspectives,
- Part III: Liberation—the *Now What* we can do to work toward the attainment of social justice education and liberation as an individual, as a group, in coalition with other individuals and other groups, and across social, physical, and national boundaries.

While the *What* and the *So What* are highlighted throughout the book, much of the *Now What* comes within the concluding chapters and within the Appendices. The researchers, theorists, and practitioners cited and referenced throughout the book represent a cross-section of pioneers and preeminent scholars in the field as well as contemporary and younger theorists, researchers, and practitioners who have built upon the foundations constructed by earlier generations.

· 2 ·

CULTURE AND IDENTITY

> There can be no justice without peace, and there can be no peace without justice.
> —Reverend Dr. Martin Luther King Jr

Peace activist and Civil Rights leader, Dr. King, chanted this statement outside a California prison, which was holding Vietnam War protesters on December 14, 1967. In his commitment and passion for justice, and in his inimical and profound way, he understood several connecting strands: "I see these two struggles as one struggle." By fighting a war "against the self-determination of the Vietnamese people," he realized that his country, the United States of America, had been proliferating injustice. While fighting for the civil and human rights of people in his home nation without opposing what King believed to be the clear exploitation of the Vietnamese people would have contradicted his declaration that "injustice anywhere is a threat to justice everywhere." Throughout his life, he invoked his vibrant image of the "inescapable network of mutuality" that links all of humanity (in King, 2001).

Dr. King is but one of literally countless social justice worriers, known and unrecognized throughout the ages across our remarkable planet. They have placed their values and their very lives on the line to ensure a better, more peaceful, and equitable world for themselves and their descendants, a world highlighted by a more level playing field between people of every identity and background, and one where a safety net catches people who have hit tough times and people with limited abilities to meet their needs.

Because of their courageous dedication to the concept of fairness and justice in the relationship between the individual and the state and between states, in their devotion to obliterating the barriers of social mobility by working actively for equality of opportunity and economic justice, they have given us so much. But as we know, the struggle for social justice is ongoing, for the journey must continue before we collectively reach our ultimate destination.

Equitable v. Equal

What: When asked by Jane Schmidt, student coordinator of the Gay/Straight Alliance at Waverly High School in Waverly, Iowa on November 30, 2011 "Why can't same-sex couples get married [throughout the United States]?," ultra-conservative then U.S. Representative from Minnesota, Michelle Bachmann, responded that gay and lesbian people should have "no special rights" to marry people of the same sex, insisting that "the laws are you marry a person of the opposite sex." She continued: "They can get married, but they abide by the same law as everyone else. They can marry a man if they're a woman. Or they can marry a woman if they're a man" (*Washington Post*, 12/1/2011).

In this discussion, Bachmann exhibits a basic misunderstanding between the terms "Equal" and "Equitable." I like to use my friend Vernon Wall's metaphor to differentiate between the terms: Being treated "equally" is providing everyone with a pair of shoes. Being treated "equitably," though, is providing everyone with a pair of shoes *that fit them.*

In her argument, Bachmann is saying that we all are being provided with a pair of shoes, and she is indeed correct. If you happen, for example, to wear a size 10 men's or women's shoe, and you are given a pair of size 10 shoes, all is possibly fine and fair if the shoes fit comfortably and you like the style and shade. However, how fine and fair is it for those who do not wear a size 10 shoe at all, or if you do, you don't like the style and shade? Though we can equally attempt to fit into these shoes, when we struggle to walk, we either inadvertently step out of the shoes and possibly fall, or we develop bruised and blistered feet.

Let's look at the following analogy to Bachmann's argument. Prior to 1967, nine states within the U.S. prevented consenting adults from engaging in sexual activities, let alone marriage, with anyone from another so-called "race." One could argue that these laws treated everyone equally: Those socially determined to be "white" adults could have consensual sex with and marry other white people, but they could not have sex with or marry people of any other so-called "race." People socially determined to be "black" adults could have consensual sex with and marry other black people, but they could not have sex with or marry people of any other so-called "race," and so on.

In the case of *Loving v. Virginia*, 388 U.S. 1 (1967), the Supreme Court of the United States, however, disagreed with the above scenarios codified in law, ruling against equality and in favor of equity. They declared the state of Virginia's anti-miscegenation statute, the "Racial Integrity Act" of 1924, unconstitutional, thereby overturning *Pace v. Alabama* (1883) and ending all race-based legal restrictions on adult consensual sexual activity and marriage throughout the U.S.

The plaintiffs in the case were Mildred Loving (born Mildred Deloris Jetter, a woman of African descent) and Richard Perry Loving (a man of white European descent), both residents of Virginia who married in June 1958 in the District of Columbia to evade Virginia's "Racial Integrity Act." Upon returning to Virginia, they were arrested and charged with violating the act. Police entered their home and arrested them while they slept in their bed. At their trial, they were convicted and sentenced to one-year imprisonment with a suspended sentence of 25 years on the condition that the couple leave the state of Virginia. At the trial, the judge, Leon Bazile, used Biblical justifications to convict the couple in Caroline County Court, 1958:

> Almighty God created the races white, black, yellow, Malay and red, and He placed them on separate continents. And but for the interference with His arrangement there would be no cause for such marriages. The fact that He separated the races shows that He did not intend for the races to mix.

On issues of marriage equality and interracial marriage, religious justifications were cited to deny people the right to shoes that fit them.

So What: Can we learn any lessons here? I say we can. Opponents of providing equitable treatment to transgender people, for example, argue that everyone must only use public facilities of those of the sex that was assigned to them at birth. They claim that current laws are treating people "equally." By doing so, they are forcing trans people to walk with seriously calloused and bruised feet.

Culture

What: Merriam-Webster (2018a) defines "culture" as "the characteristic features of everyday existence (such as diversions or a way of life) shared by people in a place or time." Herskovits (1955) provided a simplified way of looking at the term "culture" as "everything that is human made." In addition, Gudykunst (1994) proposed culture as "the systems of knowledge used by relatively large numbers of people" (p. 38).

According to Nieto (2010):

> Culture can be understood as the ever-changing values, traditions, social and political relationships, and world view created and shared by a group of people bound together by a combination of factors that can include a common history, geographic location, language, social class, and/or religion, and how these are transformed by those who share them. (p. 138)

Some of the component parts of cultures include the symbols, language, material items, norms, and the values of a people. Though all cultures are heterogeneous to some extent, social scientists talk about national cultures—for example, a "United States" culture, a "Chinese" culture, a "Chilean" culture. In some countries, there is more than one overriding culture. Canada and Switzerland, for example, are said to constitute two cultures: for Canada, English and French; for Switzerland, French and German.

According to Bonvillain (2003): "Culture is communication and communication is culture" (p. 213). Of course, one must consider individual personality types (Keirsey & Bates, 1978), personal learning styles (Kolb, 1981), cognitive development (Perry, 1981), and personal histories, but in addition, our culture enormously influences the way we communicate, and the reverse, our communication influences our culture.

Within cultures, there are groups, called "subcultures" whose members share some of the component values of the dominant culture, but also have several traits and values that differ from the larger culture ("cultural pluralism"). Some of these subcultures are based on social identities, for example, related to race, ethnicity, religion, sexual identity, gender identity, ability, sex assigned at birth, socioeconomic class, age, and others. They can also be organized around occupations or interests. Primarily, when I refer to "social identities" throughout this book, I am referring to the former category.

Identity[1]

What: Most people hold concurrent "social identities" (consciously or unconsciously) based on *socially constructed* categories: for example, on our personal and physical characteristics, on our ages, abilities, genders, sexes assigned at birth, class backgrounds, and on our cultural, racial, ethnic, sexual and affectional, and religious identifications. Identities can also be determined by our relationships to other people (e.g., "parent," "daughter," "lover/partner"), our occupations, interests, or organizational positions ("politician," "athlete," "construction worker," "artist," "management supervisor," "tailor"), and our educational backgrounds. Sometimes these identities are ascribed to us by others (often at birth); sometimes identities are achieved later in life; some are permanent, lasting a lifetime; others are temporary or transitional. Some identities are more salient than others to an individual at any given time and in any given social situation.

Erikson (1950/1963), the preeminent developmental psychologist, asserted that individuals possess an *innate drive* for identity, an inborn lifetime quest to know who they are, which powers their personality development.

Identity can be defined as:

> … the organization of the individual's drives, abilities, beliefs, and history into a consistent image of self. It involves deliberate choices and decisions, particularly about work, values, ideology, and commitments to people and ideas. (Woolfolk, 2004, p. 68)

In a basic sense, then, identity is the detailed and multifaceted answer to the question, "Who am I?"

Foundational to Erikson's theory of psychosocial development is that throughout life individuals progress through a series of eight discrete periods or stages. During each they confront "identity crises" (or "developmental crises") that they must successfully negotiate and resolve to advance to the next stage. "Healthy development" at any one stage rests on meeting the challenges posed by the crises at previous stages.

For example, in Erikson's "Stage 1" of the first year of life, infants are challenged to develop a primary sense of trust with the world around them. Depending on how they resolve this life stage, they will go on to either view the world as a predictable and manageable place, which they can influence (basic trust), or as an unpredictable and volatile place over which they have little control (mistrust). In Erikson's "Stage 5," between the ages of 13–18 ("Identity v. Role Confusion"), people address the question of "Who am I now?" "Who was I before?" "Who will I become?" A crisis in the Eriksonian sense, however, need not be considered negative.

Hardiman and Jackson (1997) divided identity into two levels: personal and social. The "personal level" they define as the ways in which the individual recognizes aspects of their personhood including all the aspects of personality, character, tastes, and interests. The "social level" refers to the role of others in society in defining these aspects, especially around the individual's participation and membership in the social group. Social identity, then, includes:

> … all the various social groups that an individual consciously and unconsciously has membership in and the conscious and unconscious use of a social frame of reference in self-perception, social perception or in social interaction. (Hardiman & Jackson, 1997, p. 76)

Leading social researcher Tajfel (1982) discussed the self as composed of numerous, or multiple, identities, and he subdivided these identities, as did Hardiman and Jackson, into two types: the personal and the social. Tajfel proposed what he called an "interpersonal-intergroup continuum" representing the two-way direction that social behavior continually travels—from interpersonal to intergroup—and a shift from one's awareness from personal identity to social identity. Tajfel acknowledged that most behavior would be considered "mixed" (interpersonal *and* intergroup), and many times would appear toward the middle of the continuum. In addition, in highly collectivist and interdependent societies such as Japan, for example, this distinction between "individual" and "group" would be understood very differently. I would add that for many cultures (e.g., collectivist in tradition) *within* the several Western countries, this individual/group separation does not exist to the extent it does among assimilated peoples of European heritage.

Intersectionality

> My husband, Martin Luther King Jr., once said, "We are all tied together in a single garment of destiny … an inescapable network of mutuality. … I can never be what I ought to be until you are allowed to be what you ought to be." Therefore, I

appeal to everyone who believes in Martin Luther King Jr.'s dream to make room at the table of brotherhood and sisterhood for lesbian and gay people.
—Coretta Scott King (2000)

So What: Within a patriarchal system of male domination, cisgender heterosexual male bodies matter more, while "othered" bodies matter less. These "othered" bodies include female and intersex bodies, and bodies that violate the "rules" for the reproduction and maintenance of the dominant patriarchal system, such as transgender, gender non-conforming, gender diverse, and gay, lesbian, and bisexual bodies, and bodies with disabilities. In addition, within many Western societies, non-European-heritage bodies are regarded also as abject bodies—bodies that, to use theorist Butler's (1993) phraseology, do not matter, or, at least, do not matter as much as "white" bodies.

Butler (1990) reminds us that the term "abjection" is taken from the Latin, *ab-jicere*, meaning to cast off, away, or out. On a social level, abjection designates a degraded, stigmatized, or cast out status. In psychoanalytic parlance, this is the notion of *Verwerfung* (foreclosure). Butler states that "we regularly punish those who fail to do their gender right" (p. 140), and similarly punish those who fail to do their "race" right. *Doing* one's "race" right often depends on *doing* one's socioeconomic class right. The regulatory regimes of "sex," "sexuality," "gender," "ability," "race," and "class" are inimically connected, and these connections are discursively maintained.

What: Critical race theorist, Crenshaw (1995), coined the term "intersectionality" or "intersectionalism" to apply to the multiple social identities and group memberships of each individual, and how these together impact peoples' lives. Crenshaw originated the theory of intersectionality when examining the realities of black women's lives as a core concept of women of color feminist theory.

Each person is composed of multiple identities that interconnect. Depending on time and location, some of these identities may seem more or less important to the individuals. Most people in most societies have some identities accorded more social privileges, while simultaneously having some identities accorded less social privileges.

Tatum (1999) asks us to question who we are regarding Erikson's (1968) phrase "in the core of the individual and yet also in the core of his communal culture" (p. 22). Kirk and Okazawa-Rey (2013) talk about identity formation as "… the result of a complex interplay among individual decision and choices, particular life events, community, recognition and expectations, and societal categorization, classification and socialization" (p. 8). They list three various levels of identity. At the first level, the Macro Level, individuals feel most comfortable *as* themselves. They can describe themselves with several personal characteristics. On the micro level we choose to "define ourselves and structure our daily activities according to our own preferences" (p. 10). The next level involves community recognition, expectations, and interactions in which big life events demonstrate how individuals think about themselves. In this Meso Level, individuals determine their relationships with others. At the Macro and Global Levels, individuals are placed by their society into certain categories based on several characteristics based on deep-rooted systems of classification and structural inequality. These systems may change depending on where a person resides globally. "Thus social categories such as gender, race, and class are used to establish and maintain a particular kind of social order" (p. 54).

So What: Asking ourselves who we are aids us in understanding our social privileges that come with some of our identities, lesser privileges with other identities, while giving us further insight into the topic of dominant and subordinate groups.

What: A dominant group, according to Tatum, is "systematically advantaged by the society because of group membership" while a subordinate group is "systematically disadvantaged." Almost every person belongs to a certain system of privilege as well as suffers from oppression. It is often difficult for privilege to be understood as "the dominant group is seen as the norm for humanity" while the subordinate groups "… internalize the images that the dominant group reflects back to them … [and] may find it difficult to believe in their own ability" (p. 23). Lorde (1984) discusses what she called a "mythical norm" of identity in Western countries such as white, thin, male, young, heterosexual, Christian, and financially secure.

As a concept in Critical Transgender Politics (CTR—a form of critical theory, see, e.g., Stryker & Whittle, 2013), let us imagine identity intersectionality something like a room with multiple sides with each side representing one of our many social identities. A floor-to-ceiling mirror has been attached to each of the multiple sides. When we direct our gaze toward one side (mirror), we focus on one of our identities and the form of oppression under which it may fall. For example, we see (or understand if we have limited vision or if we are blind) that we are female living in a sexist society, and therefore, the ways society subordinates us. Though we are facing this one mirror, we can simultaneously see in this mirror, reflections of differing angles of our other identities.

Let's take another example. If we move our bodies to face another side (mirror), we can now perceive our racialized identity. If we are white, we can see that we have white privilege within a racist society that privileges white people and subordinates people of color.

So What: The point of this metaphor is to demonstrate that all the forms of oppression are related and that they each impact our social identities. Chase Catalano (2018) demonstrates this intersectionality:

> For example, youth pregnancy can be conceptualized as anti-heteronormative because of how [adultism or] youth oppression (youth should not be sexual beings) interacts with sexism (cisgender females are supposed to be responsible for pregnancy prevention). Thus, while pregnancy is often seen as a heteronormative expectation, youth pregnancy is actually a demonstration of gender deviance. CTP gives us the ability to attend to the power of institutional and cultural hegemony, such as how pregnant youth are tracked or rebuked through a school system. The pregnant youth may see herself as a woman, heterosexual, youth, or any other social identity so the view in the mirror are constantly in flux, impacted by self-identification, as well as perception and organized by individuals, institutions, and cultural norms. In this conceptualization we are able to understand how shifting our view from one mirror to another does not mean the other images go away, but that our view of them differ.

Border Identities

> The U.S-Mexican border es *una herida abierta* where the Third World grates against the first and bleeds. And before a scab forms it hemorrhages again, the lifeblood of two worlds merging to form a third country—a border culture.
>
> Borders are set up to define the places that are safe and unsafe, to distinguish us from them. A border is a dividing line, a narrow strip along a steep edge. A borderland is a vague and undetermined place created by the emotional residue of an unnatural boundary. It is in a constant state of transition. The prohibited and forbidden are its inhabitants.
>
> —Anzaldúa (1987, p. 25)

What: "Border Identities" exist outside binary frames and include identities socially constructed as, for example, "biracial," "bicultural," "bisexual," "intersex," "cross-racial adoptees," and others. Border identities may confuse or challenge the binary constructions of privilege and disadvantage, dominant and subordinated. Sometimes people occupy *intermediary* locations by association: for example, a white man married to a black woman, a parent of a transgender child, and a heterosexual woman married to a bisexual man.

Here is another example of border identities:

> We continually negotiate our identity, every day of our lives, every time we open our mouths. My name is Enrique Lamadrid. I'm from New Mexico. Every time I open my mouth, I have to decide whether to talk to people in Spanish or English. When I was growing up, to some people I was Rick, to other people Enrique. It's a dual identity, but it's not cut in the middle. Both of these ends meet, and there is a unity to all of that. All of us have experienced that, I'm sure.
>
> Smithsonian Institution Center for Cultural and Folklife Heritage (2009)

So What: What does Enrique mean to "negotiate our identity"? And consider how we (you) "negotiate" your identities, in Enrique's words, "every day of our lives. ..."

Note

1. See Appendix A: Multiple Identities Essay.

· 3 ·
SOCIAL CONSTRUCTION OF IDENTITIES AND OTHER FORMS OF "DIFFERENCE"

So What: The societies and the times in which we live determine the extent to which we are accorded or denied privileges based on our socially constructed identities. Yes, *socially constructed*. For example, a woman who lived her entire life in a small African village surrounded by a community of people like herself may never have given much thought about being "black" since her society did not construct identity in terms of her skin color. When she takes a trip to Poland, for example, she discovers that she is a "black African" since that society constructs identity based on skin color and country of origin. She "learned" in Poland that she "is black." Therefore, societies determine the systems of privilege and oppression we encounter.

I offer first an introductory example of a socially constructed identity that has changed and diminished over time.

Left-Handedness: A Case Study of the *What*, the *So What*, and the *Now What*

What: Estimates suggest that one in ten people is left handed. In fact, this number probably holds true for all places during all times (Kens, 2017). Left-handed people have existed throughout the ages in all cultures, in all races, in all social classes, and in every country. Even the earliest cave drawings show left-handed figures.

Though it may seem obvious, it is not always easy to determine who is left handed. Some people, for example, use different hands for different activities. Former U.S. President Gerald Ford used his left hand to write while sitting, and his right hand to write on chalkboards while standing. Some people can successfully manage with either hand. In fact, it is probably true that most people are not exclusively right or left handed. Many people, though, define their handedness in terms of whichever hand they use most, especially in writing. Nevertheless, people in general exhibit a vast variety of hand skills covering a broad continuum between exclusive left to exclusive right handedness.

Although you might not think your friend, or mother, or classmate is all that different because they are left handed, such tolerance or support has not always been the case. In fact, for centuries, left-handed people were viewed with scorn and even, at times, with fear. People often justified this disparagement with references to religious texts such as the Bibles, both the Jewish Bible and Christian Testaments, though primarily the Christian Testaments, which consider "the left" as the domain of the Devil, whereas "the right" as the domain of God. For this reason, Jesus told his followers to "not let thy left hand know what thy right hand doeth" (Matthew 6:3).

Jesus also described God's process for separating good from evil in the Last Judgment: "… the King [shall] say unto them on His right hand, 'Come, ye blessed of my Father, inherit the Kingdom prepared for you from the foundation of the world. …' Then shall He say unto them on the left hand, 'Depart from me, ye cursed, into everlasting fire, prepared for the devil and his angels …'" (Matthew 25:32–41). Early Christians applied these categories so strictly that they even held that the saints, while still infants, were so holy that they would not suckle from the left breasts of their mothers.

Not only do the Bibles condemn left handedness, but so did several ancient societies. The ancient Greeks and Romans shared this attitude as well. For example, the philosopher Pythagoras argued that left-handedness was synonymous with "dissolution" and evil, and Aristotle described good as "what is on the right, above, and in front, and bad what is on the left, below, and behind." The Romans further reinforced these beliefs by standardizing the right-handed handshake, and in Western countries, alphabets favor right-handed people in being written from left to right. Hebrew and Arabic, written from right to left, also favored right-handed people when, in ancient times, writing was often done on stone tablets in which they held the chisel with the left hand and the hammer with the right.

Later, in the Middle Ages, left-handed people were sometimes accused of being witches, sorcerers, or as fathered by the Devil. The present-day wedding custom of joining right hands and placing the gold ring on the third finger of the left hand began with the superstition that doing so would *absorb* the evil inherent in the left hand.

Even our terminology reflects anti-left-hand bigotry. Words like *"sinister"* ("left" in Latin) and *"gauche"* ("left" in French) suggest a moral evil or physical awkwardness associated with left-handedness. Their opposites, however, *"dexter"* ("right" in Latin) and *"droit"* ("right" in French) mean "skillful," "artful," "clever," "correct," "adroit," or "lawful." The English word "left" comes from the old Dutch word, *"lyft,"* meaning "weak" or "broken," whereas "right" derives from an Anglo-Saxon word, *"riht,"* meaning "straight," "erect," or "just." The term "ambidextrous" literally means "being right-handed on both sides." Phrases like "left-handed compliment" are insults to left-handed people.

It is difficult to determine precisely why a little more strength in one hand over the other has been used as the basis of wide-scale persecution of a group of humans. Some people argue that the preference for right-handedness began with the military. If all soldiers were right-handed, they would all pass to the right of their enemy, keeping the enemy on their left side, where they held their shields thereby enabling them to maintain a uniform defensive posture. This practice extended to rules of the road, except in countries such as England, where they drive on the left side of the road. But even there, the practice was established from a right-handed preference. Knights on horseback would keep their opponents to their right with their lances when jousting.

What "righties" usually take for granted often involves awkward adjustments for "lefties." Most tools and utensils and most packaging of products are designed for the ease of right-handed people. These include scissors, power saws, corkscrews, sewing machines, and even gum wrappers. Left-handed pilots have not been allowed in the past to sit on the right side of the cockpit to reach the controls in the center, even though to do so would make it easier for them. And writing from left to right accommodates right-handed people, while forcing left-handed people to make difficult adjustments. Stereotypes have circulated about hand-handed people as willful and stubborn. Some people even incorrectly believe that left-handed people are at greater risk of committing criminal offenses. This all brings to light the realities of right-hand privilege, which includes unearned advantages bestowed on right-handed people that often are invisible to those who have them.

So What: So why does this matter anyway? Well, it matters to some who believe that left-handedness is intrinsically evil or unnatural. This attitude has led many theorists to propose tactics for changing an exhibited hand preference.

They have urged parents to encourage young people to emphasize their right hands, especially in writing. In some schools, teachers have tied young students' left hands and arms behind their backs or made them sit on their left hands to promote use of the right hand. This treatment often resulted in emotional outbursts, speech impairments such as stuttering, reading problems, and other learning disabilities. Some left-handed people have tried to conceal their hand orientation and to "pass" as right-handed to fit in and to avoid social sanctions.

Now What: Over the years, activists have challenged societies to become aware and acknowledge that oppression toward left-handed people falls into issues of civil rights. They have fought to make physical accommodations to left-handed people and to reject all prejudices that prevent full support and social inclusion for them. More recently, some individuals have created organizations to ensure rights for left-handed people. In fact, centuries ago the left-handed artist, Michelangelo non-violently and surreptitiously challenged the Catholic Church for its anti-left-hand condemnations. When he painted his famous ceiling in the Sistine Chapel at the Vatican, he portrayed God giving life to Adam through Adam's *left* hand.

As other minoritized groups, left-hand social movement activists cite examples of famous members of their group throughout history including Alexander the Great, Judy Garland, Gerald Ford, Marilyn Monroe, Ben Franklin, King George VI, Jimi Hendrix, Babe Ruth, Cole Porter, Pablo Picasso, Lefty Gomez, Henry Wallace, Queen Victoria, Barack Obama, and many others.

"Racialized" Social Constructions

What: Looking over the historical emergence of the concept of "race," critical race theorists remind us that this *concept* arose concurrently with the advent of European exploration as a justification and rationale for conquest and domination of the globe beginning in the 15th century of the Common Era (CE), and reaching its apex in the early 20th century CE (see, e.g., Smedley & Smedley, 2005). Geneticists tell us that there is often more variability *within* a given so-called "race" than between "races," and that there are no essential *genetic* markers linked specifically to "race." They assert, therefore, that "race" is discursively constructed—a historical, "scientific," biological myth, an idea—and that any socially conceived physical "racial" markers are fictive and are not concordant with what is beyond or below the surface of the body (see, e.g., Rutherford, 2017).

Carl Linnaeus (1707–1778), born Carl Linné, (whom we call today the "Father of Scientific Racism"), a Swedish botanist, physician, and zoologist, developed a system of scientific hierarchical classification. Within this taxonomy under the label *Homo sapiens* ("Man"), he enumerated five categories based initially on place of origin and later on skin color: *Europeanus, Asiaticus, Americanus, Monstrosus,* and *Africanus*. Linnaeus asserted that each category was ruled by a different bodily fluid (Humors: "moistures"), represented by blood (optimistic), phlegm (sluggish), cholor (yellow bile: prone to anger), melancholy (black bile: prone to sadness).

Linnaeus connected each human category to a respective humor, thereby constructing the Linnaeus Taxonomy of humans in descending order:

- *Europeanus*: sanguine (blood), pale, muscular, swift, clever, gentle, acutely inventive, with abundant, long hair, blue eyes, covered with close vestments and regulated by laws;
- *Asiaticus*: melancholic, yellow, inflexible, severe, avaricious, dark-eyed, black hair, governed by opinions;
- *Americanus* (indigenous peoples in the Americas): choleric, copper-colored, straightforward, eager, combative, governed by customs;
- *Monstrosus* (dwarfs of the Alps, the Patagonian giant, the monorchid Hottentot): agile, fainthearted; and,
- *Africanus*: phlegmatic, black, slow, relaxed, negligent, black frizzled hair, silky skin, flat nose, tumid lips, females without shame, mammary glands give milk abundantly, crafty, sly, careless, anoints himself with grease, governed by impulse.

Voltaire, 18th century French Enlightenment philosopher was a polygenist (human "races" are from different origins—different Adams and Eves). He asserted: "The Negro race is a species of men different from ours as the breed of spaniels is from that of greyhounds" (Voltaire in Smith, 2015, p. 236).

The British psychologist, Francis Galton (1822–1911)—a cousin of Charles Darwin—was a founder of the "Eugenics" Movement. In fact, Galton coined the term "eugenics" in 1883 from the Greek word meaning "well born." Eugenicists attempted to improve qualities of a so-called "race" by controlling human breeding. It was based on the theory that genetic predisposition determined human behavior. Galton also profited greatly from the slave trade. He stated:

> I do not join in the belief that the African is our equal in brain or in heart; I do not think that the average negro cares for his liberty as much as an Englishman, or as a self-born Russian; and I believe that if we can in any fair way, possess ourselves of his services, we have an equal right to utilize them to our advantages. (Galton in MacKeller & Bechtel, 2015, p. 16)

The modern-day Eugenicist, William Shockley (Shurkin, 2006), asserted that black Americans suffered from "dysgenesis," or "retrogression evolution."

> My research leads me inescapably to the opinion that the major cause of the American Negro's intellectual and social deficits is hereditary and racially genetic in origin and, thus, not remediable to a major degree by practical improvements in the environment. (Firing Line, 1974)

Shockley proposed eliminating the public welfare system to be replaced with a "voluntary sterilization bonus plan."

The highly charged racist stereotype of black men as oversexed and sexually insatiable predators of white women and girls persists today, as does the myth that black men are more highly endowed genitally than their white counterparts.

Throughout the history of the United States, for example, vicious white gangs have beaten and lynched black men and boys on charges, bogus or not, of even looking at white women or girls. White vigilantes killed black residents and burned down the town of Rosewood, Florida on the false charge by a white woman that a black man had raped her. A band of white men in Mississippi viciously tortured and lynched Emmett Till, a 14-year-old black teenager, for allegedly flirting with a white woman.

"Racialization" of Nationality, Language, and Religion

What: As an aspect of the social construction of "race," we can list how nationality, language, and religion have at times become "racialized" in various societies and time frames. Take, for example, the following examples:

1. A married Jewish couple of German birth and descent flee Germany during the rise of the Nazis in 1933 and immigrate to Colombia in

South America. Within 5 years after arriving, they produce and raise three children. Colombian society defines this family as European-heritage white. One of the children comes to the United States to attend college. When she enters the U.S., she suddenly becomes "Latina" owing to her country of birth and her first language of Spanish. Not only does language through discursive regimes racialize, but also, in many instances, language *itself* is racialized.
2. A white woman of English, Irish, and Swedish heritage grows up in a home in Iowa following the tenets of the Christian Methodist faith. When she was 32-years-old, she met, fell in love with, and married an Iranian professor from a nearby university who teaches Islamic Culture and Religion and is himself a Muslim. Before their marriage, the woman studied and converted to Islam, and now she wears the traditional *hijab*, the veil customarily worn by some Muslim women covering the head and chest. Many people now consider this woman as no longer "white," but, rather, as a person of color by converting to Islam and marrying a man of Iranian descent. This example underscores the racialization of religion.

Performativity of "Race" and "Gender"

What: Within academia and activism, greater emphasis and discussion is centering on what has come to be called "queer studies" and "queer theory" and "critical race theory" (areas of critical theory) where writers, educators, and students analyze and challenge current notions, categorizations, and repressive binary frames of sexuality and gender constructions and race. Queer theory, for example, is founded on the principle that "identities" are not fixed or inflexible and are instead socially rather than biologically determined. Queer theorists have insisted that identities comprise many and varied components, and that it is inaccurate and misleading to collectively categorize people on the basis of one single element (e.g., as "lesbian," "gay," "bisexual," "heterosexual," or as "woman," "man," and others).

According to author and theorist Halperin (1997):

> Queer is by definition whatever is at odds with the normal, the legitimate, the dominant. *There is nothing in particular to which it necessarily refers*. It is an identity without an essence. "Queer" then, demarcates not a positivity but a positionality *vis-à-vis* the normative. (p. 62)

Wittig (1992), for example, asserts that the terms "woman" and "man" constitute *political* rather than eternal or essentialized categories. Preeminent scholar and social theorist Butler (1990) addressed what she refers to as the "performativity of gender" in which "gender" is basically an involuntary reiteration or reenactment of established norms of expression, an act that one performs as an actor performs a script that was created before the actor ever took the stage. The continued transmission of gender requires actors to play their roles so that they become actualized and reproduced in the guise of reality, and in the guise of the "natural" and the "normal."

> The act that one does, the act that one performs, is, in a sense, an act that has been going on before one arrived on the scene. Hence, gender is an act, which has been rehearsed, much as a script survives the particular actors who make use of it, but which requires individual actors in order to be actualized and reproduced as reality once again. (Butler, 1990. p. 272)

Several theorists argue that the notion of "gender" is a concept that is taught and learned and sustained in the service of maintaining positions of domination and subordination. Not only are the categories man/woman, heterosexual/homosexual and bisexual, and gender conforming/gender non-conforming binary frames inaccurate and constraining for the complexities and diversity of human bodies and lives, but they also leave no space for intersex people—the estimated one in 2000 people born with either indeterminate or combined male and female sexed bodies—and transgender people. In the case of gender, the binary imperatives lock all people into rigid gender-based roles that inhibit creativity and self-expression, and therefore, we all have a vested interest in challenging and eventually obliterating the binaries.

Transgender people are increasingly coming out of another closet in large numbers. Many include young people emerging from a new generation of activists who are on the cutting edge in the movement for equality and pride. They are making the links between transgender oppression, heterosexism, sexism, and other forms. The increased visibility and activism of transgender activists (including within popular media and academic discourse) has had the effect of shaking up traditionally dichotomous notions of male/female and gay/straight. They are creating a vision of social transformation as opposed to mere reform by contesting and exploding conventional gender constructions, most notably the limiting and destructive binary conceptualizations and definitions of "masculinity" and "femininity."

The American Psychiatric Association, in its DSM-V, the diagnosis of "gender identity disorder," which the manual imposed upon transgender people since it published DSM-III in 1980, changed to the designation, "gender dysphoria," which APA considers as a descriptive term rather than as diagnostic and pathologizing.

Throughout Judith Butler's (see, e.g., 1990, 1993, 1997, 2000, 2010) work, she explicates the performativity (a forced reiteration of norms) of gender. Yet even in an early work, however, she asks the question: "What other foundational categories of identity," which Butler sees as a stylized repetition and reiteration of acts, "can be shown as productions that create the effect of the natural, the original, and the inevitable?" (1990, p. viii). While focusing much attention on discursive constructions (processes of reiteration) and representations of "sex," Butler sees subjects as *multiply constituted*. Eliciting Friedrich Nietzsche's notion of there being no doer behind the deed, Butler claims that there is neither gender identity behind the expression of gender nor racial identity behind the expression of "race."

We are "gendered" at once from the time the physician announces, "it's a girl." Thus, according to Butler, "begins the long string of interpellations by which the girl is transitively *girled*" (1997, p. 49). Butler likewise, argues that the subject is "raced"—acted upon and constructed by racialized and racist speech.

> "Race" is partially produced as an effect of the history of racism, that its boundaries and meanings are constructed over time not only in the service of racism, but also in the service of the contestation of racism. (Butler, 1993, p. 20)

In addition to her discussions regarding the performativity of gender, she writes that "'race' might be construed as performative" (1993, p. 275, fn 4). According to Butler,

> [P]erformativity must be understood not as a singular or deliberate "act," but, rather, as the reiteration of a norm or set of norms and citational practice by which discourse produces the effects that it names. (p. 2)

The meaning of "race" is reiterated and regulated through an ongoing process, a racial history of being "acted upon."

> [W]e can see that institutional exercises repeatedly construct race within a set of differentials that seek to maintain and control racial separateness. This could also be described as part of the performativity of race. (Butler, in Breen & Blumenfeld, 2005, p. 11)

Butler considers "race" and also "gender" not as nouns but rather as verbs, and, therefore, as actions. Butler emphasizes that the power *to gender* as well as the power *to race* precedes the speaker. The speaker, nonetheless, appears to have this power.

In addition, Butler (1993) focuses on the concept of "matter" as signification. "Materiality," for Butler, "will be rethought as the effect of power—power's most productive effect" (1993, p. 2). She explores the body as discursive, insisting that there is no access to a pure materiality outside of language—that accessibility to anatomy always takes place in language through an "imaginary schema." She contends, therefore, that pure matter or anatomy can never be reached, that the body is always a "matter of signification" (p. 66).

"Race Passing"

What: Butler (1990, 1993) discusses a hegemonic cultural discourse that sets a binary framework of gender, and a binary framework of "race," that is "white" / "persons of color," that is constituted within a white-supremacist signifying economy. This racial binary frame not only demarcates "whites" from "people of color," but in effect differentiates whites as fully human from those who are less-than-human, or lower or less evolved developmentally. In this regard, the concept of "race passing"—attempting to be perceived by others as a "race" outside of one's "assigned race," in most instances, "passing" as "white"—is to pass *as* fully human. As Butler argues that there is no sexuality outside of power, likewise, there is no "race" or "racial" crossings outside of power as well. Can, then, "passing" be used as parodic repetition that troubles, disrupts, or subverts dominant interpolating ideologies of "race," and if so, how and under what circumstances?

In discussing the topic of "race passing," we can make a distinction between, on one hand, "passing" by endeavoring to avoid detection and bypass injustice, stigma, harassment, discriminatory actions, death, while still desiring to maintain some degree of interior identification with the "non-passing" self, "identity," and on the other hand, the transitional location of passing in an effort to *become* the other by relinquishing the past self and the past identification.

Schlossberg (2001) reminds us that we commonly denote terms of sight to signify concepts related to understanding, knowledge, and truth. On one hand, we use what could be considered as ablest terms such as, for example, "to have vision" or "to be a visionary," "to be perceptive," "insightful," "to have clear vision," "to have 20/20 vision or hindsight," and on the other hand such terminology as "to be shortsighted," "myopic," "to have no vision," "to be blind or blind to the truth," and so on. She asserts that in Western societies, identity is primarily "structured around a logic of visibility" (p. 1). In this regard, on the issue of "passing":

> Because of this seemingly intimate relationship between the visual and the known, passing becomes a highly charged site for anxieties regarding visibility, invisibility, classification, and social demarcation. (p. 1)

For Butler (1990, 2010), the performative of passing has the potential of counteracting the logic of visible markers, of removing corporeality, the phenotypically visible, from essentialist interpellations of "race." "Race passing" has a subversive *potential* by calling into question the efficacy of the binary frame by exciting racial anxieties concerning the very stability of "whiteness" and the indefinite boundaries separating "white" from "black," or separating "white" from "persons of color."

Jews and Jewishness

What: Charles Darwin, in his pioneering book *On the Origin of Species* published in 1859, posited an evolutionary theory of plant and animal development. Within his larger theory, he held that the physical, mental, and moral characteristics of the human species had evolved gradually over large expanses of time from our ape-like ancestors. Although Darwin himself did not assert this, some of Darwin's successors (some of whom were referred to as "Social Darwinists") extended his ideas to theorize that black Africans, Jews, and other groups (including homosexuals) were throwbacks to earlier stages of human development. They fostered a so-called "racial" hierarchy placing "Aryans" on the top end, black Africans at the lower end, and other "races" (including Jews) at various points in between (Greenberg, 1988; Gilman, 1991, 1993).

In 1853, the French writer de Gobineau (1853/1967) published his theories of a supposed "Aryan" race. He referred to "an original tribe" that resided in the Himalayas, which, he asserted, was the cradle of the Caucasian race. The French writer, Renan (1882/1996), stated that the [Jewish or] "Semitic" mind is superficial, while that of the "Aryan" is natural and wise. Later these theories would be expanded representing Jews as subhuman species, and as a symptom of racial impurity and decay. Darwin (1871/2009) believed that Jews have a "uniform appearance" independent of geographic location. So-called Social Darwinists extended Charles Darwin's theories to claim that Jews comprise much more than a separate religious, ethnic, or political group, but they, along with black Africans and homosexuals comprise a lower or earlier form of human species, and are, therefore, distinct "racial" types.

Francis Galton asserted that Jews are of a lower racial form, and that they could be easily recognizable in their bodies:

> Who has not heard people characterize such and such a man or woman they see in the streets as Jewish without in the least knowing anything about them? The street Arab who calls out "Jew" as some child hurries on to school is unconsciously giving the best and most disinterested proof that there is a reality in the Jewish expression. (Galton in Salaman, 1912, p. 190)

Marks (2002) emphasized that "[d]ividing human populations into a small number of discrete groups results in associations of populations and divisions between populations that are arbitrary, not natural" (pp. 65–66).

This supposed "racialization" of the Jews was codified in Grant's (1916) influential book, *The Passing of the Great Race*, in which he argued that Europeans comprised four distinct races. Sitting atop his racial hierarchy were the superior "Nordics" of northwestern Europe. Lower inferior races included the "Alpines" and the "Mediterraneans" of Southern and Eastern Europe. On the bottom were the most inferior—the Jews. Analogous to the notion in the United States that "one drop" of "black African" blood makes a person black, according to Grant: "the cross between any of the three European races and a Jew is a Jew."

In European society, according to social theorist and author Gilman (1991), Jews were interpellated as the "white Negroes" by the prevailing dominant discourses: "In the eyes of the non-Jew who defined them in Western [European] society the Jews became the blacks" (Gilman in Thandeka, 1999, p. 37). Thandeka adds that "the male Jew and the male African were conceived of as equivalent threats to the white race" (p. 37).

Although Jews are members of every so-called "race," the supposed "racial" characteristics of Jews were thought to be evident in their physiognomy. By the end of the 19th century CE, the popular image of the "Jewish type" (portrayed invariably as the Jewish male) consisted of a hooked nose with curling nasal folds, prominent thick lips, receding forehead and chin, large ears, curly black hair, dark "swarthy" skin, stooped shoulders, weak flat feet, deflated rump, and piercing bulbous eyes. In addition, the gaze of the Jew was said to be pathological, searing, cunning, cold, and piercing (Gilman, 1991, 1993). Jews are also stereotyped as having a heavy interest in money. Phrenologists (Phrenology: an offshoot of Eugenics) traced this interest to a specific, "abnormally" developed section of the "Jewish" or "Hebrew" brain.

Fearing a continued influx of immigrants, legislators in the United States Congress in 1924 enacted an anti-immigration law ("Origins Quota Act," or "National Origins Act") setting restrictive quotas of immigrants from Asia and Eastern Europe, including those of the so-called "Hebrew race." Jews continued to be, even in the United States during the 1920s, socially constructed as non-white. The 1924 law, on the other hand, permitted large allotments of immigrants from Great Britain, Ireland, and Germany. This law, in addition to previous statutes (1882 against the Chinese, 1908 against the Japanese) halted further immigration from Asia and excluded blacks of African descent from entering the United States. It is interesting to note that during this time, Jewish ethnic/racial assignment was constructed as "Asian":

> Jews were called Asiatic and Mongoloid, as well as "primitive, tribal, Oriental." Immigration laws were changed in 1924 in response to the influx of these undesirable "Asiatic elements." (Gilman, 1991, p. 117)

Thus, during the 1920s, a series of Jim Crow segregation laws were passed and rigidly enforced, because, as Lewis and Ardizzone (2001) contend, "Racially ambiguous Americans complicated and potentially threatened the logic of Jim Crow and the definition of race that underlay it" (p. 109). Jews, they posited, comprise a separate "race," one that is a "mixed" of "bastardized race" that crossed "racial" barriers by interbreeding with black Africans during the Jewish diaspora. Francis Galton claimed in a letter he sent to Swiss botanist Alphonse de Candolle in 1884 that "The Jews are specialized for a parasitical existence upon other nations" (Galton in Gilman, 1991, p. 456).

Jews were viewed as murderers of Christian children and seducers of Christian women. In 1144 began the so-called "Blood Libel" in England when Christian leaders accused Jews of slaying William of Norwich, a Christian male child, to use his blood in the making of the sacred Jewish *matzos*. Many Christians believed that Jews used the blood of Christian youth because it was virginal and innocent and, therefore, was the most potent medication to heal hemorrhoids, to relieve pain during circumcision, to increase fertility, and to cure the so-called "stink of the Jews."

Also, it was used to replenish the body after menstruation. Because Jewish men are circumcised, the belief was that they, therefore, were feminized males who themselves menstruated. The charge of ritual murder continued into the 20th century C.E. Christian clergy have also accused Jews of imposing circumcision on Christian infants as a means of inflicting involuntary conversion to Judaism ("recruitment").

So What?: The case of the supposed "racialization" of Ashkenazi (European-heritage) Jews demonstrates and challenges the falsehood of conceptualizing a bipolar or binary perspective of "race" whereby "white" people are placed on one side and "people of color" are placed on the other side. Rather, "race" and privilege are charted along a wide continuum considering time, context, and identity intersectionalities.

Disabilities

What: The concept of human "disabilities" is also socially constructed. During various historical eras and in several countries, people with disabilities suffered harsh and even deadly treatment:

> Historically, disability was perceived through a religious lens and considered an unchangeable condition that resulted from sin (Kaplan, 2000). In Western societies, infants with disabilities were dropped off balconies to their death; children with disabilities were abandoned and left to live on the streets where they had no choice but to beg for food and money to survive (Wood & Associates, 1998). The term *handicapped* emerged in England from people with disabilities who used their cap in hand on street corners to plead for money (Castañeda, Hopkins, & Peters, 2013, p. 462).

Several nations forced people with disabilities into prisons or institutional asylums under unimaginably harsh conditions. Sometimes their "handlers" paraded them out at paid "freak shows" for the entertainment of the public. By the middle to the end of the 19th and into the 20th century, the scientific community, which included leaders in the Eugenics movement, "medicalized" people with disabilities thereby further denying them the right of defining themselves or having power over their life decisions.

Francis Galton's work heavily impacted the development of mandatory involuntary sterilization laws in the U.S. and Germany on people considered "less suitable" for offspring (the so-called "feebleminded," those "prone to criminality," and the "mentally insane"). Though later legislative initiatives and some accommodations helped to guarantee some degree of civil protections, discrimination, however, remains prevalent toward people with disabilities.

Table 3.1. Lenses of Perception in Understanding the Social Construction of Disability and Issues of Ableism.

Medical Model	Wellness Model
Disability	Differently Abled
Disorder	Identity
Defect	Difference
Deficiency	Diversity
Condition	Variation
Abnormality	Normal for Us
Ailment	What's the Big Whoop?

The left side includes some of the lenses or filters of perception by which the medical profession and thereby the larger society have constructed people and entire communities whose physical, emotional, and/or mental abilities have differed from the socially established norm at any given point in time.

The right side includes some of the ways people and entire communities who vary from these socially established norms understand and define themselves as disability rights organizations and larger movements have gained strength and impact.

Sexual Identities

The histories of homosexuality and bisexuality are filled with incredible pain and enormous pride, of overwhelming repression and victorious rejoicing, of stifling invisibility and dazzling illumination. Throughout the ages, same-sex love and relationships and gender diversity have been called many things: from "sins," "sicknesses," and "crimes" to "orientations," "identities," and even "gifts from God."

Many historians believe that although same-sex attraction and behavior and gender diversity have probably always existed in human history, the concepts of sexual and gender identities in general and the construction of these identities and sense of community based on these is a relatively modern Western invention. A historic shift occurred in the early- to mid-19th century C.E., brought about by the growth of industrialization, competitive capitalism, and the rise of modern science, which provided people with more social and personal options outside the home (D'Emilio, 1993).

As more people moved away from their rural agricultural communities where survival depended upon large interdependent nuclear and extended family units, to the growing cities where individuals entered into employment founded on wage labor, they were given the opportunity to meet and relate with others who recognized their sexual and emotional desires for their own sex (D'Emilio, 1993). Only within the last 150 or so years has there existed an organized and sustained political effort to protect the rights of people with same-sex and all-sex attractions, and those who cross traditional constructions of gender expression of all backgrounds and ages.

Similarly, from the Eugenics movement some members of the scientific community viewed people attracted to their own sex as constituting a distinct biological or racial type—those who could be distinguished from "normal" people through anatomical markers. For example, Dr. G. Frank Lydston, U.S. urologist, surgeon, and Professor from Chicago, in 1889 delivered a lecture at the College of Physicians and Surgeons in Chicago in which he referred to homosexuals as "sexual perverts" who are "physically abnormal."

The U.S. medical doctor, Allan McLane Hamilton (1896), wrote in 1896 in a publication titled the *American Journal of Insanity* that "The [female homosexual] is usually of a masculine type, or if she presented none of the 'characteristics' of the male, was a subject of pelvic disorder, with scanty menstruation, and was more or less hysterical and insane" (p. 505). Physician, Perry M. Lichtenstein, who co-published *A Handbook of Psychiatry* in 1943, previously in 1921 wrote that: "A physical examination of [female homosexuals] will in practically every instance disclose an abnormally prominent clitoris." And he expressively added, "This is particularly so in colored women" (1921, p. 372).

In 1857 in France, Ambroise Tardieu wrote that: "This degeneracy is evidenced in men who engage in same-sex eroticism by their underdeveloped, tapered penis resembling that of a dog, and a naturally smooth anus lacking in radial folds" (1857, p. 236). The Swiss psychiatrist, August Forel, wrote that "the [sexual] excesses of female inverts [homosexuals] exceed those of the male" and that "this is their one thought night and day almost without interruption" (Forel, 1907, p. 252). He also claimed that male homosexuals "feel the need for passive submission" and "occupy themselves with feminine pursuits," while "nearly all [female and male] inverts are in a more or less marked degree psychopaths and neurotics" (pp. 243–244). And Dr. Havelock Ellis, by current standards in relative terms was one of the more "progressive" physicians who did not consider same-sex sexuality as a disease, in a 1902 article titled "Dr. Havelock Ellis on Sexual Inversion" [*inverting* the "normal" gender expectation] concluded that "Women's colleges are the great breeding ground of lesbianism. ... They learn the pleasure of direct contact ... and after this, the normal sex act fails to satisfy them" (in Shufeldt, 1902).

Karoly Maria Benkert, also known as Karl Maria Kertbeny, coined the terms "homosexual" and "heterosexual" in 1869 in Germany in his attempt to convince the religious, legal, and scientific communities that same-sex attractions, though not the norm, were widespread and therefore should not be legally penalized.

Although, in the overwhelming majority of cases, those who abuse and molest youth the most include close family members, primarily men who identify as heterosexual (Jenny, Roesler, & Poyer, 1994; Jacob Wetterling Resource Center), the cultural perception persists that they are primarily gay and bisexual men. For example, Focus on the Family, a conservative Christian media ministry organization, asserted in published accounts that gay rights advocates are forcing their viewpoints (their so-called "gay agenda") in schools in the guise of bullying prevention. Spokesperson, Candi Cushman, asserted that gay activists are the real schoolyard bullies while conservative Christians are the victims. According to Cushman,

> We feel more and more that activists are being deceptive in using anti-bullying rhetoric to introduce their viewpoints, while the viewpoint of Christian students and parents are increasingly belittled. (*Denver Post*, 2010)

The first *Diagnostic & Statistical Manual of Mental Disorders* (DSM-I) (the American Psychiatric Association-sponsored and endorsed handbook of mental disorders) published in 1952 listed homosexuality, for example, as "Sociopathic Personality Disorder." The "updated" 1968 DSM-II described homosexuality as "Sexual Orientation Disorder (SOD)."

The U.S. physician Irving Bieber co-authored a study in 1962, *Homosexuality: A Psychoanalytic Study of Male Homosexuals* sponsored by the New York Society of Psychoanalysts, in which he concluded that homosexuality constituted a psychopathology that could be cured or prevented with psychoanalysis. Bieber later said in an interview in the *New York Times*, Dec. 23, 1973: "A homosexual is a person whose heterosexual function is crippled, like the legs of a polio victim" (p. 109).

In addition, the psychiatrist Charles Socarides, another co-founder of NARTH, argued that homosexuality is an illness, a neurosis, possibly caused by an over-attachment to the mother, which he too argued could be treated. Bieber and Socarides became the "authoritative" and often-referenced researchers in causation and "treatment" of homosexuality.

(As a side note, Socarides' son Richard came out as gay and served as a White House counselor and principle advisor on LGBT rights to President Bill Clinton.)

By 1973, the American Psychiatric Association had finally changed its designation of homosexuality for those comfortable with their sexual orientation, now asserting that it does not constitute a disorder. Two years later, in 1975, the American Psychological Association followed suit and urged mental health professionals "to take the lead in removing the stigma of mental illness that has long been associated with homosexual orientations." It declared: "[H]omosexuality *per se* implies no impairment in judgment, stability, reliability, or general social or vocational capabilities" (adapted January 24–26, 1973).

· 4 ·
SOCIALIZATION

What: Tatum (1999) states that identity is shaped by several factors, including individual characteristics, family dynamics, historical factors, and social and political contexts. Everywhere a child is born—for example, Atlanta, New Guinea, Moscow, and Tokyo—all children undergo the process of socialization, which can be defined as the life-long process through which people acquire personality and learn the values, attitudes, norms, and societal expectations of their culture. Though the content varies from one culture to the next, the process of socialization is very similar. Through this process, people come to understand their culture, begin to develop a sense of who they are, and come to know what is expected of them in terms of their social role. While an acorn will inevitably become an oak tree, humans require socialization to realize their humanity. Cooley (1918) talks about the "looking glass self," whereby other people are the mirrors through which we see ourselves.

A social role is any pattern of behavior that an individual in a specific situation is encouraged to perform. The term comes from the language of the theater, being derived from the French role, referring to the "roll" of paper containing an actor's part. A role is not the same as the person who is performing it at the moment—just as the role of Macbeth has been played by countless actors over the centuries. Macbeth has certain characteristics, which, regardless of the particular actor who plays the part, enable the audience to recognize him as "Macbeth." Yet, as a stage role leaves some room for interpretation, so too most social roles involve general guidelines, but not precise behaviors.

Individuals play many different social roles. One can, for example, play the role of daughter, mother, student, friend, patient, and professional. Each of these roles has a set of expectations associated with it. The role of student, for example, involves coming to class on time, treating teachers respectfully, participating in class discussions, doing homework on time, and so forth. Our understanding of these expectations enables us to recognize "inappropriate" behavior.

Though we have the capacity to reflect on these roles, most of us do not even notice them. The roles represent our socialization. Actors receive their roles by the person in charge of casting, instructed by the director, and handed the part to memorize. In learning a social role, however, we have a variety of teachers and models.

When infants are born, they are very limited in their understanding of the ways of the world. For the young child, the most important agents of socialization are parents or guardians who consciously and unconsciously model certain behaviors while teaching all sorts of roles: "No dear, not like that, like this." As roles become more and more sophisticated, people may begin to learn them from others who are already performing them. For example, a first-year middle school student may "learn" how to be a middle school student from observing members of the senior class in the school.

When a young child enters school, teachers are not merely the transmitters of knowledge, but they also serve to continue and supplement the process of socialization. It is in these early years of school when the child learns many of the "rules" of behavior and becomes a social being to an even greater extent. Later, peer relationships play a more significant position in the socialization process.

> Social agents whose importance should not be underestimated are the media. From the television tube, the radio or iPod speakers, the movie screen, the pages of newspapers, books, and magazines, the internet, and billboards come the messages that help formulate or reinforce our attitudes and value systems. The media expose people to the latest concepts of style, beauty, morality, and social behavior. Other social institutes that reinforce the socialization process include the schools, religion, law, businesses, science, the government, and others. (Harro, 2013a)

People often learn their roles by playing complementary roles, which are then interdependent. Juliet, for example, learns to play her part by taking cues from Romeo, and vice versa. Social roles are similar; there cannot be parents without children, teachers without students, leaders without followers.

Our socialization begins before we are born, with no choice on our part. No one brings in a survey in the womb inquiring into which gender, class, religion, sexual orientation, cultural group, ability status, or age we might want to be born. These identities are ascribed to us at birth through no effort or decision or choice of our own; there is, therefore, no reason to blame each other or hold each other responsible for the identities we have. This first step in the socialization process is outside our control. In addition to having no choice, we also have no initial consciousness about who we are. We don't question our identities at this point. We just are who we are (Harro, 2013a, p. 47).

Urie Bronfenbrenner's Bioecological Model of Human Development

What: Developmental psychologist, Bronfenbrenner (1981), provides a Bioecological Model of Human Development, a systems model of human behavior composed of three major aspects:

1. The Mind or Human Personality involving Cognition (thinking, knowing, and understanding), Affect (attitudes, predisposition, emotions, and feelings), and Conation (volition, will, intentions to act, reason for doing). The mind receives information and it manifests actions through …
2. The Body: Biological or genetic influences bodily functioning of overt behavior or output. There is feedback between overt responses—behavior—and the resulting stimuli from the environment.
3. The Spirit: In addition to the biological component, the spiritual component influences the development and functioning of the components of the mind.

Bronfenbrenner theorizes that several interacting social contexts affect personal-social development, the Bio- (people bring their biological selves) Ecological (to social contexts, "ecosystems") in which they interact and influence others. These ecosystems comprise:

1. The Microsystem: The level that has the most immediate and earliest influence on the individual including family, friends, teachers, the local neighborhood, and community.
2. The Mesosystem: The intermediate level of influences including the set of interactions and relationships among all the elements of the microsystem: family members interact with each other or with teachers: the ways the teacher influences the parents or guardians, and the ways the parents or guardians influence the teacher. In addition, other social interactions are involved: media organizations, entertainment, transportation, and more.
3. The Exosystem: All the social settings that affect the individual, even though the individual is not a direct member of the system. Examples include teachers' relationship with administrators and the school board, parents' or guardians' employment, community resources regarding health, employment, recreation, religions and houses of worship.
4. The Macrosystem: The larger society, its values, laws, norms, traditions, history. The most removed influences on the individual include such things as international or global conditions like the paradigm shift from agricultural to industrial and information-age economies.

The Family as Early Socializing Institution

For infants and young children, the initial and most important agents of socialization include parents or guardians and other members within nuclear as well as extended families. When we discuss the units we call "the family"; however, we enter into a virtual battlefield of contested and opposing forces arguing for differing definitions and functions.

Drawn from sociological theory known as "functionalism" (or "structural functionalism"), this views each aspect of society as interdependent and contributing to a holistic functioning of society held together by social consensus. A proponent is Coser (1956) who defined "family" as:

> ... a group manifesting the following organizational attributes: It finds its origin in marriage; it consists of husband, wife, and children born in their wedlock, though other relatives may find their place close to it this nuclear group, and the group is united by moral, legal, religious and social rights and obligations (including sexual rights and prohibitions as well as such social patterned of love, attraction, piety, and awe). (p. xvi)

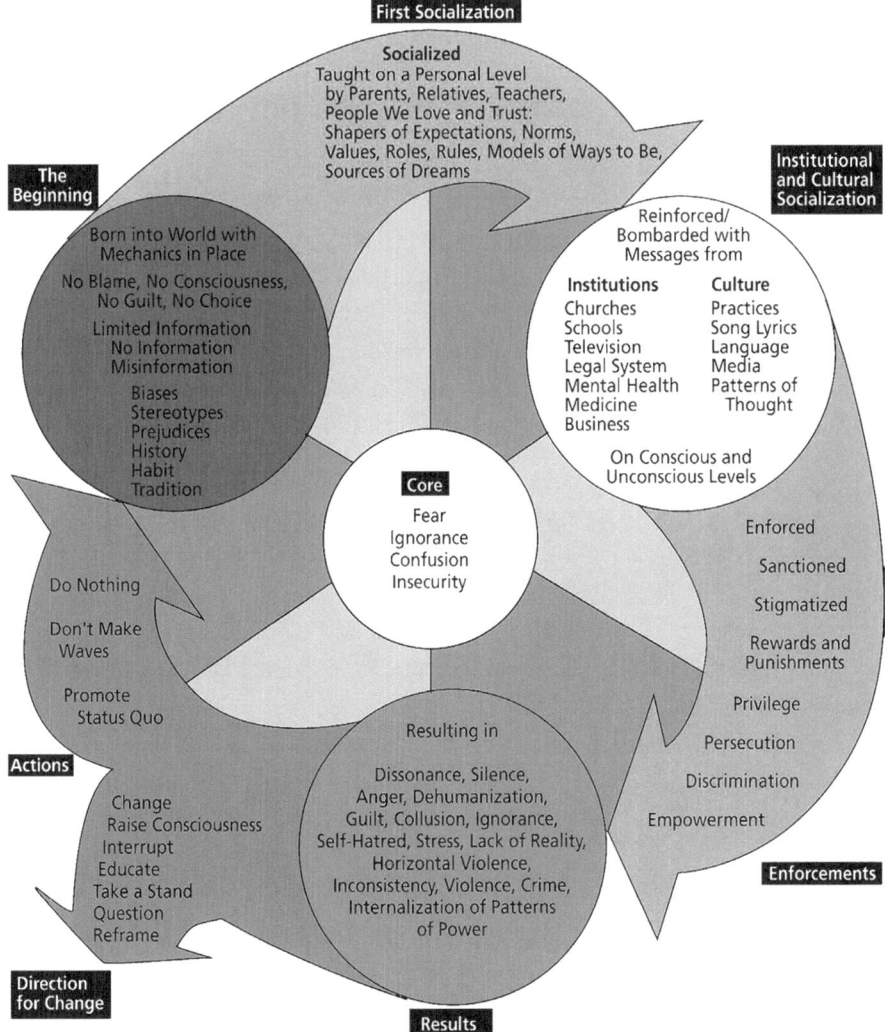

Figure 4.1. "Cycle of Socialization" by Bobbie Harro. Reproduced with permission.

Talcott Parsons, also a "functionalist," faults some in the claims for the universalization of the "nuclear family," which Parsons argues has not and is not always the case in all societies.

> From the perspective of Marxism, on the other hand, the family, by socializing the young in accepting and following authority and a hierarchal structure within the family unit, prepares their eventual acceptance of authority within the workplace. Families are expected to socialize their members into an appropriate set of

"family values" that simultaneously reinforce the hierarchy within the assumed unity of interests symbolized by the family and lay the foundation for many social hierarchies. In particular, hierarchies of gender, wealth, age, and sexuality within actual family units correlate with comparable hierarchies in U.S. society. (Collins, 1998, p. 64)

Whereas Functionalism views the socialization process as it works within the family unit as promoting conformity to desirable norms and values that enhance overall social stability, Marxism argues that the socialization process within the family (as well as within other social institutions such as schools, religion, the media) transmits "a ruling class ideology whereby individuals are deceived into accepting the capitalist system and the dominance of the capitalist class more or less without question" (Holborn & Steel, 2012).

Bobbie Harro's "Cycle of Socialization"

What: Harro (2013a) details the process by which individuals learn the overarching values regarding issues of domination and subordination of their societies in what she calls her "Cycle of Socialization." (In Part III, we introduce Harro's "Cycle of Liberation" (2013b).)

Bobbie Harro's model comprises six stages:

1. The Beginning
2. First Socialization
3. Institutional and Cultural Socialization
4. Enforcements
5. Results
6. Actions

A seventh component of Harro's model, "The Core," includes the individual's emotions, which serve to keep the cycle in place.

Harro's first stage, "The Beginning," discusses that in the womb even before the person is born, society ascribes a collection of identities that will eventually shape their dominant or subordinate statuses within existing systems of privilege and oppression. Since humans are born with no consciousness or self-awareness, they do not have an initial basis upon which to challenge or dispute the identities ascribed to them.

During First Socialization, Harro's second stage that happens as soon as we are born, humans are taught by their caretakers (i.e., immediate family, guardians) what roles they are expected to play, the rules they are expected to follow, and the norms to which they are expected to adhere. This happens on two levels, the intrapersonal level, which refers to how humans think about themselves, and the interpersonal level, which refers to how humans relate to others. At this stage, members of subordinate groups are initially taught what it means to be members of those groups, which reflects the hegemony of the larger dominant culture. Although this may result in them learning and accepting their subordinate social roles, this is not always the case, especially when the individual's initial caretakers have critically reflected on and consciously challenged the dominant ideology. (For example, Hindu families maintaining and teaching about the values and cultural heritage of their religious traditions.)

During Stage three, Institutional and Cultural Socialization, the bases of socialization broaden to include the institutions and cultural contexts by which people are surrounded. Harro states:

> The media (television, the Internet, advertising, newspaper and radio), our language patterns, the lyrics to songs, our cultural practices and holidays, and the very assumptions on which our society is built all contribute to the reinforcement of the biased messages and stereotypes we receive. (p. 48)

At this stage, Harro asserts that the opportunities for transmission or contradiction of oppressive messages arises more frequently from increasingly numerous places, and that these oppressive messages are "woven into every structural thread of the fabric of our culture" (p. 48). Members of subordinate groups are, therefore, surrounded and immersed within an atmosphere that consistently reflects and reinforces their subordinate status.

Harro's fourth stage in the Cycle of Socialization, Enforcements, comprise all the rewards and/or punishments that confirm members of subordinate groups to follow prearranged roles in oppressive systems. Members of subordinate groups who observe their roles and follow the status quo are thus rewarded for abiding. For example, people who accept and behave according to their given gender scripts are accorded more benefits and privileges by society and are considered as "normal." On the other hand, members of subordinate groups who somehow contest their prescribed gender roles or refuse to obey the status quo are summarily punished, sometimes subjected to violence, and even murdered.

Harro's fifth stage, Results, explains the outcomes of the socialization process. Harro states:

> By participating in our roles as targets, we reinforce stereotypes, collude in our own demise and perpetuate the system of oppression. This learned helplessness is often called internalized oppression because we have learned to become our own oppressors from within. (p. 49)

At this stage of the socialization process, society teaches and enforces members of subordinate groups to more completely internalize their oppression within overarching systems of oppression. Harro labels specific behaviors and emotions including anger, low self-esteem, guilt, hopelessness, and self-destructive behaviors.

In the final stage of the Cycle of Socialization, Actions, people make decisions, sometimes unconsciously, regarding which way to go with the results of their socialization process. Harro views the options as twofold: Either choose a direction for change or accept and eventually maintain and perpetuate the cycle. Harro states:

> We fail to realize that we have become participants just by doing nothing. This cycle has a life of its own. It doesn't need our active support because it has its own centrifugal force. It goes on and unless we choose to interrupt it, it will continue to go on. (p. 50)

Indoctrination and Surveillance

So What: The family, by socializing the young to accept and follow authority and the hierarchal structure within the family unit, prepares the individual's eventual acceptance of authority within the workplace and within the social order. Hierarchies in terms of wealth, race, culture, ethnicity, gender, and other social identities in the workplace parallel equivalent hierarchies within society at large.

The socialization process within the family (as well as within other social institutions such as schools, religion, the media, and others) transmits "a ruling class ideology" (Hamadi, 2007) in which people become deceived into agreeing to the capitalist system and the dominance of the capitalist class without questioning that system.

Engels (1884) saw how economic developments encouraging the accumulation of private property required the fortification of the monogamous family to guarantee that men's property would be inherited by their biological heirs. Engels represented one of the first to argue that women's subordination was not the result of any biological dispositions, but rather, caused by the efforts of men to attain their demands for controlling women's labor and their sexual faculties, which have over time become solidified and institutionalized in the nuclear family.

Foucault's (1975) concept of "Panopticon" (in Greek mythology, the monster with 100 eyes) helps us to understand the function and effectiveness of regulatory surveillance first initiated through the "parental gaze," and reinforced by official social actors such as police officers. Foucault took the term from the structure of institutional buildings such as prisons first designed by philosopher Jeremy Bentham. Cells within these prisons radiate from a central watch station permitting a single guard to observe all inmates (though not simultaneously), without these inmates having the ability to see the guard or to know exactly when this observer gazes upon them. This arrangement effectively forces inmates to assume that the watchperson inside the station is constantly watching them. The Panopticon metaphor represents the omnipresent nature of being watched and monitored by society.

Foucault maintains that all socially constructed hierarchal systems demand forms of surveillance, whether actual or imaginary, to preserve dominant and subordinate positions according to those upholding authority or power. Surveillance maintains and extends power by exercising subtle, often imperceptible, as well as not-so-subtle signs and warnings that one is being watched. Through Panopticon, people conduct themselves in ways that anticipate negative consequences from those they perceive as having authority over them.

· 5 ·
BINARIES

Binaries Defined

What: The human brain, through millennia of its evolutionary process, has developed a capacity to categorize reality into easily digestible morsels in its attempt to absorb and make sense of a complex world. We have seen the perennial theme, for example, of Good versus Evil surface throughout the human condition as far back as over 3000 years in Zoroastrianism as valued by Zarathustra, and the theme has reappeared in literary and religious discourses ever since. In some monotheistic religions, within the overarching theme of dualism, for example, God is good, while the Devil is bad; the "right" side (the side of God) is good, while the "left" side (the side of the Devil) is bad; and white is good, while black is bad.

Philosopher and exponent of "objectivism," Ayn Rand, described anyone who does not view issues upon a binary frame, but rather perceives a continuum with its nuances, as "evil." According to Rand's (1957) hero John Galt in her novel *Atlas Shrugged*:

> There are two sides to every issue: one side is right and the other is wrong, but the middle is always evil. The man who is wrong still retains some respect for truth, if only by accepting the responsibility of choice. But the man in the middle is the knave who blanks out the truth in order to pretend that no choice or values exist, who is

willing to sit out the course of any battle, willing to cash in on the blood of the innocent or to crawl on his belly to the guilty, who dispenses justice by condemning both the robber and the robbed to jail, who solves conflicts by ordering the thinker and the fool to meet each other halfway. In any compromise between food and poison, it is only death that can win. In any compromise between good and evil, it is only evil that can profit. (p. 1054)

So What: So, let us consider the implications, the inevitable extensions, of a binary/dualistic/objectivist world perspective in which one side is good, one side is bad, and the middle is evil, in which the following could be constructed as "evil": people of mixed or multiple so-called "races"; intersex people; transgender people, gender fluid people; bisexual and pansexual people; people who do not have a hand preference ("*ambidextrous*" literally meaning "having two or multiple *right* hands"); people following no religious faiths, which, by the way, included Ayn Rand herself.

Unfortunately, this good/bad/evil worldview stands much more than a mere philosophical exercise, but it has real-life, and often tragic, consequences. The natural world has never conformed to our human notions of only "two sides" to everything. Nature shows many hues and forms along a seemingly endless continuum or spectrum, where white and black function amazingly in company with wide-ranging tones of grey; where polychrome rainbows of infinite colors excite the Earth and the entire universe; where some animals, including coral reef fishes, come into the world as one sex and change to another in the course of their lives; where the determinant of behavior resides within individuals' inner sense rather than on socially predetermined scripts.

The socially constructed binary and hierarchical views within a Western cosmology represent a major connecting factor within the varying forms of oppression. The socially constructed "races" of "white" is seen as good, "people of color" as bad, and "light" as good or adroit (whose root comes from *droit*, in French meaning "right") and "dark" as bad and sinister (*sinister* comes from Latin for "left"); "male" depicted as leader and good, "female" as subservient and inferior; "heterosexual" as good, "homosexual" as bad, and "heterosexual" perceived as love and "homosexual" as sex; "Christian" considered good in a Western context, "non-Christian" judged bad; "rich" as good and virtuous, "poor" as bad and lazy; people of, say, 21 to about 50 as good and in their "prime" versus under 21 as irresponsible and untrustworthy and elders as "over the hill" and "no longer sexual" or "valuable"; "able bodied" as good, "people with disabilities" as unfortunate, once also seen as punished by the Devil for past transgressions, possibly in a former life; and I could go on in this vein virtually forever.

We have seen the many and severe consequence of bifurcated world views, where historically governmental and religious authorities have literally killed people for stepping out of their prescribed roles (e.g., Joan of Arc for transgressing her assigned gender expression, and left-handed people whom the Church viewed as Devil-inspired); where parents and doctors physically mutilated intersex infants in their misguided attempts to "fix" them into one "side" or the "other" into a gender binary; where doctors and family members involuntarily committed lesbian, gay, bisexual, and transgender people to psychiatric wards, forced "hormone" treatments, electroshock therapy, and even frontal lobotomies.

In many quarters of our society, we still hear individuals loudly proclaim that compromise (a middle perspective) equals surrender, which in the real world has resulted in a freezing or even reversing of political, economic, and social advancements; where "my way or the highway" has set the stage for war and other human tragedies; where my belief system is right and your belief system is wrong, and, therefore, I have the "right" to impose my system onto you and upon your country in the form of colonialism, land and property theft, slavery, forced religious conversion, territorial expulsion, rape, and murder.

Binaries: Polytheism and Monotheism

> … Then that little man in black there, he says women can't have as much rights as men, 'cause Christ wasn't a woman! Where did your Christ come from? Where did your Christ come from? From God and a woman! Man had nothing to do with Him.
>
> —Sojourner Truth, "Ain't I A Woman?" speech, 1851

What: Many ancient and non-Western cultures—including, for example, Hinduism, most Native American, Mayan, and Incan cultures—base their religions on polytheism (multiple deities). In general, these religious views seem to attribute similar characteristics to their gods. Particularly significant is the belief that the gods are created, and they age, give birth, and engage in sex. Some of these gods even have sexual relations with mortals. The universe is seen as continuous, ever-changing, and *fluid*. These religious views often lack rigid categories, particularly gender categories, which become mixed and often ambiguous and blurred. For example, some male gods give birth, while some female gods possess considerable power.

Figure 5.1. The Androgynous Form of Shiva and Parvati (Ardhanarishvara). India, Rajasthan, 11th century, Sculpture Black schist, Ancient Art Council and the Indian Art Special Purpose Fund, Los Angeles County Museum of Art (LACMA).

Hindu example of deity transcending gender norms and manifesting multiple combinations of sex and gender.

In contrast, monotheistic Abrahamic (Judaism, Christianity, Islam) religions view the Supreme Being as without origin, for this deity was never born and will never die. This Being, viewed as perfect, exists completely independently from humans and transcends the natural world. In part, such a Being has no sexual desire, for sexual desire, as a kind of need, is incompatible with this concept of perfection. This accounts for the strict separation between the Creator and the created. Just as the Creator is distinct from *His* creation, so too are divisions between the Earthly sexes in the form of strictly defined genders and gender roles. This distinction provides adherents to monotheistic religions a clear sense of their designated *socially constructed* roles: the guidelines they need to follow in connection with their God and to other human beings.

So What: In San Francisco Roman Catholic Archbishop Cordileone's (2015) statements, he asserted: "When the culture can no longer apprehend those natural truths, then the very foundation of our teaching evaporates and nothing we have to offer will make sense." Cordileone concluded that the inevitable result "is a reversion to the paganism of old, but with unique, postmodern variations on its themes, such as the practice of child sacrifice, the worship of feminine deities, or the cult of priestesses" (n.p.).

Now What: Women's equality, lesbian, gay, and bisexual equality, transgender equality, and equality of people of color all challenge the hierarchal binary structure entrenched within patriarchal and white supremacist systems of domination because when people fight for and achieve the right to control their bodies, this in turn better guarantees them the freedom to control their own minds.

Stigma

What: Officials in 17th-century C.E. Puritan Boston coerced Hester Prynne, of Nathanial Hawthorn's classic novel *The Scarlet Letter* (1850) into permanently affixing the stigma of the scarlet letter onto her garments to forever socially castigate her for her so-called "crime" of conceiving a daughter in an adulterous affair. Stigmata include symbols, piercings, brands, or special clothing used throughout recorded history to mark an outsider, offender, outcast, the enslaved, or animal.

Though Nathaniel Hawthorne's novel is a work of fiction, members of several minoritized communities continue to suffer the sting of metaphoric stigmata forced onto their skin, birth sex, sexual and gender identities and expressions, religious beliefs and affiliations, countries of origin and linguistic backgrounds, (dis)abilities, ages, and so on.

So What: Stigmatized groups live with the constant fear of random and unprovoked systematic violence directed against them simply because their social identities. The intent of this xenophobic (fear and hatred of anyone of anything seeming "foreign") violence is to harm, humiliate, and destroy the "other" for the purpose of maintaining hierarchical power dynamics and attendant privileges of the dominant group over minoritized groups.

Terrorism and Violence

What: Terrorism has been described generally as the use of violence, or the threat of violence, to accomplish a political, religious, or ideological purpose (Fortna, 2015).

There is a long-standing tradition in the western part of the United States of ranchers killing a coyote and tying it to a fence to scare off other coyotes, and to keep them from coming out of their hiding places. That's what Matthew Shepard's killers did to him in 1998. They smashed his skull and tied him to a fence as if he were a lifeless scarecrow, where he was bound for over 18 hours in near-freezing temperatures. The message to the rest of us in the LGBTQ community from these killers was quite clear: stay locked away in your suffocating and dank closets, and don't ever come out.

Well, in his brief time with us, Matthew Shepard also changed lives. His caring soul transformed the people he met. Though his attackers may have succeeded in devastating his body, they did not and will never succeed in destroying his gentle spirit, or in extinguishing the heart of a community and a movement for social justice, for Matthew's spirit continues, inspiring a people, a nation, a world. We can take solace in the words of Judy Shepard, Matt's mother, when she told us at his memorial service: "Go home, give your kid a hug, and don't let a day go by without telling them you love them."

The World Health Organization defines violence rather broadly as:

> … the intentional use of physical force or power threatened or actual, against oneself, another person, or against a group or community, which either results in or has a high likelihood of resulting in injury, death, psychological harm, maldevelopment, or deprivation. (2013, n.p.)

"Power" in this sense can situate itself on physical power, but it can also include the power of dominant authority figures and social institutions to impose physical as well as emotional and even coercive power onto individuals and groups of lower social rank, the "psychological harm, maldevelopment, or deprivation."

Bullying and Cyberbullying

Ross (2002) defines bullying as a form of terrorism since it involves an "unprovoked attack" upon another person or persons with the intention of causing harm. While bullying and harassment have long been problems for young people in our nation's schools at every level, advanced information and communication technologies bypass, filter, and thus mitigate social cues that act in ways to constrain bullying. At the same time, these information and communication technologies extend abusive and destructive bullying practices to virtually all aspects of a person's life. Thus, cyberbullying takes bullying to a more destructive and protracted level.

The American Psychological Association passed a resolution (2004) calling on educational, governmental, business, and funding agencies to address issues of face-to-face and cyberbullying. In the resolution, they particularly addressed acts of harassment "about race, ethnicity, religion, disability, sexual orientation, and gender identity" (p. 1).

Young people and even adults continue to endure schoolyard and workplace bullying and harassment. Bullying—also termed "face-to-face" ("f2f"), "real life" ("RL,"), "traditional," "in-person," or "offline" bullying—involves deliberate and repeated aggressive and hostile behaviors by an individual or group of individuals intended to humiliate, harm, and/or control another individual or group of individuals of lesser power or social status (JAMA, 2001). Bullying is a specific type of aggression in which (1) the behavior is intended to harm or disturb, (2) the behavior occurs repeatedly over time, and (3) there is an imbalance of power, with a more powerful person or group attacking a less powerful one (Garret, 2003; Orpinas & Horne, 2006; Ybarra & Mitchell, 2004). This asymmetry of power may be physical or psychological, and the aggressive behavior may be verbal (e.g., name calling, threats, taunting, malicious teasing), physical (e.g., hitting, kicking, spitting, pushing, taking personal belongings), or psychological (e.g., spreading rumors, engaging in social exclusion, extortion, or intimidation). In our era of advanced information and social communication technologies, however, a new variation has emerged, for we now live in the age of cyberbullying.

Cyberbullying occurs over information and social communication technologies such as Internet websites, e-mail, chat rooms, mobile phone and text messaging, and instant messaging, and includes instances such as: (1) people sending hurtful, cruel, and oftentimes intimidating messages to others (e.g., "Flame Mail") designed to inflame, insight, or enrage; (2) "Hate Mail" (also known as "Cyberharassment"), which constitutes hate-inspired and oppressive harassment based on actual or perceived social identities in terms of race, ethnicity, religion, sex, gender, sexuality, physical and mental abilities, socioeconomic class, and others; (3) people stealing other peoples' screen names and sending inflammatory messages under those screen names to others; (4) anonymous postings of derogatory comments about another on web journals called "blogs" or on Facebook or Twitter; (5) young people creating online polling booths, for example, to rate girls and boys as the "hottest," "ugliest," "most boring," "biggest dyke," or "wimpiest fag" in the school; (6) individuals taking pictures of others in gymnasium locker rooms with digital phone cameras and sending those pictures to others, or posting them on Internet websites (a form of "sexting"); (7) people creating websites with stories, cartoons, caricatures, pictures, or "jokes" ridiculing or mocking others; (8) posting material about a person involving private, sensitive, or embarrassing information, for example, "outing" a person's sexual identity to classmates and sometimes to the targets' parents or guardians; (9) sending intimidating or threatening messages (also known as "Cyberstalking"); (10) intentional interruption and harassment on gaming websites (so-called "Griefing") causing grief to website players; or (11) actions designed to isolate and exclude a person from online social communication technologies.

The Psychology and Sociology of Cyberspace

Psychology and sociology, as ever-expanding fields, have connected and redeployed their theories and concepts of human behavior to the virtual realities of cyberspace. What follows includes some of the theoretical foundations that may hold promise in addressing abuse of human–computer interactions.

The "Online Disinhibition Effect"

Several similarities and differences exist between face-to-face (f2f) or real life (RL) bullying and cyberbullying. Both are about human relationships, power, and control, and actions can occur on numerous occasions. Also, both may involve what psychologists call the "leveling effect": people who cyberbully often do so to diminish others to inflate their own egos reflecting their insecurities. In addition, both do not simply involve those who abuse and those who are abused (the "dyadic view") but rather involve a number of "actors" or roles in polyadic relationships across the social/workplace/school environment (see, e.g., Sutton & Smith, 1999).

The very nature of social communication technologies, however, establish the conditions that make it possible for users to perform and act in cyberspace in ways they would not ordinarily act in f2f interactions. Suler (2001) proposes a conceptual framework enumerating many basic psychological features when taken individually and in differing synergistic combinations within various online environments, help to explain how people experience themselves and others. Taken together, these elements explain what Suler (2001) terms the "online disinhibition effect": the nature of social communication technologies combined with the relative anonymity of cyberspace creates the conditions for users to experience less behavioral inhibitions than in RL f2f situations.

The online disinhibition effect can manifest itself in positive as well as negative ways. For example, through the anonymity of cyberspace, users can exhibit extraordinary acts of kindness or charity that they may have felt *inhibited* from expressing in RL. Suler describes this as "benign disinhibition." For example, an individual can initiate a kind or charitable action pulling in a seemingly endless number of others from distances great and near anonymously that if identified might make the benefactor or the recipient uncomfortable. On the other hand, this anonymity and altered psychological environment may allow users to communicate more objectionable needs and desires onto others, Suler's expression of "toxic disinhibition."

Cyberbullying is a particularly cowardly form of abuse. Social communication technologies permit people who engage in cyberabuse to hide in the anonymity of cyberspace. With anonymity, those who cyberabuse do not have to "own" their actions, and they often do not fear being punished. The technology can also shelter the user from tangible feedback about consequences of one's actions, which can result in minimized empathy or remorse for the target of the bullying (Media Awareness Network). In cyberspace, according to Suler, the user experiences reduced or filtered sensual input, often unable to see or hear the person or people on the other end: no facial expressions signaling emotional output, no ability to see or read body language or hear voice intonations. This is particularly evident in print e-communications: texting, instant messaging, website blogs, email, chat rooms, social media like Facebook, and others. Even when employing audio and visual means of communication such as videoconferencing, podcasting, and Internet phoning, much of the sensory input remains limited at best. Therefore, people who engage in cyberbullying can inflict pain without having to see the effects, which can result in a "deeper level of meanness" (Harmon, 2004). In addition, people who cyberbully can also communicate their hurtful messages to a wider audience (even thousands of people simultaneously near and far) with incredible speed.

Much of cybertime exists asynchronously (Turkle, 1995), that is, people often do not have to interact in real time, which can add to the disinhibition effect when one does not have to deal with the immediate reactions of others. Cyberspace also transcends distance by virtually shrinking space making geography irrelevant. This feature has advantages and disadvantages. It can bring people closer together, but for those with anti-social motives, the nature of social communication technologies can enable the user to abuse others not only next door, but also clear on the other side of the planet.

Freud Peering from the Computer

What?: The concept of "transference" (as introduced by Sigmund Freud, 1912) refers to an individual's unconscious redirection of feelings from one person to another. Kapelovitz (1987) defines transference as "the inappropriate repetition in the present of a relationship that was important in a person's childhood" (p. 66). Taking this concept into the realm of social communication technology interactions, Suler (2005) makes clear that though the technology is certainly not a past or current member of our human family, "… but rather we recreate in our relationship with the computer some aspect of how we related to our family members" (p. 2). Often, and primarily on an unconscious level, the very nature of the information and social communication technologies provide the (cyber)space for individuals to recreate and replay past relationships, and also to satisfy unmet, frozen, or thwarted needs from childhood. In addition, Suler discusses the notion of "erotic transference," which he makes clear does not consist of sexual feeling *per se* toward computers, "… but rather the perception of the computer as powerful, perhaps in ways similar to how parents are perceived as powerful" (p. 4). Related to cyberbullying, social communication technologies provide the users the means to act out unmet needs for power and control over others, or to transfer frozen needs for attention or acknowledgement not sufficiently satisfied within the family constellation.

Marshall Brain and Wesley Fenlon (n.d.) theorize that perpetrators of computer-generated abuse, and, the production and transmission of computer viruses, do so for a number of psychological motivations. Some may transmit viruses simply for the emotional "rush" or thrill, much the same way as would an individual who vandalizes or intentionally sets destructive fires. In addition, creating and transmitting a computer virus works much the same as an explosion for someone who finds joy in watching cars crash or bombs explode. Another reason is simply finding adventure in and claiming bragging rights for exploiting security holes in computer systems before someone else beat them to it.

The same emotional thrill and sense of adventure can result for perpetrators of cyberbullying, possibly to the same degree as those fashioning and disseminating explosive computer viruses. By posting a hurtful or threatening message through social communication technologies, the perpetrator places an emotional bomb on an unsuspecting potential victim.

Social communication technology users now have the potential to cyberbully any time and to any place. Home, therefore, is no longer a refuge from this abuse. Although perpetrators of cyberbullying often do so outside the parameters of the school grounds or workplace, it invariably affects the overall school and workplace climate and environment, and the individuals' educational or work performance, as well as their short- and long-term psychological states. Policies and legislation have not always caught up with cyberabuse, for it is often outside the legal reach of workplaces, schools, and school boards when it occurs outside the workplace site or off school grounds.

Cyberbullying and face-to-face bullying are similar in that both are associated with higher rates of mental health problems. Low self-esteem, feeling of loneliness, depression (e.g., Rigby, 2002); suicidal ideation, and anxiety disorders (Bond, Carlin, Thomas, Rubin, & Patton, 2001; Kim, Koh & Leventhal, 2005; La Greca & Harrison, 2005; Prinstein, Boergers, & Vernberg, 2001; Swearer, Grills, Haye, & Cary, 2004) have been shown to be some of the most common mental health outcomes related to being the target of abusive behaviors. These targets may also experience increased school and workplace absenteeism (Owens, Shute, & Slee, 2000) and they often find it difficult to concentrate on schoolwork (McClure & Shirataki, 1989). Studies report that between 5% and 10% of students stayed at home to avoid being bullied (Rigby & Slee, 1999; Smith et al., 1999). Also, a study, conducted by Education Statistics Services Institute found that student targets of bullying were more likely to receive lower grades than their non-bullied counterparts.

Targets of both direct and indirect bullying were more likely to receive mostly Ds and Fs than those bullied either directly only or indirectly only (DeVoe, Kaffenberger, & Chandler, 2005). "Indirect bullying" includes actions such as social isolation, spreading rumors, and others.

So What?: Overall, related to those who have suffered as the targets of bullying and cyberbully, in some cases, students have turned into the perpetrators of school violence. For example, this was indeed the case in 75% of school shootings during the 1990s and early 2000s (Pescara-Kovach, 2006). In addition, students who were bullied at least once a week experienced poorer health. Garrett (2003) provides a comprehensive list of symptoms and disorders, including constant high levels of stress and anxiety; frequent viral infections, aches and pains in the joints and muscles with no obvious cause; also back pain with no obvious cause, which will not go away or respond to treatment; headaches and migraines; tiredness, exhaustion, constant fatigue; insomnia; poor concentration; and other symptoms. Face-to-face bullying and cyberbullying can also lead to suicidal ideation, attempts, and completion as noted earlier.

With all of this considered, it becomes clearer that cyberspace can also inhibit a user's sense of responsibility for actions online. Researchers (e.g., Staub, 1978 in Harrington, 1995) suggest that denial of responsibility (RD) can be seen as an enduring human trait measured along a wide continuum from high to low. Those low in RD tend to accept responsibility for their actions, while those closer to the high side of the scale tend to deny responsibility, tend not to be responsible for the well-being of others, and are likely not to follow societal or personal rules. BloomBecker (1990 in Harrington, 1995), who has investigated computer-related crimes, found that this denial of responsibility is a major factor leading to computer abuse. For example, BloomBecker profiled Robert Morris, a graduate student who lacked a sense of responsibility (high RD), though he was raised in a family where considerable attention focused on his moral development. Morris, who methodically infected a large number of computers with his Internet worm, when discovered and apprehended, rationalized his actions as being beneficial in that he contributed to the identification of weaknesses in the nation's computer networks and systems. He justified his actions as providing a valuable service.

In a study of cyberbullying (Blumenfeld & Cooper, 2010), a perpetrator, when identified and asked why he sent abusive messages to others online retorted, for example, "I was only telling the truth. She is ugly, and I felt she had to know it!" (from unpublished transcripts). His rationalization—denial of responsibility—centers on offering the target of his abuse supposed needed and useful "information."

Scapegoating

What: The origin of the scapegoat dates to the Book of Leviticus in the Hebrew Bible (16:20–22). On the Day of Atonement, a live goat was selected by lottery. The high priest placed both hands on the goat's head and confessed over it the sins of the people. In this way, the sins were symbolically transferred to the animal, which was then cast out into the wilderness. This process thus purged the people, for a time, of their feelings of guilt (Blumenfeld & Raymond, 1993). A crucial point in the psychology of scapegoating is the representation of minoritized "others" as violent predators resolved to ensnare, torture, and devour primarily women and children of the dominant group. And when demagogues play on people's fears and prejudices by invoking these images for their own political, social, and economic gains, the result in more instances than not amounts to loss of civil and human rights, harassment, violence, and at times, death of the "other."

Researchers have proposed several conditions necessary for specific people or groups to be singled out as scapegoats in contemporary society:

- Prejudice and stereotyping must already exist against the particular group(s) before the scapegoating commences (Saenger, 1953).
- The group(s) in question must appear to be too weak to fight back successfully when attacked (Saenger).
- The society must sanction the scapegoating through its own institutional structures (Saenger).
- Such groups must be visible and easily distinguished from the ingroup (Young, 1932).
- Outgroups perceived as most frustrating will be more hated by the ingroup (LeVine & Campbell, 1972).
- The nearer the outgroups in terms of having the *opportunity* to frustrate, the more hated they will be (LeVine & Campbell).
- The stronger outgroup, in terms of having more *capacity* to frustrate, will be more hated (LeVine & Campbell).
- The outgroup on which aggression and hostility has most recently and severely been carried out will be more hated (LeVine & Campbell).
- Those outgroups that are intermediate in similarity to the ingroup sources of frustration will be the most likely target of aggression (LeVine & Campbell).

· 6 ·

OPPRESSION

Oppression Defined

What: "Oppression," a noun, means "the unjust or cruel exercise of authority or power," coined sometime in the 14th century, CE. (Merriam-Webster). For Bell (2007), "The term oppression encapsulates the fusion of institutional and systematic discrimination, personal bias, bigotry, and social prejudice in a complex web of relationships and structures that shade most aspects of life in our society" (p. 3).

The concept of oppression, however, constitutes more than only the cruel and repressive actions of individuals upon others. It involves an overarching *system* of differentials of social power and privilege by dominant groups over subordinated groups based on ascribed social identities and reinforced by unequal social group status. And this is not merely the case in societies ruled by coercive or tyrannical leaders, but it occurs as well within the day-to-day practices of contemporary democratic societies (Young, 1990).

For example, Tocqueville, French political scientist and diplomat, traveled across the United States for nine months between 1831 and 1832 conducting research for his epic work, *Democracy in America* (1835). He was astounded to find a certain paradox: on one hand, he observed that the

United States promoted itself around the world as a country where freedom and tolerance were among its defining tenets, but on the other hand, he witnessed a certain intolerance against those with minority beliefs or identities. Though he favored U.S.-style democracy, he found its major limitation to be in its stifling of independent thought and independent beliefs. In a country that promoted the notion that the majority rules, this effectively silenced minorities by what Tocqueville termed the "tyranny of the majority." This is a crucial point because in a democracy, without specific safeguards for minority rights, there is a danger of domination or tyranny over minoritized groups and individuals.

Hegemony

What: The concept of "hegemony" (Gramsci, 1971/written between 1929 and 1935) describes the ways in which the dominant group successfully disseminates dominant social realities and social visions in a manner accepted as common sense, as "normal," as universal, and as representing part of the natural order, even at times by those who are marginalized, disempowered, or rendered invisible by it (Tong, 1989). Hegemony maintains the marginality of already marginalized communities. Dominant groups, by establishing and maintaining higher degrees of social power, are therefore able to project and transmit *their* beliefs, values, and perspectives (through hegemonic discourses) thereby rendering subordinated groups virtually invisible while simultaneously constructing stereotypes about these groups.

What: Hegemony is advanced through "discourses" (Foucault, 1980), which include the ideas, written expressions, theoretical foundations, and language of the dominant culture. These are implanted within networks of social and political control, described by Foucault as "regimes of truth" (p. 133), which function to legitimize what can be said, who has the authority to speak and be heard, and what is authorized as true or as the truth (Kreisberg, 1992, in Bell, 2007).

Colonization

What: In this regard, the verb "to colonize" can be described as the process of appropriating a place or domain to establish political and economic control. Throughout history, nations have invaded not only their neighbors' lands, but also territories clear across the globe for their own use. During the practice, the dominant nation attempts to colonize not only indigenous peoples' domains (territorial imperialism), but also their minds, their customs, their language, in fact, their very way of life. In countries with a historical legacy of colonization, and even in those without this history, members of dominant groups have accumulated unearned privileges not accorded to others. Though the official terms "colonization," "colonizer," and "colonized" may have changed somewhat, nowhere in the world have we experienced a truly post-colonial society. The imperialism remains, though at times possibly in less visible forms.

One form it has taken centers on the way some members of dominant groups, with their sense of entitlement and privilege, take it upon themselves to lecture minoritized people when and how they should or should not speak out against the marginalization, degradation, discrimination, and oppression they face. Dominant groups often simply do not want to understand or be reminded about the privileges they have simply because of their dominant identities. They don't want to acknowledge the reality of social inequality.

Prejudice and Discrimination and a Case Study

What: The classic definition of prejudice was put forth by the famous Harvard psychologist, Gordon Allport, who published his groundbreaking *The Nature of Prejudice* in 1954: "Prejudice is an antipathy based on faulty and inflexible generalization. It may be felt or expressed. It may be directed toward a group or an individual of that group" (p. 7). The term "prejudice" comes from the Latin *praejudicium* meaning "prejudgment." It is a feeling held by an individual toward another individual or group without just reason or before acquiring sufficient information. For example, a person is said to be prejudiced if they believe that all people within a given group—say, Muslims—are inherently inferior.

What: When individuals' prejudiced feelings or beliefs move into the realm of behavior, the result is discrimination. Discrimination involves denial to individuals or groups of people equality of treatment. Therefore, it is discriminatory for parents not to allow their children to play with Muslim children or for other children to taunt and harass others simply because they adhere to the tenets of Islam, and for legislators to vote to deny Muslims access to certain careers, such as teaching. We can distinguish between two primary types of discrimination: *de jure* and *de facto*.

What: De jure discrimination constitutes a formalized system, which exists by law.

Legal Case Studies

So What: For example, the 1896 the United States Supreme Court decision *Plessy v. Ferguson* ruled that segregated facilities did not constitute a violation of the United States Constitution. Not until 1954, in *Brown v. Board of Education*, was the ruling overturned, and the Court decided that the concept of "separate but equal" was inherently unequal.

The Louisiana General Assembly passed in 1890 the "Separate Car Act" granting railroad companies the right to provide separate railway cars for the "white" race and the "colored" race. On June 7, 1892, Homer Plessy, a shoemaker, was jailed for sitting in a "white" car on the East Louisiana Railroad. Though demographically he was defined as one-eighths black and seven-eighths white, he was required to sit in the "colored" car under the so-called "one drop" rule—one drop of "black" blood makes you "colored."

Homer Plessy sued Louisiana in 1892 claiming in state court that the Separate Car Act violated the 13th (abolition of slavery) and 14th (equal protection) Amendments of the U.S. Constitution. Judge John Howard Ferguson ruled against Plessy by declaring that the state could indeed regulate railroad companies operating within Louisiana.

Now What: Plessy appealed to the Louisiana state Supreme Court, which upheld Judge Ferguson's decision. As his final recourse, Homer Plessy took his case to the U.S. Supreme Court. In 1896, in *Plessy v. Ferguson*, in what became a deep-seated stain on the cause for human and civil rights until it was reversed in *Brown v. Board of Education* (1954), the Supreme Court, by a ruling of 7–1, upheld the lower court's decision. Writing in 1896 for the majority, Justice Henry Brown asserted:

"That [the Separate Car Act] does no conflict with the Thirteenth Amendment, which abolished slavery ... is too clear for argument. ... A statute which implies merely a legal distinction between the white and colored races—a distinction which is founded in the color of the two races, and which must always exist so long as white men are distinguished from the other race by color—has no tendency to destroy the legal equality of the two races. ... The object of the [Fourteenth Amendment] was undoubtedly to enforce the absolute equality of the two races before the law, but in the nature of things it could not have been intended to abolish distinctions based upon color, or to enforce social, as distinguished from political equality, or a commingling of the two races upon terms unsatisfactory to either."

So What: The precedent set in this ruling came to be known as the "Separate but Equal" doctrine, which argued that separate facilities for black people and white people were constitutional if they were allegedly "equal" (though in actuality, they were not). This doctrine soon spread to other areas of public life including public facilities, restaurants, theaters, hospitals, and public schools.

It also extended the "Black Codes"—the so-called "Jim Crow" laws—throughout the South. These laws were passed following the enactment of the 13th Amendment to limit rights of newly freed enslaved black people. "Jim Crow" statutes got their name from Jim Crow, a southern minstrel performer.

Now What: United States Supreme Court decision, *Brown v Board of Education* (Topeka, Kansas), was rendered on May 17, 1954. In a unanimous decision, the court ruled that the "separate but equal" clause (set down in the case of *Plessy vs. Ferguson*, 1896) was unconstitutional because it violated students' rights as covered under the 14th Amendment[1] of the U.S. Constitution when separation was solely on the classification of "race." Delivering the court opinion, Chief Justice Earl Warren wrote that the "segregated schools are not equal and cannot be made equal, and hence they are deprived of the equal protection of the laws."

The *Brown* decision rested on accumulated social science research that emphasized the detrimental effects of school segregation on students of color. Following the decision, intransigence on the part of several Southern political leaders prevented the law from fully taking effect. In fact, President Eisenhower was compelled to call out federal troops to ensure compliance in Little Rock, Arkansas in 1957. Some Southern governors chose to close some public schools in their states rather than comply with desegregation orders.

Now What: The Civil Rights Act of 1964 strengthened the *Brown* decision. Prior to this act, the 14th Amendment of the United States

> Constitution applied primarily to the actions and laws of *states*. Following the Civil Rights Act of 1964, however, this was extended to include individuals who discriminate. The United States Congress passed the law to protect the constitutional rights of all people in the areas of public facilities and public education and prohibiting discrimination in federally assisted programs. Title VI, Section 2000d of the Act stipulated: "Prohibition against exclusion from participation in, denial of benefits of, and discrimination under federally assisted programs on ground of race, color, or national origin." Title VI expressly mandated the withholding of federal funds from institutions, including public schools, which engaged in racial discrimination.

What: De facto discrimination exists more informally and is not sanctioned by law. For example, when a homeowner and real-estate agency refuse to show a residence to an African American couple, the result is that members of this group are restricted from attending certain neighborhood schools. Ultimately, these schools become segregated schools.

> [M]en cannot be oppressed as *men*, just as whites cannot be oppressed as whites or heterosexuals as heterosexuals, because a group can be oppressed only if there exists another group with the power to oppress them.
> —Rothenberg (2008, p. 120)

What: Hardiman and Jackson (1997) have devised a convenient equation to represent the concept of oppression:

$$\text{Oppression} = \text{Prejudice} + \text{Social Power (or O = P + SP)}$$

"Social Power" includes the ability of dominant groups to impose its authority and social control over subordinated groups.

Hardiman, Jackson, and Griffin (2013) show that societal privilege and oppression are constructed and maintained on overlapping and coexisting societal/cultural, institutional, and individual/interpersonal levels and on other multiple dimensions.

Oppression is an interlocking, multileveled system that consolidates social power to the benefit of members of privileged groups and is maintained and operationalized on three dimensions: (a) contextual dimension, (b) conscious/unconscious dimension, and (c) applied dimension (p. 27).

Levels of Oppression

What: These multiple dimensions all link to support and enhance each other. The contextual dimension refers to the "levels" of oppression, which can be on a scale from fully conscious to virtually unconscious by individuals and groups that oppress and takes the form within the applied dimension from attitudes (prejudice) to behaviors (acts of discrimination/oppression).

Societal/Cultural Level of Oppression

Many overt forms of oppression are obvious when a dominant group tyrannizes a subordinate group: the horrendous treatment of people of color under the system of apartheid in South Africa and of black Africans in the trans-Atlantic slave trade, the mass slaughter of Jews and other stigmatized groups in Nazi Germany, and the merciless killing of Muslims and Jews during the Christian "Crusades" are prime examples.

What: In this regard, in political terms, an "authoritarian" or "strongman" is one who leads by force within an overarching totalitarian or dictatorial regime. Sometimes the formal head of state, sometimes another political or military leader, the authoritarian exerts influence and control over the government more than traditional laws or constitutional mandates sanction.

Authoritarians situate themselves within positions along the political spectrum, usually toward the extremes on the political right and the political left. Examples of brutal authoritarians include Joseph Stalin, Benito Mussolini, Adolph Hitler, Idi Amin Dada, Juan Perón, Saddam Hussein, Manuel Noriega, Vladimir Putin, and others throughout history across the planet.

On the right-wing side of the dictatorial strongmen's political spectrum, we find the philosophy and practice of "fascism." While also deployed as an epithet by some, fascism developed as a form of radical authoritarian nationalism in early-20th century Europe in response to liberalism and Marxism on the left.

Umberto Eco, who grew up under the fascist Mussolini regime, enumerates the characteristics of what he calls "Ur-Fascism," or "Eternal Fascism" in 14 "typical" features. He stressed that "These features cannot be organized into a system; many of them contradict each other and are also typical of other kinds of despotism or fanaticism. But it is enough that one of them be present to allow fascism to coagulate around it."

1. *The cult of tradition.*
2. *The rejection of modernism.* "The Enlightenment, the Age of Reason, is seen as the beginning of modern depravity. In this sense Ur-Fascism can be defined as irrationalism."
3. *The cult of action for action's sake.* "Action being beautiful in itself, it must be taken before, or without, any previous reflection. Thinking is a form of emasculation."
4. *Disagreement is treason.* "The critical spirit makes distinctions, and to distinguish is a sign of modernism. In modern culture the scientific community praises disagreement as a way to improve knowledge."
5. *Fear of difference.* "The first appeal of a fascist or prematurely fascist movement is an appeal against the intruders."
6. *Appeal to social frustration.* "One of the most typical features of the historical fascism was the appeal to a frustrated middle class, a class suffering from an economic crisis or feelings of political humiliation and frightened by the pressure of lower social groups."
7. *The obsession with a plot.* "The followers must feel besieged. The easiest way to solve the plot is the appeal to xenophobia."
8. *The enemy is both strong and weak.* "By a continuous shifting of rhetorical focus, the enemies are at the same time too strong and too weak."
9. *Pacifism is trafficking with the enemy.* "For Ur-Fascism there is no struggle for life but, rather, life is lived for struggle."
10. *Contempt for the weak.* "Elitism is a typical aspect of any reactionary ideology."
11. *Everybody is educated to become a hero.* "In Ur-Fascist ideology, heroism is the norm. This cult of heroism is strictly linked with the cult of death."
12. *Machismo and weaponry.* "Machismo implies both disdain for women and intolerance and condemnation of nonstandard sexual habits, from chastity to homosexuality."
13. *Selective populism.* "There is in our future a TV or Internet populism, in which the emotional response of a selected group of citizens can be presented and accepted as the Voice of the People."
14. *Ur-Fascism speaks Newspeak.* "All the Nazi or Fascist schoolbooks made use of an impoverished vocabulary, and an elementary syntax, in order to limit the instruments for complex and critical reasoning." (Eco in Kottke, 2016, n.p.)

Political scientist, Britt (2003), enumerates another 14 tenets of fascism:

1. Powerful and continuing nationalism,
2. Disdain for the recognition of human rights,
3. Identification of enemies/scapegoats [of the country's problems] as a unifying cause,
4. Rampant sexism,
5. Supremacy of the military,
6. Controlled mass media,
7. Obsession with national security,
8. Religion and government are intertwined,
9. Corporate power is protected,
10. Labor power is suppressed,
11. Disdain for intellectuals and the arts,
12. Obsession with crime and punishment,
13. Rampant cronyism and corruption, and
14. Fraudulent elections.

While many governmental leaders and candidates for public office may exhibit a number of these tactics while remaining outside the definition of "fascist," the cumulative effect increases depending on the severity of and the degree to which they initiate these measures.

During the late 1940s, researchers, led by Adorno et al. (1950) studied the historical conditions that paved the way for the rise of fascist regimes in the 1930s, World War II, and the Holocaust. They theorized about individuals who supported the growth of fascism. They suggested that people of a certain personality type, which they labeled the "authoritarian personality," were most disposed to extremism, in this case, those most susceptible to believing anti-Jewish propaganda and *anti*-democratic political philosophies.

They suspended their autonomy and freedom for the promise of going back to a future reminiscent of a (mythic) idealistic past of economic, political, social, cultural, and personal security, where their "ingroup" won and led, and those "outgroups" served obediently and acquiesced to "ingroup" needs and demands.

Many forms of societal/cultural level oppression (and dominant group privilege), however, are not as apparent, especially to members of dominant groups. Oppression in its fullest sense also refers to structural/systemic constraints imposed on groups *even within constitutional democracies*, and "[i]ts causes are embedded in unquestioned norms, habits, and symbols, in the assumptions underlying institutional rules and the collective consequences of following those rules" (Young, 1990, p. 36).

What: Societal/Cultural level oppression and dominant group privilege, one of Hardiman et al.'s (2013) levels, involves the implied and explicit hegemonic cultural norms, values, and perspectives/discourses of the dominant group imposed and infused "on institutions by individuals and on individuals by institutions" (p. 19). These social and cultural principles, philosophies, and/or discourses related to how one should live one's life, definitions of good and evil, health and sickness, normality and deviancy, are often used to provide dominant group members justification and rationalization for social oppression, while often sheltering them from a conscious acknowledgment or understanding of the ways in which they are privileged based on their social identit(ies).

So What: Many social codes of behavior, while some may not be written into law, nonetheless work within a society to legitimize social oppression. Social theorist, Myrdal (1944), traveled throughout the United States during the late 1940s examining U.S. society following World War II, and he discovered a grave contradiction or inconsistency, which he termed "an American dilemma." He found a country, founded on an overriding commitment to democracy, liberty, freedom, human dignity, and egalitarian values, coexisting alongside deep-seated patterns of discrimination (especially racial), privileging white people, while subordinating people of color.

What: The theologian Tinney (1983) suggests overlapping categories under societal/cultural oppression. One form Tinney labels "Denial of Culture and Conspiracy to Silence."

So What: A form of societal/cultural oppression of many groups, is that its members often grow up within society depriving them of a historical context for their lives. The larger society perpetuates the myth that they have no culture and no history, and that they do not constitute a *bona fide* community. From Europe in the Middle Ages to the U.S. and many other countries today, there has been an active attempt to falsify historical accounts thereby making accurate reconstruction extremely difficult.

Historian Boswell (1980) has documented the various means by which this falsification has been enacted to erase lesbian, gay, bisexual, and transgender (LGBT) history, for example: through censorship, deletion, half-truths, and the changing of pronouns signifying gender. These sorts of discriminatory actions not only lead to the false conclusion that LGBT people have made no significant contributions to their societies, but also furthers the isolation and invisibility of these groups.

Boswell cites as an example of heterosexist censorship a manuscript of *The Art of Love* by the Roman author Ovid. A phrase that originally read, "A boys' love appealed to me less" (*Hoc est quod pueri tanger amore minus*), was altered by a Medieval moralist to read, "A boy's love appealed to me not at all" (*Hoc est quod queri tanger amore nihil*), and an editor's note appearing in the margin informed the reader, "Thus you may be sure that Ovid was not a sodomite" (*Ex hoc nota quod Ovidius non fuerit Sodomita*). One of the first instances of a change of gender pronouns occurred when "Michelangelo's grandnephew employed this means to render his uncle's sonnets more acceptable to the public" (Boswell, 1980, p. 18).

Now What: Every year, the American Library Association announces its list of the most challenged and banned books in schools, libraries, and within the larger society to inform people on issues of censorship.

Institutional Level of Oppression

What: Sometimes major social institutions—for example, the government, the courts, religious organizations, educational institutions, financial institutions, law enforcement, corporations, and others—enforce existing prejudices and discriminate. This is said to constitute "institutional oppression."

So What: Institutions have tremendous power and social status, and, through penalties and rewards, disapproval and approval, create incentives for conformity to dominant norms. Institutional racism has denied people of color equal opportunity. Brodkin (1998), for example, terms the nationally funded United States G. I. Bill of Rights following World War II as "affirmative action" for white people:

> The G. I. Bill of Rights, as "The 1944 Serviceman's Readjustment Act" was known, is arguably the most massive affirmative action program in American history. ... I call it affirmative action because it was aimed at and disproportionately helped male, Euro-origin GIs ... [Benefits] were decidedly not extended to African Americans or to women of any race. Theoretically they were available to all veterans; in practice women and black veterans did not get anywhere near their share. (Brodkin, p. 38, 42)

The Church of Jesus Christ of Latter Day Saints provides another example on the institutional level. LDS President, Brigham Young instituted a policy on

February 13, 1849 emanating from "divine revelation" and continuing until as recently as 1978 forbidding ordination of black men of African descent from the ranks of LDS priesthood. In addition, this policy prohibited black men and women of African descent from participating in the temple endowment and sealings, which the Church dictates as essential for the highest degree of salvation. The policy likewise restricted black people from attending or participating in temple marriages.

Young attributed this restriction to the so-called sin of Cain, Adam and Eve's eldest son, who killed his brother Abel: "What chance is there for the redemption of the Negro?" stated Young in 1849 following declaration of his restrictive policy. "The Lord had cursed Cain's seed with blackness and prohibited them from the Priesthood." While making a speech to the Utah Territorial Legislature in 1852, Young further asserted: "Any man having one drop of the seed of [Cain] ... in him cannot hold the Priesthood, and if no other Prophet ever spoke it before, I will say it now in the name of Jesus Christ. I know it is true and others know it" (in Harris & Bringhurst, 2015, p. 99).

In another instance, Young continued:

> You see some classes of the human family that are black, uncouth, uncomely, disagreeable and low in their habits, wild, and seemingly deprived of nearly all the blessings of the intelligence that is generally bestowed upon mankind. ... Cain slew his brother. Cain might have been killed, and that would have put a termination to that line of human beings. That was not to be, and the Lord put a mark upon him, which is the flat nose and black skin ... that they should be the "servant of servants"; and they will be, until that curse is removed. ... (in Kick, 2003)

Joseph Fielding Smith, Tenth Prophet and President of the LDS Church wrote in 1935 that, "Not only was Cain called upon to suffer, but because of his wickedness, he became the father of an inferior race. A curse was placed upon him and that curse has been continued through his lineage and must do so while time endures ..." (in Harris & Bringhurst, 2015, p. 60). And in 1963 he asserted: "Such a change [in our policy] can come about only through divine revelation, and no one can predict when a divine revelation will occur" (in Lund, 1967, p. 45).

Now What: It seems that the Twelfth LDS Church president, Spencer W. Kimball, who served from 1973 to his death in 1985, was touched with such a "vision" and, therefore, reversed the ban, referring to it as "the long-promised day." We can ask today whether "revelation" or mere pragmatism was the determining factor in permitting black people full membership rights in the Church at a time of ongoing and heightened civil rights activities in the

United States and an increase in LDS missionary recruiting efforts throughout the African continent. We can also ask whether "revelation" or mere pragmatism was the motivating consideration for abandoning its promotion of polygamous marriages at a time when the United States Congress demanded this as a condition for the admission of Utah as a state within the United States.

Personal/Interpersonal Level of Oppression

What: Allport (1954) theorized that both internal and external forces influence an individual's behavior and effect personality development. He termed these forces as genotypes and phenotypes. *Genotypes* encompass internal forces that effect how a person processes and stores information, and then uses it to interact with the world. *Phenotypes* comprise external forces that relate to the way people accept their surroundings and how others influence their behavior.

Referred to as "Allport's Scale of Prejudice and Discrimination" or "Allport's Scale of Prejudice" created in 1954, its rankings go along a continuum from stages 1 to 5.

1. Antilocution happens when an "ingroup" freely confers negative expressions of an "outgroup." An example at this stage is hate speech, including stereotypical "ethnic jokes."
2. Avoidance ("social exclusion") occurs when members of the ingroup consciously or unconsciously avoid contact with individuals in the outgroup, resulting often in the isolation of outgroups.
3. Discrimination (the active result of prejudice) by the ingroup occurs against the outgroup denying its members equality of opportunities in achieving their goals as well as being accorded the granting of material and other services. Sometimes forms of discrimination are informal (*de facto*) while in many instances codified (*de jure*) as official policies and laws (e.g. U.S. "Jim Crow" laws, Statute of Kilkenny in British Ireland, Apartheid in South Africa, "Nuremberg" anti-Jewish laws in Nazi Germany).
4. Physical Attack includes vandalism and destruction of outgroup property by the ingroup and violent attacks upon individuals and groups. These can range from the singling out of isolated members of the outgroup, or highly organized attacks such as pogroms targeting Jews in Europe, lynchings of black people in the United States, and violence against Hindus in Pakistan.

5. Extermination (in its current sanitized terminology "ethnic cleansing") attempts to remove and murder members of outgroups by ingroups resulting in the genocide of a people. Examples include the Armenian genocide, Jewish genocide, Cambodian genocide, genocide of the Hellenes, genocides in Bosnia, Rwanda, Ukraine, and U.S. genocide of First Nation and African heritage peoples, among others throughout history.

Dominant Group Privilege and the Myth of Meritocracy

> The trouble that surrounds difference is really about privilege and power—the existence of privilege and the lopsided distribution of power that keeps it going. The trouble is rooted in a legacy we all inherited, and while we're here, it belongs to us.
>
> —Johnson (2006, p. 13)

What: Privilege can be a difficult term to understand. Johnson provides the following definition:

> Privilege generally allows people to assume a certain level of acceptance, inclusion, and respect in the world, to operate within a relatively wide comfort zone [and] privilege grants the cultural authority to make judgments about others and to have those judgments stick. (p. 17)

Depending on our many social identities, we are simultaneously granted certain societal privileges and socially marginalized established solely on these identities. Based on McIntosh's (1988) pioneering investigations of white and male privilege, we can understand dominant group privilege as constituting a seemingly invisible, unearned, and largely unacknowledged array of benefits accorded to members of dominant groups, with which they often unconsciously walk through life as if effortlessly carrying a knapsack tossed over their shoulders.

So What: This system of benefits confers dominance on certain social identity groups, for example, in a Western context, males, European-heritage people, heterosexuals, cisgender people, Christians, upper socioeconomic classes, temporarily able bodied people, people of a certain age range (young adults through the middle years), native born, dominant language as first language speakers, people who fall into socially defined standards of attractiveness, beauty, and body size, while subordinating and denying these privilege to other groups, for example, females and intersex people, racially minoritized peoples, lesbians, gays, bisexuals, and transgender people, those who do not hold to Christian beliefs, working class and poor people, people with disabilities, young and old people, non-native born, non-dominant as first language speakers, people who do fit socially defined standards of attractiveness, beauty, and body size, and others. These systemic inequities are pervasive throughout the society. They are encoded into the individual's consciousness and woven into the fabric of social institutions, resulting in a stratified social order privileging dominant groups while restricting and disempowering subordinated group members.

So What: Through the socialization process, dominant group members *internalize* (internalized dominance), consciously though largely unconsciously, the "normalization" of the socially established privileges they are granted. The relative invisibility of these privileges to members of dominant social identities helps to keep this system firmly in place.

I often use the analogy of dominant group privilege as the water in an aquarium in that the fish do not see or even feel because it is so pervasive. For our society to move forward with greater equity, however, we need to be conscious of the water of dominance, oppression, and privilege that saturates our environments.

Now What: I conduct an activity each semester in my university classes, which I learned from my friend Jackson Katz, to expose the water of male privilege. I ask all my students the following question: "What do you do daily to prevent yourself from being sexually harassed or raped?"

Within seconds, cisgender female and transgender students raise their hands and say things such as: "I never walk alone at night," "I sometimes dress down as not to call attention to myself," "I carry a set of keys between my fingers to use as a weapon if I'm attacked," "I am taking a self-defense class," "I carry pepper spray." The vast majority of cisgender men in the class, on the other hand, usually remain silent except for the occasional, "Well, I never really think about it."

And that is the point! Cisgender males have the privilege of not having to think about it, which is one of the many benefits associated with cisgender male privilege. The entrenched human mechanism of denial acts as an additional factor that maintains this system of dominance and privilege. Members of dominant social identities often resist, deny, and refuse to accept the fact of their privilege, while viewing it as, to borrow former Vice President Al Gore's term, an "inconvenient truth" to hear and even consider or acknowledge the ways in which their privileges marginalize and oppress others.

With the above as a starting point, though, I caution us not to conceptualize dominant group privilege monolithically, for we must factor into the equation issues of context and intersectionality of identities. We need to view forms of privilege along a *continuum* or *spectrum* rather than conceiving them as binary opposites. Though we can never fully quantify privilege, by discarding the bifurcated polar perspective while charting privilege along a continuum considering context and identity intersectionality, we will come to a fuller and deeper awareness of issues of power and privilege, marginalization, and oppression as we work toward a more socially just society and world.

What: Meritocracy[2] is the idea that individuals are basically born onto a relatively level playing field, and that success or failure depends on the individual's personal merit, motivation, intelligence, ambition, and abilities. Those who are, however, born into or enter difficult circumstances can choose to "pull themselves up by their boot straps" (the so-called "Horatio Alger" myth), and they can rise to the heights that their abilities and merit can take them. People, therefore, possess "personal responsibility" for their life's course. This, however, gives the rationalization to ignore, deny, or address systemic oppression and inequity.

> It takes money to make money (inheritance); It's not what you know but whom you know (connections); What matters is being in the right place at the right time (luck); the playing field isn't level (discrimination); and he or she married into money (marriage). (McNamee & Miller, 2009, p. 1)

This concept of "meritocracy" is founded on the premise of "personal responsibility," and those who do not achieve success must accept personal responsibility for their failures. Maybe they did not try hard enough. Maybe they failed to scale any barriers that could have been placed in their way because they did not have enough will and self-control, fortitude, intelligence, character, or because they simply made bad choices.

So What: While of course we are all accountable and liable for our actions, what impact do the social conditions of our nation have on our personal success? This very question triggers immediate reasons in many people, for it challenges the foundation of many Western democracies as meritocratic nations by asking:

How can patterns of systemic oppression operate within a system of meritocracy? How can I have certain unearned dominant group privileges when I was taught to believe that my success or failure rests totally within my own personal control?

Rather than having to sit with and attempt to understand the cognitive dissonance and sense of narcissistic injury these questions raise, many people negatively react, resist, deny, and sometimes vehemently attack the very notion of dominant group privilege and those who carry the message. The promotion of the idea of meritocracy has been used as a common strategy in the psychology of dominant group privilege denial that everything they may have gained was brought about by their own hard work and talents, which did not come from some kind of unearned privilege based on any of their social identities.

Notes

1. All persons born or naturalized in the United States and subject to the jurisdiction thereof, are citizens of the United States and of the State wherein they reside. No State shall make or enforce any law which shall abridge the privileges or immunities of citizens of the United States; nor shall any State deprive any person of life, liberty, or property, without due process of law; nor deny to any person within its jurisdiction the equal protection of the laws.
2. See Appendix C: Meritocracy Activities.

· 7 ·

WHAT CAUSES PREJUDICE AND DISCRIMINATION?

The song "You've Got to Be Carefully Taught," from the Broadway musical *South Pacific* is preceded by the line that prejudice is "not born in you! It happens after you're born." Though the lyrics in this song referred to racism and ethnic biases ("You've got to be taught/to hate and fear") it can and does refer to other forms of social prejudices and discrimination as well (Rogers & Hammerstein, 1949).

Young children through their socialization learn the values and attitudes of people and later the larger society around them. Within this process, children also learn prejudices and how to discriminate through observing others around them, and through reinforcement, and modeling.

> Children begin developing attitudes about various groups in society as early as ages three or four. Initially such attitudes are quite flexible. However, as children grow older such attitudes become more difficult to change. (Byrnes, 1995, p. 3)

Overall, individuals maintain oppressive behaviors to gain certain rewards or to avoid punishment, to protect their self-esteem against psychological doubts or conflicts, to enhance their value systems, or to categorize others to comprehend a complex world.

Social Learning Theory

What: Social Learning Theory, sometimes referred to as "Social Cognitive Theory" or "Social Modeling Theory," proposes that individuals learn by observing and associating with others (modeling), and through the process of reinforcement, one's beliefs and actions are in some way supported by others'.

Sidebar Questions:
Think back in your life to any role models (however you define this) you may have had.

- Who were they?
- How did they serve as role models?
- What skills, knowledge, behaviors, views, perspectives, outlooks, feelings, etc. did you gain from them?
- How have they impacted the course of your life?

Social Modeling Theory: Albert Bandura

Bandura (1965), proposed that children learn primarily through observation, and that one's culture transmits social mores and what he called "complex competencies" through social modeling. As he noted, the root meaning of the word "teach" is "to show." Others, including Diane Maluso, propose that parents teach prejudice through their beliefs and actions, and through the process of reinforcement:

> Parents play important roles in prejudice acquisition. The relationship between parents' and children's attitudes toward members of outgroups is consistent. Not only do parents teach prejudice directly through reinforcement but children often learn their parents' prejudiced attitudes by simply observing their parents talking about and interacting with people from other groups. (Maluso, 2007, n.p.)

Bandura, on the other hand, asserted that the process of modeling alone—*free* from social reinforcements—can, in fact, be enough for children to incorporate and act on their own beliefs and behaviors. Bandura, and educational psychologist Vygotsky (1978), posited that positive modeling by knowledgeable or advanced peers/classmates, can develop even higher efficiency and cognitive developmental competencies than teachers modeling the same activities.

Vygotsky asserted that schools are major socializing agencies whereby students learn further their *expected* social roles, including expressions of gender and sexual identity. For Vygotsky:

> Every function in the child's cultural development appears twice: first on the social level, and later on the individual level; first, between people (interpsychological) and then inside the child (intrapsychological). This applies equally to voluntary attention to logical memory, and to the formation of concepts. All the higher functions originate as actual relationships between individuals. (1978, p. 57)

Vygotsky claimed that the child's understanding of society is shaped through the process of social learning, and at the same time, the individual retains the ability to think independently while growing in experience throughout life. Society at large, adults, and peers present an array of modeling, a continuum from very productive and affirming to very biased, aggressive, and destructive. Modeling to Albert Bandura includes much more than simple observation of concrete actions followed by imitation ("response mimicry"), but also included what he called "abstract modeling" of such abstract concepts as following rules, taking on certain values and beliefs, and making moral and ethical judgments. On the negative side of the modeling continuum, for example, Bandura concluded that young children act out aggression modeled by adults in their homes. This finding contradicted the premise that parental/guardian punishment would inhibit children's aggressive behaviors.

To test his hypothesis that social modeling had a primary impact on children's learning and on their behaviors and beliefs, Bandura, Ross, and Ross (1961) developed the "Bobo Doll" experiments. The purpose of the experiment was to determine whether adult modeling resulted in either aggressive or non-aggressive behaviors by the young children in the study. Research participants included 36 boys and 36 girls, with a control group of 24 children. The participants ranged in age from 3 to 6 years, with an average age of 4 years and 4 months, all from the Stanford University Nursery School in California. The researchers investigated and were knowledgeable about each participant's prior behavioral history, and this they factored into the final data analysis.

Each child was taken individually into a playroom filled with a variety of "non-aggressive toys" including a tinker toy set, and "aggressive toys" including a wooden mallet and a Bobo Doll: a large inflatable clown weighted on the bottom so it could stand unaided, approximately the size of a pre-adolescent child of 5 feet. The experimenter told each child participant that the toys were only for the adult model to play with, and that the child was to watch the adult. The children in the control group, however, were each told individually that they could play with the toys. No adult model was to enter their playroom.

For half of the participants, the adult model initially played with the tinker toys for one minute, then for nine minutes, attacked the Bobo Doll with a sequence of verbal insults and physical violence including kicking, punching, and hitting about the head with the wooden mallet. For the other half of the participants, the adult model played with the tinker toys and ignored the Bobo Doll for the entire 10-minute duration of this phase of the experiment.

Following their observations, each child was taken individually by the experimenter into another playroom with an assortment of toys, which included an airplane, a fire engine, a Bobo Doll set with clothes and carriage, and others. To instill a certain degree of anger and frustration, the experimenter told each child that they could play with the toys in this room for a very short time, and that these toys were reserved for other children.

The children were then taken individually to a third playroom and left alone for 20 minutes to play with aggressive and non-aggressive toys. The aggressive toys included the Bobo Doll, a wooden mallet, two dart guns, a tetherball with a face painted on it, and others. Among the non-aggressive toys were paper and crayons, a tea set, two dolls, a ball, cars and trucks, and plastic farm animals. Experimenters observed each child behind a one-way mirror and evaluated their behaviors on a series of specific measures of aggressive behavior.

Bandura and his researchers found that the children who observed the aggressive adult model were much more likely to exhibit both imitatively physical and verbal aggressive behaviors when left alone in the third playroom, as opposed to children who were exposed to the non-aggressive model or no model. In addition, Bandura's initial assumption that children were more highly influenced by same-sex models was validated. Both the males and the females exhibited higher degrees of aggressive verbal and physical behaviors following modeling by a same-sex experimenter than by an experimenter of the other sex. Finally, overall, males tended to behave more aggressively than females in the study.

Bandura and his associates succeeded in supporting their theory of social learning. Children, they found, can indeed learn specific behaviors, such as forms of verbal and physical aggression, by observing and imitating others. This was found to be true even in the *absence of behavioral reinforcements*. Bandura concluded that children are highly influenced by observing adult behaviors, leading them to believe that such behavior is acceptable, and, in this instance, freeing their own aggressive inhibitions. They are then more likely to behave aggressively in future situations.

Social Rank Theory

What: Social Rank Theory, as used by Hawker and Boulton (2001), proposes that aggressive individuals actually hold a higher rank, power, or status within a social group. Therefore, aggressive behavior, and bullying, may be reinforced, and it provides those who engage in aggressive behaviors a sense of belonging. Hawker and Boulton contend that peer victimization serves many functions. First, it establishes and maintains a social hierarchy within a given group (an "ingroup"), and second, it maintains distinctions between members of the ingroup, from members of other groups ("outgroups").

Both individual and situational factors related to ethical decision-making must be considered when attempting to explain oppressive beliefs and actions. Salancik and Pfeffer (1978) found that an individual's values, attitudes, and behaviors are greatly impacted by coworkers and peers. Even when individuals judge a behavior or action to be morally wrong, the organizational environment—that is, the perceived attitudes and behaviors of peers or coworkers—can severely "neutralize" their previously held moral judgments. They then often take on the actions consistent with the perceived organizational climate, especially individuals who are particularly susceptible to social influences, what Snyder (1979) refers to as those high in "self-monitoring" who rely on cues from social interactions to shape appropriate attitudes and behaviors ("social cognitive theory"). In this sense, then, behavior is not always an indication of beliefs or values, for an individual may take on actions in accordance with perceived accepted organizational or peer actions, even when those actions run counter to the individual's ethical judgment.

Psychodynamic Theories

Some theorists argue that the denial of basic (and often intangible) psychological needs for security, identity, recognition, and participation underlie prejudiced beliefs (e.g. Azar & Burton, 1986; Schirch, 2005). Helmreich and Marcus (1998) asserted that one must look at the underlying psychological bases of social interactions. They proposed that the conflict is not *over* anything. At the core of the conflict "are feelings of insecurity and mistrust, competing claims to greater suffering, and issues of envy, resentment, and otherness" (p. 28).

What: Since the 1930s, many theories to explain prejudice and conflict through psychological factors operating in a social context are placed under the general category of "Frustration-Aggression-Displacement Theory" (or FADT). These theories made assumptions about *social* structures and *social* processes based on several hypotheses:

- Individuals are concerned with gratifying their own needs, but are, to one extent or another, inhibited by social or communal restraints.
- Ingroup norms and discipline require self-denial, postponement of gratification, and/or repression of certain impulses and needs, which can be *frustrating* to the individual.
- Such frustration can generate retaliatory impulses directed toward the perceived source of the restraint, which is often from *ingroup* members (Berkowitz, 1962).
- Opposition itself can give one inner satisfaction and a sense of direction and relief (Simmel, 1955).
- In terms of the ingroup, the expression of hostility and aggression on the direct source of restraint can inhibit or reduce cooperation and cohesion.
- Thus, the hostility and aggressiveness directed toward the stimulus object can also be expressed against *other* objects. This principle is known as "stimulus generalization."
- The transfer of hostility and aggressiveness from the original instigating stimulus object onto another object is called "displacement" and the "displacement mechanism."
- Ingroups tend to institutionalize the displacement of hostility and aggression onto outgroups. This displacement is often rationalized and justified as appropriate by the ingroup. LeVine and Campbell (1972) called this process the "socially institutionalized displacement target mechanism," which they defined as "a verbal tradition leading ingroup members to perceive outgroups as the cause of their frustrations" (p. 123).

Additional propositions that increase ingroup displacement include:

- The more frustrating the environment, the more likely will be the displacement onto outgroups.

- The more ingroup cohesion and discipline, the more likely the hostility will be directed toward outgroups.
- The more domineering and autocratic the ingroup authorities, and the more obedience that is required of ingroup member, the more hostility will be directed toward outgroups (Adorno, Frenkel-Brunswik, Levinson, & Sanford, 1950; Barry, Chold, & Bacon, 1959).

So What: Ethnocentrism to Freud (1930) carried with it the social "function" of displacement of aggression from the in-group to the out-group. In fact, for Freud, a group's "displacement of aggression" function helps to explain, in part, the history of antisemitism. To borrow a chapter title from Wistrich (1991), the displacement function partially explained a history "from the cross to the swastika":

> When once the Apostle Paul has posited universal love between men as the foundation of his Christian community, extreme intolerance on the part of Christendom toward who remained outside it became the inevitable consequence. ... Neither was it an accountable chance that the dream of the Germanic world-dominion called for anti-Semitism as its complement. (Freud, 1930, pp. 114–115)

In addition, Wurzel (1986) maintains that people maintain prejudicial attitudes to gain certain rewards and to avoid punishment; what he refers to this as the "Utilitarian Function" of prejudice. People generally want to be liked and, therefore, will take on the prejudices of others, including family member and peers. In doing so, they are consolidating their personal and social relationships, and in turn enhancing their own self-concept. Also, when a leader exploits a prejudice widely held by their constituency, group members may experience a heightened sense of purpose and a stronger feeling of community while at the same time solidifying the leader's position.

Wurzel (1986) also contends that people treasure their own particular sets of values and modes of living, and there may be some insecurity surrounding anything that is different from those standards. For any difference may be construed as a threat to those frameworks, a threat that would undermine the security their social norms provide. Consequently, any group perceived as challenging one's values one may consider as inferior and threatening. Prejudice against people who maintain values different from one's own tends to strengthen the values of those who hold the prejudice. Wurzel calls this the "Value-Expressive Function" of prejudice. Seeing even imaginary threats to one's shared values may not only increase animosity toward those who are perceived as threats, but also make the values appear to be worth defending.

· 8 ·

ELEMENTS, CHARACTERISTICS, AND "FACES" OF OPPRESSION

Returning to the image of the wheel in which each spoke represents the various forms of oppression, we can understand the rim circling and connecting the spokes as comprising the many components of oppression common to each form or spoke. To place a bright spotlight on what comprises the rim linking the spokes together and begin imaging what a socially just world might be, I employ at least five different but overlapping theoretical organizers: Lee Anne Bell's "Defining Features of Oppression," Suzanne Pharr's "Elements of Oppression," Iris Marion Young's "Faces of Oppression."

Lee Anne Bell's "Defining Features of Oppression"

> We use the term oppression rather than discrimination, bias, prejudice, or bigotry to emphasize the pervasive nature of social inequality woven throughout social institutions as well as embedded within individual consciousness.
> —Bell (2007, p. 3)

What: Bell discusses additional defining features of oppression including the ways it restricts individual self-development and self-determination owing to its structural and material constraints. Oppression also signifies the hierarchical relationships among groups in which those of dominant status gain the benefits and privileges, often unconsciously, due to the disempowerment of minoritized group. Since individuals hold membership in several social groups, oppression is also complex and intersectional in which relative privilege or disadvantage exist differently depending on context. In addition, the numerous forms of oppression all contain several distinctive as well as shared characteristics and histories among and between them.

Suzanne Pharr's "Elements of Oppression"

In her pioneering book, *Homophobia: A Weapon of Sexism* (1988), Suzanne Pharr describes a series of elements she finds common to the multiple forms of oppression.

What: Defined Norm: Pharr explains as "… a standard of rightness and often of righteousness wherein all others are judged in relation to it. This norm must be backed up with institutional power, economic power, and both institutional and individual violence" (p. 53).

Pharr emphasizes that though it is an established norm, this does not necessarily mean that it is the norm of most people in terms of numbers. The norm was formed by those with the power to maintain control over others. This power must have become "institutionalized."

Now What: To expose the defined norm of heterosexuality, for example, Rochlin (1971) created an assessment turning around questions that gay, lesbian, and bisexual people commonly are asked:

Heterosexual Questionnaire
by Martin Rochlin, Ph.D.

1. What do you think caused your heterosexuality?
2. When and how did you first decide you were a heterosexual?
3. Is it possible that your heterosexuality is just a phase you may grow out of?
4. Is it possible that your heterosexuality stems from a neurotic fear of members of the same sex?
5. Isn't it possible that all you need is a good same-sex lover?

6. If heterosexuality is normal, why are a disproportionate number of mental patients heterosexual?
7. To whom have you disclosed your heterosexuality? How did they react?
8. The great majority of child molesters are heterosexuals (95 percent). Do you really consider it safe to expose your children to heterosexual teachers?
9. Heterosexuals are noted for assigning themselves and each other to narrowly restricted, stereotyped sex roles. Why do you cling to such an unhealthy form of role playing?
10. Why do heterosexuals place so much emphasis on sex?
11. There seem to be very few happy heterosexuals. Techniques have been developed that you might be able to use to change your sexual orientation. Have you considered aversion therapy to treat your sexual orientation?
12. Why are heterosexuals so promiscuous?
13. Why do you make a point of attributing heterosexuality to famous people? Is it to justify your own heterosexuality?
14. If you've never slept with a person of the same sex, how do you know you wouldn't prefer that?
15. Why do you insist on being so obvious and making a public spectacle of your heterosexuality? Can't you just be what you are and keep it quiet?

What: Institutional Power: This includes power in the social institutions including resources, laws, policies, political clout, political representation. Institutional power in Pharr's sense means that power has become systemic across and within social institutions. This institutional power is backed up economically.

What: Economic Power: Pharr argues that "Once economic control is in the hands of the few, all others can be controlled through limiting access to resources, limiting mobility, limiting employment options" (p. 54). In this way, people compete with one another, they are "pitted against one another," through the myth of scarcity.

What: Myth of Scarcity: The socially created fear and alarm that there are not enough resources to go around. "…[W]hich suggests that our resources are limited and blames the poor for using up too much of what little there is to go around" (p. 54). In this way, those in power can demand restricted immigration with resonance that people are trying to enter your country to take your jobs, destroy your schools and other social institutions, which are already suffering under the weight of economic distress, ruin your neighborhoods, and bring in crime and drugs. This myth of scarcity is used by those in power to pit people against one another on the basis of race, ethnicity, and socioeconomic class.

What: Violence and Threats of Violence: Systemic and individual power and control is backed up by the threat and use of violence by dominant groups who have defined and imposed the social norms upon those who do not or will not conform to these norm, and includes the implicit or explicit societal messages intended to make people afraid, to fear harm, pain, suffering, etc. if they advocate for themselves or challenge oppressive conditions. This type of violence is often sanctioned within the criminal "justice" system. It is also supported by the threat to use the military to quell uprisings.

What: Othering: This to Pharr involves treating some people and groups "as abnormal, deviant, inferior, marginalized, not 'right'" (p. 58), or different related to the defined norm, even if they are the numerical majority like women and girls. "Those who seek their rights, who seek inclusion, who seek to control their own lives [and bodies] instead of having their lives controlled are the people who fall outside the norm. ... They are 'the Other'" (p. 58).

Poet, novelist, and anthropologist Mackey (1992) discusses how "othering" is something people *do*, and therefore, "to other" must be seen as a verb, an action. An "other" is someone or a group that has been *acted upon*, constructed as a *minoritized* "outgroup." Likewise, "to minoritize" is also something people *do*, and it must be seen as a verb, as an action.

But this othering discourse is nothing new. A Butte, Montana editorial in the *Butte Bystander* (1873) represents the exclusionist sentiments toward Chinese people held by many white U.S. citizens at that time:

> The Chinaman's life is not our life, his religion is not our religion. His habits, superstitions, and modes of life are disgusting. He is a parasite, floating across the Pacific and thence penetrating into the interior towns and cities, there to settle down for a brief space and absorb the substance of those with whom he comes into competition. His one object is to make all the money and return again to his native land dead or alive. ... Let him go hence. He belongs not in Butte. (February 11, 1873, n.p.)

The editorial also argued that: "The Chinaman is no more a citizen than a coyote is a citizen, and never can be."

What: Lack of Prior Claim: This, according to Pharr, "… means that if you weren't there when the original document (the Constitution, for example) was written, or when the organization was first created, then you have no right to inclusion. … Those who seek their rights, who seek inclusion, who seek to control their own lives instead of having their lives controlled are the people who fall outside the norm. … They are *the Other*" (p. 57).

In the original and unamended version of the U.S. Constitution, for example, since only European-heritage male landowners had the right to vote, all *Others*, including women and people of color (those outside the defined norm and who lacked prior claim) had to fight long and difficult battles against strong forces to gain access to the voting booth, often under the threat of and actual violence inflicted against them. Some who oppose marriage equality for same-sex couples, because it lacked prior claim argue that this would undermine the sanctity of marriage, and possibly lead to the destruction of society itself, often using religious sanctions as their justification.

For example, responding at a press conference to the state of Vermont's Civil Unions legislation in 2000, Catholic Cardinal Bernard Law reflected the opinion of the delegation of New England Cardinals and Bishops:

> The Legislature of the State of Vermont, by passing the Civil Unions Bill [countering the defined norm and lack of prior claim], has attacked centuries of cultural and religious esteem for marriage between a man and a woman and has prepared the way for an attack on the well-being of society itself [by these *Others*].

Similarly, Dabney, Professor of Theology at Union Seminary in Virginia, warned:

> What then, in the next place, will be the effect of this fundamental change [countering the defined norm and lack of prior claim] when it shall be established? The obvious answer is, that it will destroy Christianity and civilization in America [by these *Others*]. (1871, n.p.)

Cardinal Law and Professor Dabney engaged in similar dire predictions, but, and here is the key, they are referring to two *different* events—the Cardinal referred to marriage for same-sex couples, Dabney, who lived from 1820 to 1898, referred to women's suffrage—but they forewarned similar consequences: the destruction of the family and civilization.

Since the power structure of the United States has excluded transgender and intersex people from the category of "defined norms" by viewing transgender and intersex people as the *Other*, and the founding national and institutional policy documents have likewise excluded transgender and intersex peoples' civil and human rights from a prior claim, a spate of state legislatures have either passed or have considered passing laws prohibiting transgender (and by implication, intersex) people from entering public facilities that align most closely with their gender identities and expressions, but may differ from the sex assigned to them on their birth certificates. Transgender people have been banned from military service until recently in the United States and other countries, and the ban remains in many others.

What: Invisibility: Those in power continually attempt to omit, delete, minimize, distort, and completely erase the contributions, presence, and existence of individuals and groups as if they have made no significant and important contributions. The result often is that many groups' histories, stories, and voices have gone underrepresented. Therefore, "[t]he Other's existence, everyday life, achievements are kept unknown through invisibility" (Pharr, 1988, p. 58).

What: Distortion: The invisibility of the "Other" reflecting their incomplete, inaccurate, or thoroughly false histories provides a distorted overall picture of their existence. Within this environment of virtual invisibility and distortion, conditions are ripe for the creation, maintenance, and extension of stereotyping.

What: Stereotyping: A stereotype is an oversimplified, preconceived, and standardized conception, opinion, affective attitude, judgment, or image of a person, group, etc., held in common by members of other groups. Originally referring to the process of making type from a metal mold in printing, social stereotypes can be viewed as molds of regular and invariable patterns of evaluation of others. Pharr discusses the ways that stereotypes depersonalize and dehumanize people and their ideas, in effect seeing individuals largely as members of a group and not as individuals with unique and distinctive qualities and attributes. This often results in the tendency to diminish the humanity of people by relegating them to the category of "Other," and as "different."

Hewstone and Giles (1986) isolate three fundamental facets of stereotypes: (1) categorizing others based on easily identifiable characteristics; (2) assuming that certain attributes apply to most or all of the people in the category, and that people in the category are different from people in other categories with respect to these attributes; and (3) assuming that individual members of the category have the attributes associated with their groups.

Stereotypes may have originally contained some small grain of truth, but that element has since been exaggerated, distorted, or in some way taken out of context. Stereotypes, therefore, may be based on false generalizations derived from very small samples or even from a unique case. Some stereotypes have no foundation in fact at all. When stereotyping occurs, people tend to overlook all other characteristics of the group. Individuals sometime use stereotypes to justify the subjugation of members of that group. In this sense, stereotypes conform to the literal meaning of the word "prejudice," which is a *pre*judgment.

Are There "Positive" Stereotypes?

When people, for example, carry the stereotypes that all gay males have a great fashion sense and are well groomed, that all lesbians are mechanical and strong, that all Asians have a special aptitude for mathematics and physics, all Jewish men are doctors or lawyers, or that all African-heritage people have superior athletic abilities, the person is placing members of these groups—from different social identities—into limited boxes, perpetuating stereotyping, while neglecting to view each person's individual abilities, talents, and learning styles. Basically, they are still "othering" them. Thus, all stereotypes—whether considered "positive" or "negative"—imprison individuals and erase diversity and individuality.

What: Blaming the Victim: In this element of oppression, Suzanne Pharr discusses how perpetrators of oppression attempt to portray targets as somehow deserving the treatment they receive; that the problems people face are the result of individual behaviors and failures of character, motivation, culture, and others causes.

> Blaming the victims for their oppression diverts attention from the true abuser or the cause of the victimization. For example, a commonly held belief is that people are poor because they are unwilling to work. The belief is supported by the stereotypes that poor people are lazy, abuse welfare, etc. What goes unnoted is the necessity for poverty in an economic system in which wealth is held and controlled by the few. (Pharr, p. 60)

Teräshjo and Salmivalli (2003) contend that those who bully fulfill the social "function" of establishing and reinforcing social norms. They found that students often justify bullying behaviors by blaming the targets of their attacks and emphasizing that they somehow deserve the peer aggression or that they in some way deviate from the established peer social norms. This is a form of "ruthless socialization." The element of blaming the victim often leads to the targets of oppression coming to believe they somehow deserve the treatment they receive in which they may act complicit with those who are advantaged within the society.

Internalized Oppression and Domination

This can result in people and groups believing the falsehoods, derogatory characterizations, stereotypes, and myths society perpetuates about them and their group. They may find it difficult not to internalize society's negative notions of themselves. Internalized oppression can be defined as the internalization, consciously or unconsciously, of external attitudes, myths, and stereotypes of inferiority, inadequacy, self-hatred, and sense of "otherness" by the targets of systematic oppression. Internalizing these external negative societal messages is not their fault, for they too have been socialized within the systemic framework of oppression. There are, however, steps we can take to reduce, or even eliminate internalized oppression, though working to end this internalization is a lengthy process.

What: Members of subordinate groups as a community carry with them an "oppression mentality," an "enemy memory" (Shelby Steele, in Berman, 1994), or a "siege mentality" (Hertzberg, in Feagin & Feagin, 1993, p. 167), which is the intense awareness that oppression can surface again at any time, regardless of how "good" conditions may appear at the moment.

What: Claude Steele (1997) coined the term "stereotype vulnerability" referring to when students of color fear conforming to the myth of intellectual inferiority. They, therefore, sometimes decrease their academic efforts in an attempt to protect themselves psychologically from the potentially devastating prospects of trying hard with poor results.

Poet and essayist Rich (1983) discusses internalized oppression and the desire to "fit in" and assimilate:

> The pressure to assimilate says different things to different people: change your name, your accent, your nose; straighten or dye your hair; stay in the closet; pretend the Pilgrims were your fathers; become baptized as a christian, wear dangerously high heels, and starve yourself to look young, thin, and feminine; don't gesture with your hands; value elite European culture above all others; laugh at jokes about your own

people; don't make trouble; defer to white men; smile when they take your picture; be ashamed of what you are. To assimilate means to give up not only your history but your body, to try to adopt an alien appearance because your own is not good enough, to fear naming yourself lest name be twisted into label. (p. 142)

An essential tenet of liberation is having the power and freedom to define ourselves!

Preeminent social science researcher Allport (1954) states that people respond in a vast variety of ways when confronting oppression. He terms these "traits due to victimization" (p. 138) or "persecution-produced traits." Many of Allport's traits are usually very destructive and psychologically damaging. Some, though, can be constructive and creative, for example, (1) strengthening ties with members of one's minoritized group, (2) having sympathy with and support for other minoritized peoples; (3) developing enhanced motivation, ambition, and assertiveness by seeing oppression as an obstacle or challenge to be surmounted; and (4) challenging the status quo in a variety of ways and refusing to "take it any longer," which can effect progressive social change.

Systems of oppression operate most "efficiently" when the targets as well as those who are advantaged internalize their assigned "roles" and accept the hierarchal positions in which they have been placed. Bell (2007) distinguishes between two types of "internalization." She defines "internalized subordination" as "the ways in which the oppressed collude with their own oppression." Memmi, in his pioneering book *The Colonizer and the Colonized* (1957), terms this "psychological colonization."

What: Bell refers to "internalized domination":

Through internalized domination individuals in the advantaged group incorporate and accept prejudices against others and assume that the status quo is normal and correct. They learn to look at themselves, others, and society through a distorted lens in which the structural privileges they enjoy and the cultural practices of their group are represented as normal and universal. (p. 12)

Bell brings up the example of the ways men have been socialized to interrupt and take over when women speak in conversations, while stereotyping women as constantly chattering.

What: According to Lipsky (1977) referring to internalized racism, which can also apply to other forms of internalized oppression:

The result has been that these distress patterns, created by oppression and racism from the outside, have been played out in the only two places it has seemed "safe" to do so. First, upon members of our own group—particularly upon those over whom we have some degree of power or control. ... Second, upon ourselves through all manner of self-invalidation, self-doubt, isolation, fear, feelings of powerlessness, and despair. (p. 5)

So What: In my studies and professional and personal work, I have compiled a list of some forms internalized oppression has taken. This includes, but is not limited to, the following:

- Denial of one's minoritized identity(ies) to oneself and others
- Attempts to alter or change one's identity(ies)
- Attempts to "pass" as a member(s) of a dominant group(s) to gain social approval
- Feeling one is never "good enough" (sometimes a tendency toward "perfectionism")
- Engaging in obsessive thinking and/or compulsive behaviors
- Under-achievement as a sign of resignation or giving up; or over-achievement as a bid for acceptance
- Delayed or postponed emotional and/or cognitive development
- Low self-esteem and/or body image
- Contempt for the more "open" or "obvious" members of your identity community(ies)
- Contempt for those at earlier stages of the identity developmental process (The "I am prouder than thou" attitude)
- Denial that oppression against minoritized peoples and communities are serious social problems
- Contempt for those who are *not just like* ourselves; and/or Contempt for those who seem *like* ourselves
- Becoming psychologically and/or physically abusive; or remaining in an abusive relationship
- Increased fear and withdrawal from friends and relatives
- Shame and/or depression
- Defensiveness
- Anger and/or bitterness
- School truancy and/or dropping out of school; workplace absenteeism/reduced productivity, resigning
- Continual self-monitoring of one's behaviors, mannerisms, beliefs, and ideas
- "Minstrelizing" or clowning as a way of acting out society's negative stereotypes of your minoritized identity(ies)

- Mistrust and destructive criticism of "activist" community leaders ("eating one's own")
- Reluctance to be around or have concern for children of dominant groups for fear of being considered a "pedophile"
- Conflicts with the law as a reaction to oppression, sometimes as a conscious or unconscious cry for help
- Unsafe sexual practices and other destructive risk-taking behaviors (including risks for pregnancy, sexually transmitted diseases (STDs), and HIV infection)
- Separating sex and love, and/or fear of intimacy; Sometimes low or lack of sexual drive
- Substance abuse (including food, alcohol, drugs, and others), or obsessive/compulsive behaviors
- Suicidal ideation, attempts, completion
- Projection of prejudice onto other minoritized group(s), reinforced by society's existing prejudices ("horizontal hostility")

What: Horizontal Hostility and Horizontal Violence: Stemming from her terms "horizontal violence" and "horizontal hostility," Pharr means having prejudice for and discriminating against other members of one's own marginalized or subordinated group rather than lodging anger toward dominant groups responsible for the subordination. Horizontal hostility also refers to hostility and/or competition with others who are also oppressed rather than joining in solidarity and coalition with other marginalized and underrepresented individuals and groups.

What: Isolation: Horizontal hostility results in circumventing, interfering with, and ultimately preventing solidarity and coalitions among groups and individuals, and/or taking advantage of the lack of solidarity among underrepresented groups and individuals. This amounts to a "divide and conquer" tactic by keeping people who come from marginalized group backgrounds virtually separated and apart physically, emotionally, and politically.

By keeping them divided, the chances of joining together to challenge the people and the policies that keep them disadvantaged (the Vertical Oppression) becomes difficult. For example, when working-class people of every social identity are taught they must compete with others for low wages rather than joining together to fight for higher wages, by doing so, they are made to work against their own economic self-interests, which supports the wages and profits of the already economically secure. What I refer to as a "join and share strategy," however, can supplant divide and conquer, justice can supersede inequality, and sharing power *with* others can surpass the oppressive power *over* others.

What: Assimilation and Tokenism: A few of the more imperceptible or subtle ways the larger society employs to maintain the systemic nature of oppression while suppressing solidarity between subordinated groups includes the tactics of assimilation and tokenism. Society imposes enormous pressure on all minoritized or subordinated groups to relinquish their cultures and "fit in" to an overarching dominant cultural standard or norm, to some amorphous undefined brew within a cultural "melting pot." This is true especially for all immigrant groups. This "assimilation" demands individuals to surrender their past and abandon their people to "blend in" to the greatest extent possible.

After an individual meets this compulsory requirement by embodying a socially fabricated "model" representative of their group, sometimes they are rewarded with a certain level of workplace advancement and other forms of social recognition resulting from the dominant group attempting to discredit or dispute any claims of and challenges to oppression.

Pharr (1988) states that:

> Tokenism is a form of co-optation. It takes the brightest and best of the most assimilated, rewards them with positions and money (though rarely genuine leadership and power), and then uses them as a model of what is necessary to succeed, even though there are often no more openings for others who may follow their model. (p. 63)

Jones and Calafell (2012) discuss tokenism in higher education content areas:

> The academy will gladly open up a small and tolerated space for alternative discourses. However, it should never be forgotten that the space has been granted as a placation, in an attempt to legitimate, sanitize, surveil, and perhaps co-opt. (p. 971)

What: Individualized Solutions: By holding up the few from minoritized groups who have "made it" socially and financially expands the larger societal narrative that individuals advance or fail due to their personal motivation and abilities, and not because of systemic inequity. This represents the societal response to systemic problems by purporting that individuals must simply work harder to proceed forward. In this way, society attempts to undercut the development and growth of groups and social movements that challenge the systemic nature of oppression. Individuals are, therefore, encouraged to *identify with* and (falsely) believe in those in positions of power to act in their best interests. This rests on the foundation of the myth of meritocracy.

Iris Marion Young's "Five Faces of Oppression"

Young's (1990) taxonomy of oppression addresses dominant group privilege and systemic oppression involving a constellation of conditions divided into five categories (or "faces") listed as exploitation, marginalization, powerlessness, cultural imperialism, and violence.

Exploitation

What: Young views the major feature of exploitation, one of her five "faces" of oppression, as "a steady process of the transfer of the results of the labor of one social group to benefit another" (p. 39). This results in the injustice of wide socioeconomic class divisions in which very few have enormous wealth while most have very little. Systemic exploitation particularly impacting people of color, women, young, and old people restricts groups of people from the freedom and status to achieve their full potential. They are among the social groups exploited by an economic and social system dominated by a white Christian male power structure.

Marginalization

What: Marginalization is the process whereby dominant social groups restrict entire categories of people from meaningful involvement in the social life of the community and nation. They are subjected to acute economic deprivation and even annihilation. Young (1990) defines marginals as "people the system of labor cannot or will not use … most of whom are racially marked" (p. 41). Young lists also people with disabilities that societies often marginalize. This marginalization can have very serious implications on individuals' sense of self and on their identity development, for they begin to view themselves through the lens of the dominant group. When this occurs, the targets of marginalization and systematic oppression remain susceptible to the effects of internalized oppression, whereby they internalize, consciously or unconsciously, attitudes of inferiority or "otherness."

Powerlessness

> Washing one's hands of the conflict between the powerful and the powerless means to side with the powerful, not to be neutral.
> —Freire (1985, p. 122)

What: Subordinated groups have less social power than members of dominant groups to engage in the decision-making process that affects the course of their lives or even to name the terms of their existence. "The powerless are ... those over whom power is exercised without their exercising it; the powerless are situated so that they must take orders and rarely have the right to give them ... and they rarely command respect" (Young, 1990, p. 43). In modern society, nonprofessional workers take orders from and lack the authority and status of those in professional ranks.

Cultural Imperialism

What: Young states that "[c]ultural imperialism involves the universalization of a dominant group's experiences and culture, and its establishment as the norm" (p. 45). Cultural imperialism is a form of hegemony. This often results in what Spring (2004) terms "cultural genocide" defined as "the attempt to destroy other cultures" (p. 3) through forced acquiescence and assimilation to majority rule and cultural and religious standards. This cultural genocide works through the process of "deculturalization," which Spring describes as "the educational process of destroying a people's culture and replacing it with a new culture" (p. 3).

A more extreme example of "deculturalization" and "cultural genocide" can be seen in the case of Christian European American domination over First Nation peoples, whom European Americans viewed as "uncivilized," "godless heathens," "barbarians," and "devil worshipers" (Takaki, 1993; Zinn, 1980). White Christian European Americans deculturalized indigenous peoples through many means: confiscation of land; forced relocation; undermining of their languages, cultures, and identities; forced conversion to Christianity; and the establishment of Christian day schools and off-reservation boarding schools far away from their people (Spring, 2004).

> Spreading Anglo-Saxon civilization and Protestantism provided the justification for English imperialism into the Americas, Africa, and Asia. Simply put, many English believed they could save the world by the imposition of their culture and religion. Many English during the colonial period believed that they were a people chosen by God to protect and spread the Protestant version of Christianity and that the English had a divine mission to spread doctrines of political liberty. Therefore, concepts of political liberty and racial superiority coexisted in English thought.
>
> —Spring (p. 4)

A Case Study of Cultural Imperialism

Between 1879 and 1905, 25 Indian boarding schools operated throughout the United States. The first off-reservation Indian boarding school was established in Carlisle, Pennsylvania in 1879 and run primarily by white Christian teachers and administered by Richard Pratt, a former cavalry commander in the Indian Territories. At the school, Indian children were stripped of their culture: the males' hair was cut short, all were forced to wear Western-style clothing, they were prohibited from conversing in their native languages and English was made compulsory, all their cultural and spiritual symbols were destroyed, and Christianity was imposed. As Pratt related to a Baptist audience: "[We must immerse] Indians in our civilization, and when we get them under, [hold] them there until they are thoroughly soaked" (Pratt, 1892) and "We must kill the Indian in him to save the man."

"Civilizing" Indians became a euphemism for Christian conversion. Christian missionaries throughout the United States worked vigorously to convert Indians. A mid-19th century missionary to the Sioux, Stephen Riggs, wrote: "As tribes and nationals the Indians must perish and live only as men, [and should] fall in with Christian civilization that is destined to cover the earth" (Riggs in Berkhofer, 1972, p. 7).

School lessons primarily centered on preaching, catechizing, and prayers (Perlmutter, 1992), which called for freedom from "the delusion of the Devil, the malice of the heathen [indigenous peoples], the invasions of our enemies, and mutinies and dissensions of our own people" (Cremin, 1970, p. 10). A number of Catholic parishes established parochial or parish schools, partly "because Protestant assumptions pervaded the public school curriculum and instruction" (Lippy, 2004, p. 114). Throughout the Alaska territory, Christian missionaries, including Presbyterians, Catholics, and Moravians vied to win converts. Simultaneously, the United States government issued laws barring Alaskan Indian ceremonies regarded as "pagan" and contrary to the spread of Christianity (Hinckley, 1967).

What: The expansion of the republic and movement west was in part justified by the overriding philosophical underpinnings since the American Revolution. Called "Manifest Destiny," it was based on the belief that God intended the United States to extend its holdings and its power across the wide continent of North America over the native Indian tribes from the east coast to the west.

"The doctrine of 'manifest destiny' embraced a belief in American Anglo-Saxon superiority. ... 'This continent,' a congressman declared, 'was intended by Providence as a vast theatre on which to work out the grand experiment of Republican government, under the auspices of the Anglo-Saxon race'" (quoted in Takaki, 1993, p. 176).

During the early years of the new republic, with its increasing population and desire for land, political leaders, such as George Washington and Thomas Jefferson, advocated that Indian lands should be obtained through treaties and purchases. President Jefferson in 1803 wrote a letter to then Tennessee political leader, Andrew Jackson, advising him to convince Indians to sell their "useless" forests to the U.S. government and become farmers (Takaki, 1993). Jefferson and other government leaders overlooked the fact that this style of individualized farming was contrary to Indian communitarian spiritual and cultural traditions.

Later, however, when he inhabited the White House, Jackson argued that white "settlers" had a "right" to confiscate Indian land. Though he proposed a combination of treaties and an exchange or trade of land, he maintained that whites had a right to claim any Indian lands that were not under cultivation. Essentially, Jackson recognized as the only legitimate claims for Indian lands those on which they grew crops or made other "improvements" (Spring, 2004). The Indian Removal Act of May 28, 1830 authorized President Jackson to confiscate Indian land east of the Mississippi River, "relocate" its former inhabitants, and exchange their former land with territory west of the River. The infamous "Trail of Tears" during Jackson's presidency attests to the forced evacuation and redeployment of entire Indian nations in which many died of cholera, exposure to the elements, contaminated food, and other environmental hazards.

The Naturalization Act of 1790 also excluded First Nation peoples from citizenship, considering them, paradoxically, as "domestic foreigners." They were not accorded rights of citizenship until 1924 when Congress passed the Indian Citizenship Act, though Asians continued to be denied naturalized citizenship status.

Violence

What: Several social theorists, including Pharr (1988) and Young (1990), list violence among the prime "elements" or "faces" of oppression. Many groups live with the constant fear of random and unprovoked systematic violence directed against them simply because of their social identities. The intent of this xenophobic (fear and hatred of anyone or anything seeming "foreign") violence is to harm, humiliate, and destroy the "other." Young claims that all the faces of oppression are connected, and, in particular, cultural imperialism and violence:

> The culturally imperialized may reject the dominant meanings and attempts to assert their own subjectivity, or the fact of their cultural difference may put the lie to the dominant culture's implicit claim to universality. The dissonance generated by such a challenge to the hegemonic cultural meanings can also be a source of irrational violence. (p. 47)

One year before the death of our slain leader, gay San Francisco City Supervisor Harvey Milk recorded a will that was to be played in the event of his assassination. In it he stated that he never considered himself simply as a candidate for public office, but rather, always considered himself as part of a movement: a liberation movement for lesbian, gay, bisexual, and transgender people—and a liberation movement for all people. Each time Harvey spoke in front of a crowd, he urged people to come out everywhere and often: "Tell your immediate family," he would say, "tell friends, neighbors, people in the stores you shop in, cab drivers, everyone." And he urged heterosexual people to be our allies, to interrupt derogatory remarks and jokes, to support us and offer aid when needed. If we all did this, he said, we could change the world.

All the numerous spokes on the wheel of oppression attempt to maintain control and power over others in the use of violence in which members of subordinated groups are viewed by many of higher status as less worthy and in cases, as less human.

· 9 ·

THE MANY SPOKES ON THE WHEEL OF OPPRESSION

What: We can perceive "oppression," and its attendant dominant group privileges, as comprising a metaphorical wheel with the numerous spokes each representing the various forms oppression takes. These include ableism, adultism, ageism, biphobia, chauvinism, cissexism, classism, environmental oppression/ecoism, ethnocentrism, heterosexism, jingoism, linguicism, lookism, racism, religious oppression, sexism, xenophobia, and more. If somehow we could dismantle or eliminate one of the spokes, the wheel will, nevertheless, continue to trample over the rights and the very lives of individuals and entire groups of people based on their many intersectional social identities.

I am reminded once again of Rev. Dr. Martin Luther King Jr.'s (1963, A letter from a Birmingham Jail, Birmingham, AL) vibrant image of the "inescapable network of mutuality" that links humanity. Hamer (1971) envisioned an inclusive model of social justice because she believed that "Nobody's free until everybody's free." Lorde reminds us in her foundational essay, "There Is No Hierarchy of Oppression" that no specific form of oppression is systemically better or worse than the others on the individuals and groups affected.

> As a forty-nine-year-old Black, lesbian, feminist, socialist, poet, mother of two including one boy and member of an interracial couple, I usually find myself part of some group in which the majority defines me as deviant, difficult, inferior, or just plain "wrong." (Lorde, 1984, p. 114)

And,

> From my membership in all of these groups I have learned that oppression and the intolerance of difference come in all shapes and sizes and colors and sexualities; and that among those of us who share the goals of liberation and a workable future for our children, there can be no hierarchies of oppression. (Lorde, 1983, p. 9)

Audre Lorde refers to the multiple forms (the spokes on the wheel) that oppression takes, which we as individuals and groups, our social institutions, and our larger societies, cultures, and planet of nations must work together to dismantle in our process toward a genuine socially just and liberated world. What follows is a summary discussion of many, though certainly not all, of the spokes on the wheel of oppression.

Ableism

What: Ableism is the system of oppression against people with disabilities while favoring (temporarily) able-bodied people. (I include "temporarily" since at some point in people's lives, they will experience a disability through illness, accident, violence, war, or growing older, with death being the disability that comes to us all.)

Ableist oppression arises frequently on the individual/interpersonal, institutional, and societal/cultural levels when perceiving people with disabilities through a "medical model," rather than a "wellness model" as applied by many disability rights advocates. I have constructed my conceptualization of the outer poles on the vast continuum between these models. (See page 35.)

So What: Many people whom society has labeled "disabled," however, find that their only "disability" is the ways their societies *react* to them and how these societies often fail to make accommodations to their differing needs. In Young's (1990) discussion of the "Five Faces of Oppression," she states that the "face" of Marginalization is very dangerous for many subordinate groups, including people with disabilities.

> A whole category of people is expelled from useful participation in social life and thus potentially subjected to severe material deprivation and even extermination. ... Material deprivation, which can be addressed by redistributive social policies, is not, however, the extent of the harm caused by marginalization. ... [T]he provision of welfare itself produces new injustice by depriving those dependent on it of rights and freedoms that others have ... [and] even when material deprivation is somewhat mitigated by the welfare state, marginalization is unjust

because it blocks the opportunity to exercise capacities in socially defined and recognized ways. (p. 39)

So What: Though each country around the world may have established varying legal definitions of "disabling conditions," the United States passed model legislation, the American with Disabilities Act (ADA, 1990, amended 2008), which prohibits discrimination against people with disabilities in employment, transportation, public accommodations, telecommunications, and government activities. The law makes it illegal to discriminate by private employers, state and local governments, employment agencies, and labor unions.

Under the ADA, a disability is defined as having at least one of the following: a physical or mental impairment that substantially limits one or more major life activities; a record of such an impairment; or being regarded as having such an impairment. The impairment must limit a person's major life activities. When one qualifies under these criteria, employers must make "reasonable accommodation" for the person with disabilities.

Returning injured veterans from the first and second World War sparked the development of rehabilitation services and devices, and a movement toward reintegration into the larger society including the Independent Living Movement and the push for the construction of all public building (Castañeda, Hopkins, & Peters, 2013), and the making of all products and environments to use "universal design" (broad-spectrum concept accommodating people with and without disabilities and of all ages).

Many countries have used legislative means in their attempts to make life better and more accommodating for people with disabilities. I include some of the legislation passed in the United States:

> Rehabilitation Act (PL 93–112), 1993: Prohibited discrimination against individuals with disabilities in programs and activities receiving federal aid. Section 504 of the law requires colleges and universities to make reasonable accommodations for students with disabilities, so they will not be discriminated against because of their disabilities.

Legislation Regarding Disabilities in Education

Education for All Handicapped Children Act (PL 94–142), 1975: This federal law contains a mandatory provision stating that to receive federal funds, every school system in the nation must provide a free, appropriate public education for every child between the ages of 3–18 (extended later to 3–21) regardless of how seriously they may be disabled.

Public Law (PL 99–457), 1986: This law stipulated that states must provide preschool services to all children with disabilities between the ages of 3–5. It also provides incentives for establishing special education programs for infants and toddlers.

Individuals with Disabilities Education Act (IDEA), 1990, 1997, (Individuals with Disabilities Education Improvement Act (IDEIA), 2004: PL 94–142 was amended in 1990 to become IDEA, and again amended in 1997. It was then amended in 2004 and renamed Individuals with Disabilities Education Improvement Act. Each state and locality must have a plan to ensure:

1. Identification of All Children & Youths with Disabilities,
2. Free, Appropriate Public Education (FAPE),
3. Due Process: Right to Information and Informed Consent,
4. Parent/Guardian Surrogate Consultation,
5. Least Restrictive Environment (LRE),
6. Individualized Education Program (IEP),
7. Nondiscriminatory Evaluation,
8. Confidentiality,
9. Personnel Development, In-Service.

IDEA requires an Individualized Education Plan (IEP) approved by the student's parent(s) or guardian(s), which is drawn up by the educational team for each exceptional child, and must include:

For All Students:

- Present Levels of Educational Performance (PLEP), sometimes referred to as Present Levels of Performance (PLOP)
- Measurable Goals and Objectives
- Assessment Status
- Participation with Nondisabled Students
- All Needed Services Fully Described (amount, frequency, etc.)
- Progress Reporting

For Some Students:

- Transition, Including Transfer of Parental Rights to Students
- Behavior Plan
- English as Second Language Needs
- Braille

- Communication Needs
- Assistive Technology

Individualized Family Service Plan (IFSP) is also mandated by PL 99–457 to provide services for young children with disabilities (under 3 years of age) and their families, drawn up by professionals and parents. This is similar to an IEP for older children.

While the U.S. federal government passed several laws (*de jure*) protecting the educational and civil rights of people with disabilities and their families in the United States and in some other countries across the globe, systematic oppression remains (*de facto*) in all levels: individual/interpersonal, institutional, and societal/cultural. The British organization, Union of Physically Impaired Against Segregation (UPIAS), in 1975 passed its *Fundamental Principles of Disability* in which it framed the basic assumption referring to the "social model" of disability:

> In our view, it is society which disabled physically impaired people. Disability is something that is imposed on top of our impairments by the way we are unnecessarily isolated and excluded from full participation in society. Disabled people are therefore an oppressed group in society. (p. 3)

Adultism

What: One of the litmus tests by which a society can be judged is the ways it treats its young people, for this opens a window projecting how that society operates generally. While some authors use the term "ageism" to apply to oppression on the general basis of age—either against the young or against older people—two terms have been increasingly employed: "adultism" regards oppression against young people by adults, and "ageism" against elders by youth and by adults (Love & Phillips, 2007). Adultism, as defined by Bell (2003) includes "behaviors and attitudes based on the assumption that adults are better than young people and entitled to act upon young people without their agreement. This mistreatment is reinforced by social institutions, laws, customs, and attitudes" (n.p.). Within an adultist society, adults construct the rules, with little or no input from youth, which they force young people to follow.

Even the terminology our society employs to refer to youth betrays a hierarchical power dynamic. For example, we refer to young people as "kids," a term originally applying to young goats. By referring to youth as farm animals provides adults cover in controlling and maintaining unlimited power over *human beings*. (We must treat and respect animals better in many instances than we do as well.) Even the term "child" implies an imbalance of power. When people refer to an individual of *any* age as "the child of," we automatically imagine and place that individual in a diminutive form.

Of course, parents and other adults have the inherent *responsibility* of protecting young people from harming themselves and being harmed by others, and of teaching them how to live and function in society within our ever-changing global community. In Freudian (1930) terms, we must develop a balance between the individual's unrestrained instinctual drives and restraints (repression) on these drives in the service of maintaining society (civilization), and to sustain the life of the individual. Society, nonetheless, must set a line demarcating protection from control, teaching from oppression, minimal and fundamental repression from what Marcuse (1961) terms "surplus repression": that which goes over and beyond what is necessary for the protection of the individual and the smooth functioning of society, and enters the realm of domination, control, and oppression.

Reading and watching *The Hunger Games* series of young adult novels by Suzanne Collins released in 2008 and transformed into a sequence of movies, I was quite fascinated by what I interpreted as a commentary on our oppressive (surplus-repressive) society. The author presents the story through the perspective of 16-year-old Katniss Everdeen, which takes place in Panem, the post-apocalyptic nation where the former countries of North America once existed. The Capitol (as it is named), a technologically advanced metropolis, exerts total political control over the entire nation. *The Hunger Games* denotes an annual event in which one young woman and one young man aged 12–18 from each of the 12 districts are selected by lottery to compete in a televised brutal and deadly battle. Of the 24 "contestants," only one will survive, though in the initial installment of the series, two *contestants contest* this rule, and they begin to forge a crack in the wall of domination.

One of the primary ways oppression in all its varieties operates is when the dominant group, in this case adults, pit members of minoritized groups, in this case youth, against one another (divide and conquer) through competition for gold stars and grades, for supposedly scarce resources, for attention, love, and affection, for financial and career success, and, in the metaphor of *The Hunger Games*, for life itself.

In addition, those of *any* age who bully often do so, though sometimes unconsciously, to reinforce dominant group scripts established and forced onto minoritized individuals and groups to memorize when they enter the stage called "life." When youth bully other youth, very often those who bully "pass down" the bullying they receive from others, often from adults. Youth killing other youth, as depicted in *The Hunger Games*, epitomizes the most extreme form of bullying.

Adultism also operates as a continuum from subtle to extreme, from adults ignoring or neglecting young people, to statements like "Children should be seen and not heard," "You're too young to do that," and "Just grow up," to "You're stupid," and "You're ugly," to "When you are living in *my* house, you follow *my* rules," to circumscribed or qualified love, to corporal punishment, and eviction by family from one's home, to sexual and other violent assaultive acts, to murder. As a society, we deprive youth of their basic civil and human rights only somewhat less than we deprive these rights from convicted prison inmates.

What if, however, youth joined together to defeat adultist oppression—the surplus repression establishing and maintaining adult privilege and control over youth? More generally, what if all minoritized groups joined together to challenge dominant group privilege and oppression in all its forms? In fact, youth and other groups of our vast society are, indeed, standing up, speaking out, and joining in coalition to contest the barriers built throughout time and space. This is true in *The Hunger Games* as it is outside of science fiction.

Ageism

What: While elders in most countries were once considered as wise and treasured members of their communities, in many contemporary societies, older people are often marginalized, stripped of their rights and responsibilities, their dignity, their voice, and the power to control their lives. Nelson (2005) explains the change in attitudes regarding elders resulting from two dramatic historical developments.

> First, the advent of the printing press was responsible for a major change in the status of elders (Branco & Williamson, 1982). The culture, tradition, and history of a society or tribe now could be repeated innumerable times, in exact detail through books, and the status and power elders once had as the village historians was greatly reduced and, in many cases, eliminated.
>
> The second major development in society that led to a shift in attitudes toward the elderly was the industrial revolution (Stearns & Tassel, 1986). The industrial revolution demanded great mobility in families—to go where the jobs were. In light

of this new pressure to be mobile, the extended family structure (with grandparents in the household) was less adaptive. Older people were not as mobile as younger people. (p. 207)

An early writer on the topic of oppression toward older people is Butler (1975) who defines "ageism" as:

> A process of systematic stereotyping of and discrimination against people because they are old. ... Old people are categorized as senile, rigid in thought and manner, old fashioned in morality and skills. ... Ageism allows the younger generations to see older people as different than themselves; thus they subtly cease to identify with the elders as human beings. (p. 12)

Gullette (2017) describes ageism as "the infliction of suffering by the mere fact of birthdate" (p. viii).

Cissexism/Transgender Oppression[1]

What: Cisgender is a term for individuals who match the sex assigned to them at birth with their bodies, and their personal gender identities. Other terms include "gender normative," "cismale," "cisfemale," and others. The Latin prefix *cis* means "on the same side (as)" or "on the side (of)" or "to/this the near side."

What: Cissexism ("Binarism," "Transgender [or Trans] Oppression," "Genderism," or "Transgenderphobia") is oppression against transgender people and comprises a conceptual structure of oppression directed against those who live and function external to the gender/sex binary, and/or the doctrine that they do not exist at all. Trans people have exposed the truth regarding this fabrication we call "gender roles" and the rigidity of gender identity as social constructions, which societies ascribe to individuals as it assigns us a sex at birth. With the label "female" assigned at birth, most societies force us to follow its "feminine script," and with "male" assigned at birth, we are handed our "masculine script" to act out.

So What: Members of trans communities often suffer the consequences of other truth tellers of the past. Nearly every three days, attackers kill a trans person somewhere in the world for expressing gender diversity. The clear majority of murders are of trans women of color. Murderers of trans people react in extreme and fanatical ways at the direction of the larger coercive societal battalions bent on destroying all signs of gender transgression in young and old alike in the maintenance of these gender scripts. We must not and cannot dismiss the murders of trans people as only the actions of a few disturbed and sadistic individuals, for oppression exists on multiple levels in multiple forms. The killers live in societies that subtly and not-so-subtly promote intolerance, spread stereotypes, impose stigmata, and perpetuate violence and the threat of violence. These incidents of murder must be understood as symptoms of larger systemic national norms.

Class and Classism

> The worship of the ancient golden calf has returned in a new and ruthless guise in the idolatry of money and the dictatorship of an impersonal economy lacking a truly human purpose. The worldwide crisis affecting finance and the economy lays bare their imbalances and, above all, their lack of real concern for human beings; man is reduced to one of his needs alone: consumption.
> —Pope Francis, 2013

What: Leondar-Wright and Yeskel (2007) define socioeconomic class as "a relative social ranking based on income, wealth, education, status, and power," and they define classism as "The institutional, cultural, and individual set of practices and beliefs that assign differential value to people according to their socioeconomic class; and an economic system that creates excessive inequality and causes basic human needs to go unmet" (p. 314).

So What: Pope Francis, in his 2013 Apostolic Exhortation *Evangelii Gaudium*, asserted his firm demand that the problems of massive structural income and wealth inequality between peoples of the world must be met with swift and appropriate measures "by rejecting the absolute autonomy of markets and financial speculation." If we do not meet this crisis, he continued, we will not be able as humans to solve any of the world's major problems. The Pope was particularly critical of unfettered Capitalist economies in his unusually descriptive remarks at a sermon delivered in Bolivia earlier in the summer of 2013 in which he quoted Saint Basil the Great:

> [B]ehind all this pain, death and destruction there is the stench of what Basil of Caesarea called "the dung of the devil". An unfettered pursuit of money rules. The service of the common good is left behind. Once capital becomes an idol and guides people's decisions, once greed for money presides over the entire socioeconomic system, it ruins society, it condemns and enslaves men and women, it destroys human fraternity, it sets people against one another and, as we clearly see, it even puts at risk [with pollution resulting in climate change] our common home.

Keynesian v. Neoliberal Economic Policies

What: In economic and political discussions and strategies within many democracies around the globe, the battle lines have clearly solidified over competing ideologies separating not only individuals, but also differentiating entire political parties and nations regarding the structure and purpose of government. One argument rests on the ideas of Keynes (1936), a bisexual British economist who theorized that economic growth and reduced unemployment can be supported through governmental fiscal policies, including spending to stimulate the economy, adjusting interest rates, and placement of certain regulations on market economics.

Another and competing philosophy has come to be known as "neoliberalism," which centers on a market-driven approach to economic and social policy, including such tenets as reducing the size of the national government and granting more control to state and local governments; severely reducing or ending governmental regulation over the private sector; privatization of governmental services, industries, and institutions including education, health care, and social welfare; permanent incorporation of across-the-board non-progressive marginal federal and state tax rates; and possibly most importantly, market-driven and unfettered "free market" economics.

As a corollary of neoliberalism, according to the so-called "Allocation Theory" of education, schooling has turned into a status competition, which confers success on some and failure on others. Our schools have morphed into assembly-line factories transforming students into workers, and then sorting these workers into jobs commanded by industry and business. In so doing, educational institutions legitimize and maintain the social order (read as the status quo). Schools drive individuals to fill certain roles or positions in society, which are not always based on the individuals' talents or interests.

So What: While there have always been familial and social pressures to perform academically, and while some people have always attempted to get or attain something with the least amount of energy expended, what effects has the age of "No Child Left Behind," an age of standardization, corporatization, globalization, privatization, and deregulation of the business, banking, and corporate sectors have on learning?

Standardized curriculum and testing were initially intended to gauge students' progress, but have, unfortunately, metastasized into benchmarks for student advancement through the levels of education, for teacher accountability, as well as criteria for school funding from the government. The Core

Standards curriculum policies, rather than improving the educational outcomes of our students, have the potential of merely reinforcing and extending the failed so-called "neoliberal" policies of the past.

The tenets of neoliberalism, taken together, claim those who favor neoliberal ideas, will ensure the continual growth of the economy, that wealth will "trickle down" from the top, while protecting individual autonomy, liberty, and freedom. Neoliberalism rests on the foundation of "meritocracy" (as described earlier). But take, for example, when during the 2012 U.S. presidential campaign at the CNN Television Tea Party-sponsored Republican presidential candidates' debate in Florida, the debate facilitator, CNN's Wolf Blitzer, asked then presidential candidate Ron Paul the hypothetical question of what we as a society should do in the case of a 30-year-old man who chooses not to purchase health insurance, and later develops a serious life-threatening disease. Before Paul had a chance to answer Blitzer's question, a number of audience members shouted "Let him die. Let him die."

Though the neoliberal battle cry of "liberty" and "freedom" through "personal responsibility" sounds wonderful on the surface, what are the costs of this alleged "liberty" and "freedom"? Pope Francis answered that question in his *Evangelii Gaudium*:

> [S]ome people continue to defend trickle-down theories which assume that economic growth, encouraged by a free market, will inevitably succeed in bringing about greater justice and inclusiveness in the world. This opinion, which has never been confirmed by the facts, expresses a crude and naive trust in the goodness of those wielding economic power and in the sacralized workings of the prevailing economic system.

Cultural Capital and Social Capital

What: French sociologist Bourdieu (1986) coined the term "Cultural Capital" to explain the cultural differences that reproduce social class division. It represents the collection of *non-economic* and *non-material* assets, such as family background, social class, varying investments in and commitments to education, different resources, etc. that influence social mobility and success within a stratified society. Bourdieu distinguishes three forms of cultural capital. The "embodied" is directly linked to and incorporated within the individual and represents what they know and can do. Embodied capital can be increased by investing time into self-improvement in the form of learning. As embodied capital becomes integrated into the individual, it becomes a type of habitus and therefore cannot be transmitted instantaneously. "Objectified" cultural capital is represented by cultural goods, material objects such as books, paintings, instruments, or machines. They can be appropriated both materially with economic capital and symbolically via embodied capital. Finally, "institutionalized" cultural capital provides academic credentials and qualifications that create a "certificate of cultural competence which confers on its holder a conventional, constant, legally guaranteed value with respect to power" (p. 248). These academic qualifications can then be used as a rate of conversion between cultural and economic capital.

Bourdieu also discusses the concept of Social Capital, which, like cultural capital also refers to *non-economic* and *non-material* assets but denotes the social networks—the who—to whom one is connected relative to gaining social advancement.

Environmental Oppression/"Ecoism"

What: Environmental oppression refers to human activities that result in contamination of the Earth the environs of space.

The United States Government (2018) released its National Climate Assessment reporting that our global climate is, in fact, changing, and this is due primarily to human activity, particularly the burning of fossil fuels. The Assessment team, composed of over 300 scientific experts assisted by a 60-member Federal Advisory Committee, investigated approximately 12,000 professional scientific journal papers on the topic of global climate change, and discovered that in the articles expressing a position on global warming, 97% fully authenticated both the reality of global warming and the certainty that humans are the cause.

So What: The report found that between the time span of 1900 to the early 1960, world temperatures remained virtually stable. However, since that time, the climate of our planet has steadily increased. Scientists who conducted the study estimated that at the current rate of increase, by the year 2100, the world's average temperatures will increase a full 9 degrees Fahrenheit relative to the early 1960s. Additional studies released after this report sighted the beginning of the depletion and ultimate total collapse of glaciers in Antarctica, which can continue to raise worldwide sea levels an additional 4 feet. This depletion is now irreversible.

Now What: In 2015, world leaders came together, and many signed the Paris Climate Accord to work on the vital issues of controlling human-made factors such as the destruction of natural ecosystems and the pumping of toxins into the ground, water, and atmosphere effecting climate change. (The U.S. was a signatory under the Barack Obama administration, but Donald Trump took the U.S. out of the agreement in 2017.) As more countries adopt policies of continued governmental *de*regulations over the corporate and other business sectors, the goals of "Paris" will ultimately fail.

The following scientifically verified consequences (Cook et al., 2013) *of human*-impacted global warming are but a few of the reasons why climate change warrants the highest of priorities:

- Increasing species extinctions
- Reduction of coral reefs, mangrove forests, and tropical rainforests
- Threats to small island states in the Pacific as sea levels rise
- Increasing drought threats in Africa
- More severe flooding in densely populated river deltas in Asia
- More severe weather in hurricane-prone zones

Returning to Merriam-Webster's dictionary, which defines "oppression" as a noun meaning "the unjust or cruel exercise of authority or power" on the individual/interpersonal, institutional, and societal/cultural levels, then human treatment of the environment certainly falls under this definition. When humans place themselves into hierarchical positions of domination and subordination, environmental degradation inevitably results. Within a patriarchal system founded on white supremacy, which must dominate these "othered" bodies, the power structure, treats the Earth itself as an abject "othered" body, which it must control to remain in power.

This is little difference in a Western context from other hierarchies of power and privilege: white people over people of color, men over women, rich over working class and poor, heterosexuals over homosexuals and bisexuals, cisgender people over transgender people, able-bodied people over people with disabilities, native-born English speakers over immigrant linguistic minorities, adults of a certain age over youth and over seniors, Christians over member of all other religious and spiritual communities as well as over non-believers, and the spokes on the oppression wheel continue to trample over people and over our environment.

A non-regulated privatized so-called "free-market" economic system lacking in environmental protections is tantamount to a social system deficient of civil and human rights protections for minoritized peoples.

I attempted to find a term for environmental oppression in parallel structure with other forms of oppression, for example, racism, sexism, heterosexism, ableism, adultism, ageism, classism, cissexism, lookism, ethnocentrism, and many others. Since "environmentalism" refers to concerns for the environment rather than signifying a form of oppression, and I have not yet found an appropriate term, I have coined the term "ecoism." By extension, actions taken by individuals, groups, organizations, nations, and humanity at large, we can consider as "ecoist" actions.

Ethnocentrism

What: "Ethnocentrism," as defined by preeminent social scientist Sumner in his classic 1906 study, *Folkways*, is:

> ... the view of things in which one's own group is the center of everything, and all others are scaled and rated with reference to it. ... Each group nourishes its own pride and vanity, boasts itself superior, exalts its own divinities, and looks with contempt on outsiders. Each group thinks its own folkways [norms] the only right ones. ... [T]he most important fact is that ethnocentrism leads a people to exaggerate and intensify everything in their own folkways which is peculiar, and which differentiates them from others. It therefore strengthens the folkways. (pp. 12–13)

Though the concept of "ethnocentrism" is used to refer to the individual's self-centered rating or scaling of values in terms of "ingroup" norms, social scientists extend the notion to account for collective actions of ingroup/outgroup polarization and hostility. In fact, Freud (1914) referred to ethnocentrism as a form of narcissism at the *collective* or group level. Freud (1930) argued that ethnocentrism "functions" to displace aggression from the ingroup to the outgroup. In Social Identity Theory, ethnocentric attitudes and expressions can be triggered by the mere understanding of the existence of ingroups and outgroups. The stronger an individual identifies with the ingroup, the greater is the tendency to perceive members of outgroups in stereotypical and undifferentiated ways.

What?: Social Identity Theory was developed by Henri Tajfel and John Turner and their colleagues at the University of Briston in the 1970s and 1980s (Tajfel, 1981; Tajfel & Turner, 1979). Henry Tajfel was a survivor of Nazi occupied France and of German prison camps during World War II. He was particularly interested in studying the psychological processes in large groups, and the conditions and consequences of intergroup conflict. Tajfel along with Turner were interested in studying people's sense of themselves (their identities) and their motivations, responses, judgments, and overall perceptions when they became members of groups. They found that an individual's general psychological processes were profoundly and qualitatively altered and transformed in group settings.

Primary to their theory was their assertion that an individual's self-definition is changed in groups. In addition, one's personal identity (one's concept of self with unique characteristics, qualities, and personality) expands to an enlarged social identity. Though the individual carries personal identities into group situations, within the group there are also possibilities for a new identity, one that carries with it the perception of oneself not only as a *member* of the group, but also as someone with the *characteristics* of the group. In this transformation from personal identity to social identity, an individual's sense of self (and by connection, self-esteem) becomes intricately entwined with the successful functioning of the group.

To paraphrase Tajfel and Turner, to have good feelings about oneself, one has to have good feelings about the group. Along these lines and considering the process of comparison described by Festinger (1954), people outside the group (e.g., outgroup members and outgroups generally) are increasingly seen as inappropriate role models and sources of information and support.

Social Identity Theory is a social psychological theory of group membership, group processes, and intergroup relations. It posits that conflict will be activated whenever social categories and group divisions are present. It emphasizes the social context as a cause of the conflict, due in part to the multiple processes of social categorization, social comparison, and social identification.

Social Categorization: Bruner (1956) stated that "the main function of categorization is to reduce the complex object world to a more simple and manageable structure" (in Taylor & Doria, 1981, p. 83). People tend to accentuate the similarities among people within their own category as well as accentuate the differences of people of different categorical groupings. This categorization process in the formation of social groupings is the same process associated with the construction and maintenance of stereotypes.

Social Comparison: Social Comparison states that identity is organized and maintained through intergroup comparison. It is the process by which individuals will pursue a positive self-identity by comparing one's sense of self with the relevant outgroup, and in the process clarifying and crystallizing one's self-identify. Therefore, for individuals to feel positive about membership in a social group, they must first feel positive about that social group. Group theorists, such as Festinger (1954), argued that "individuals are attracted to groups in which the members have opinions similar to their own so that they can evaluate their own opinions with precision." In this process, group formation is enhanced. Also, comparison with other groups can lead to the ranking of groups as better/worse, higher/lower, majority/minority, domination/subordination, and others.

A seemingly contradictory, but nonetheless, closely allied corollary to social comparison is reference-group theory (e.g., Shibutani, 1955), which asserts that aspects of outgroups are sometimes praised and held up by the ingroups as something desirable to emulate.

Social Identification: Tajfel (1982) defined "social identification" as the knowledge that one belongs to a group, along with the emotional, psychological, and value significance attached to that membership. Hurtado, Gurin, and Peng (1994) termed this "psychological work," which is "both cognitive and emotional work" undertaken by individuals "to achieve a positive sense of distinctiveness" after the processes of social categorization and social comparison (p. 131).

An individual's sense of social identity stems from three specific realms (Pliner, 1996): from self-definition, from definition by other members *within* the social group, and from definition by those *outside* the social group (p. 41). Hurtado, Gurin, and Peng maintained that those social groupings that are valued, granted a high degree of privilege, and not highly obvious to others (e.g., being "white" or heterosexual) may not become salient identities to the individuals. On the other hand:

> The groups and categories that are most problematic for a sense of positive distinctiveness—ones that are disparaged, memberships that have to be negotiated frequently because they are visible to others, ones that have become politicized by social movements, etc.—are the most likely to become social identities for individuals. (Hurtado et al., 1994, p. 132)

If an individual is a member of a low-status group relative to other groups, theorists have identified several coping strategies for individuals to maintain their self-esteem. One strategy is labeled "disidentification" by Lewin (1948) who noted that sometimes people of lower status groups attempt to "pass" as members of higher status groups. Tajfel and Turner (1979) suggested other possible approaches. One is to restrict comparisons to either similar or subordinate groups so the results of these comparisons are more favorable to the ingroup than they would be if comparisons had been made to higher-status outgroups.

So then, what constitutes group membership in terms of issues related to identity? Tajfel (1982) defined "social identity" as the "individual's knowledge that he/she belongs to certain social groups together with some emotional and value significance to him/her of the group membership" (p. 2).

For Sumner (1906), the categorization of individuals into distinct ethnic groupings originated in the first human's struggles (and competition) to meet their basic needs. Social identity theories insist, however, that the simple fact of belonging to one group over another, and the mere subdivision or categorization of persons into ingroups and outgroups, is enough to trigger ethnocentric (xenophobic, discriminatory) attitudes favoring the ingroup (Tajfel, Billig, Bundy, & Flament, 1971). This is even the case when issues of competition for scarce resources and incompatible group goals are absent.

So What?: A major premise in Social Identify Theory, as proposed by Tajfel, is that social identities themselves create and maintain attitudinal and behavioral discriminations favoring the ingroup (Tajfel, 1978, 1982; Tajfel & Turner, 1986). The stronger are the individuals' identification with their ingroup, the greater is the tendency to perceive outgroup members as undifferentiated members of another social category, and to perceive oneself and other ingroup members as different or dissimilar from the outgroup. These researchers have called this "outgroup homogeneity effect" (Quattrone, 1986). This in turn provides the basis for stereotyping outgroups and outgroup members.

Several researchers argue that the mere recognition of two groups into dichotomous social categories is sufficient for hostility. That is, group membership *itself* has profound effects on psychological functioning, irrespective of personality types and other individual differences. It is thought that the individual is transformed in group situations. People will show favoritism toward the ingroup and hostility and discrimination toward the outgroup even:

- when group membership is random and anonymous,
- in the absence of intergroup interaction,
- where there is no history of explicit intergroup competition, enmity, conflict, or status concerns,
- where no self-interest is involved (Tajfel & Turner, 1986).

Tajfel (1978) differentiated between the "objective" and "subjective" factors that give rise to intergroup conflict. His definition of "objective" factors is closely related to realistic-group-conflict theory in terms of competition for scarce resources, and to issues of exploitation and marginalization by dominant groups. He added, however, that "subjective" conditions—including life experiences related to an individual's social group membership—can, in some circumstances, impact the conflict and, therefore, must be factored into the equation.

Social Identity Theory also maintains that different facets of identity hold varying degrees of salience depending on situational factors, especially since most people in most societies hold multiple social identities and are members of several groups. Bochner (1982), in surveying the intergroup literature, concluded that social group identity becomes particularly salient in the context of intergroup conflict; an individual becomes increasingly aware of social group membership in conflictual intergroup situations, especially when group differences are the basis for such conflict. Bruner (1956) suggested that group categories most often considered salient in a given situation are those that are most "accessible" to the person at the time, those that are the closest "fit" to the stimuli the individual encounters.

Azar and Burton (1986) contend that most protracted conflicts throughout the world were social-identity related. For conflict resolution strategies to be successful, Azar and Burton (1986) emphasized that psychological needs served by social identities must be considered because these "basic psychological needs cannot be negotiated, exchanged, or bargained away" (quoted in Stephan & Stephan, 1996, p. 150).

A closely aligned spoke on the oppression wheel is xenophobia, defined as "an unreasonable fear and hatred of foreigners or strangers, or that which is foreign of strange" (WordReference.com). Like racism and sexism, for example, xenophobia includes much more than fears, for it involves attitudes and behaviors we are often taught and have learned, and, therefore, fall under the category of oppression. Xenophobia operates through the processes of stereotyping and scapegoating.

On a micro level, ethnocentrism rears its head within a nation through anti-immigrant sentiments by political leaders exerting nativist and nationalist (chauvinist, jingoist) warnings. On a macro level, ethnocentrism finds expression through the rhetoric of supposed "clashing civilizations."

Heterosexism

What: Heterosexism is the overarching system of advantages bestowed to heterosexuals. Heterosexism, which has its roots in sexism, is the institutionalization of a heterosexual norm or standard, which establishes and perpetuates the notion that all people are or should be heterosexual, thereby privileging heterosexuals and heterosexuality, and excluding the needs, concerns, cultures, and life experiences of lesbians, gay males, and bisexuals. At times subtle but often overt, heterosexism is oppression by neglect, omission, erasure, and distortion, and also by purpose and design (Blumenfeld, 2013). A related concept is heteronormativity (Warner, 1991) and compulsory heterosexuality (Rich, 1994a), which establishes the normalization and privileging of heterosexuality on the personal/interpersonal, institutional, and societal/cultural levels.

So What: When parents automatically expect that their children will marry a person of (an)other sex at some future date, and that they will produce and rear children within this union; when the only positive and satisfying relationships portrayed by the media are heterosexual; when teachers presume all their students are heterosexual and teach only about the contributions of heterosexuals—these are examples of heterosexism.

Heterosexism also takes the form of pity, when the dominant group looks upon LGB people as unfortunate human beings who "can't help being the way they are." Heterosexism forces lesbians, gays, and bisexuals to struggle constantly against their own invisibility, and makes it much more difficult for them to integrate a positive sexual identity. Though not always overt, heterosexism is a form of discrimination nonetheless. Its frequent subtlety makes it somehow even more harmful and challenging because it is harder to define and combat.

What: Heterosexism's more active and at times visible component, called "Homophobia," is oppression by intent, purpose, and design. Derived from the Greek terms *homos*, meaning "same," and *phobikos*, meaning "having a fear of and/or an aversion toward," the word "homophobia" was coined by Weinberg in his 1972 book *Society and the Healthy Homosexual*. Other terms include: "homosexphobia," "homonegativism," "lesbian-" and "gay-hatred" or "-hating," and others. Homophobia can be defined as the fear and hatred of those who love and sexually desire some others of the same sex. Homophobia includes prejudice, discrimination, harassment, and acts of violence brought on by that fear and hatred.

Some people choose not to use the word "homophobia," preferring to use "heterosexism" as a more inclusive term by expanding its traditional definition. For purposes of discussion throughout this book, I use the term "heterosexism" in its expanded and inclusive form.

What: A related term is "Biphobia," which is oppression directed against bisexuals: people who love and sexually desire some members of their same and other sexes.

In a sense, however, the terms "homophobia" and "biphobia" are inaccurate terms and possibly misnomers. As we know in psychology, a "phobia" is defined as an "irrational" or "unreasonable" fear. For example, some people have irrational fears of insects (arachnophobia), or fear open spaces or being in crowded public places like shopping malls (agoraphobia). On the other hand, some fears (and forms of prejudice) are *taught* responses between individuals and within cultures. Homophobia and biphobia fall within this latter category. Rather than existing as irrational or unreasonable attitudes and behaviors, they exist within the realm of *learned* responses.

Jingoism, Chauvinism, Nativism, Patriotism, and Nationalism

What: Jingoism (synonymous with "chauvinism") is a highly exaggerated or ultra-extreme form of patriotism with isolationist, nativist, and sometimes warlike aggressive foreign policy initiatives. Nativism in this sense, is the dogma of defending the advantages of long-established native-born citizens or already-established non-native-born residents against those of immigrants.

We need to distinguish between two terms that are often used interchangeably, but actually, while connected in some ways, are unique and distinct: the terms are "Patriot" and "Nationalist" with their corresponding concepts being "Patriotic" and "Nationalistic."

The Free Dictionary, taken from Webster's New Collegiate Dictionary, defines a "Patriot" as: "1. a person who loves, supports, and defends his or her country and its interests. 2. a person who regards himself or herself as a defender, esp. of individual rights, against presumed interference by the federal government."

A "Nationalist," according to the same dictionary is "1. a person who has devotion and loyalty to one's own nation, and 2. a person who has *excessive* patriotism or chauvinism, which is a zealous and aggressive patriotism or enthusiasm for military glory, a biased devotion to any group, attitude, or cause." This is also synonymous with "Jingoism."

Possibly what separates the Patriot from the Nationalist is that the Patriot understands and witnesses the divide or the gap between the reality with the promise and potential of their country. The Nationalist, on the other hand, is often not aware that a gap even exists between the promise and the reality. A true Patriot is one who, indeed, loves their country (though not necessarily viewing it as "exceptional"), but also one who sees the way things are, and one who works for change to make things better. A Patriot also views other countries with respect and admiration, as valued members of an interconnected and interdependent global community. My vision of a Patriot is one who embraces John F. Kennedy's challenge articulated in his Inaugural Address on the Capitol stage by "ask[ing] not what your country can do for you" but rather "ask[ing] what you can do for your country."

While many countries around the world believe they are following a noble concept, a vibrant idea, and a vital and enduring vision, as nations, though, all continue to remain as works in process progressing toward but not yet attaining and not yet reaching that concept, that idea, and that vision.

Linguicism

What: I had the pleasure of visiting my cousin Charles Mahler in Antwerp, Belgium. One sunny day as we walked the promenade in that beautiful city, Charles, a fluent speaker of seven languages, posed a riddle to me: He asked, "What is it called when someone can speak three languages?" "Trilingual?" I guessed. "Okay," he said. "Now what is it called when someone can speak two languages?" I quipped, "Bilingual!" He said, "Yes. Now what is it called when someone can speak one language?" "Monolingual?," I replied tentatively. "No," he laughed. "It's called [U.S.-] American!"

His riddle, though intended partly in jest, shot to the very heart concerning my national linguistic perceptions and policies. While people from virtually all nations reside in the United States and contribute to our collective identity and economy, a seemingly linguistic isolationist code has taken hold of its national consciousness. Though French touches its northern and Spanish its southern territorial perimeters, a long-standing nationalist jingoist ethnocentric English-as-the-only-"official"-language crusade has infused the national landscape.

So What: Then former U.S. President Theodore Roosevelt clearly and firmly articulated this ethos in a letter he sent on January 3, 1919 to the President of the American Defense Society:

> We have room for but one language in this country, and that is the English language, for we intend to see that the crucible turns our people out as Americans, of American nationality, and not as dwellers in a polyglot boarding house.

More recently, in March 2012, Republican presidential candidate and former Pennsylvania Senator Rick Santorum (Reuters, 2012) asserted that as a condition for U.S. statehood, Puerto Rico, a Spanish-speaking territory, must require English as its primary language.

Though some advocates prefer the term "Official English," the English-only campaign surfaced as a movement circa 1981 to push for a constitutional amendment banning all languages other than English in government proceedings and printed materials emanating from federal, state, and local governments. Realizing how difficult and tiresome is the process of ratifying a constitutional amendment, proponents changed tactics by lobbying Congress for a "Language of Government" law mandating official English in the federal government, though such legislation has never passed both houses of Congress by a simple majority. Since that time, movement activists have succeeded in passing laws mandating English as the "official" language in several states, including my former home state of Iowa in 2002.

The Iowa law decrees English only in the printing of all government documents and forms, except for driver's education materials, trade and tourism documents, and documents discussing the rights of victims of crimes, criminal defendants, and constitutional issues. Backers of the law argue that it not only saves tax payers the expense of printing materials in multiple languages, but that sharing a single and common language aids overall communications and brings people together into a unified "patriotic" community.

Mandating English the official language in the United States or any state is about as necessary as establishing popcorn as the official snack at movie theaters in the United States. People will eat popcorn whether we codify it as "official," just as native-born residents and immigrants to our shores understand the necessity of establishing a functional command of English as a prime requisite for success and advancement.

The "English Only" movement in the United States has the effect, however, of marginalizing and demeaning non-native English speakers, decreases the likelihood of creating and maintaining multilingual programs, and gives us all the false and discriminatory impression that languages beside English are unimportant to learn, even though most other countries on the planet promote multilingualism.

My friend, a man of Mexican descent who grew up in San Antonio, Texas, told me how the English-only mandate in his elementary school negatively and unalterably impacted his self-esteem and identity. Though fluent in English, one afternoon during recess period while playing basketball on the school yard, he alerted his friend and teammate in Spanish to get ready to catch the ball. Upon hearing this, a playground monitor ran up to him, grabbed him tightly by his left ear, and dragged him to the principal's office where he was forced to attend "Spanish detention." The overt and covert messages of this incident became crystal clear: your language and your culture are not welcome here!

A few years ago, I created an online petition directed to the Iowa House of Representative, State Senate, and Governor Terry Branstad to abolish our state's "English-only" law because I believed it falls under the definition of "linguicism" (sometimes referred to as "languagism": coined by linguist Skutnabb-Kangas (1984) and defined as "ideologies and structures that are used to legitimate, effectuate and reproduce an unequal division of power and resources between groups, which are defined on the basis of language."

The petition struck a chord with a significant list of co-signers. According to one:

> As a bilingual person, this law sickens me and demonstrates the ignorance of some Americans. Bilingualism and the use of languages other than English only promote our richness as a nation, our heritage, and ultimately help to protect our national security. No true patriot could support or tolerate this hateful law.

Lookism

What: Tietje and Cresap (2005) discuss Lookism as "prejudice toward people because of their appearance. It has been receiving increasing attention, and it is becoming an important equal-opportunity issue. People we find attractive are given preferential treatment and people we find unattractive are denied opportunities" (p. 31).

These authors argue that though the term "lookism" is of fairly recent coinage, this form of oppression based on appearance or "looks" is longstanding.

> To judge by appearances is to get entangled in the Veil of Maya [in Buddhist thought] ... From ancient times until relatively recently, there was widespread worry about lookism, because the appearance of others may deceive, especially in romance, or it may be personally or politically imprudent to judge or act on appearances. Judging by appearances was prohibited by monotheistic religions ("no graven images") and criticized in ancient and medieval philosophies. Skeptics, Stoics, Cynics, Epicureans and Scholastics elaborated various reasons to avoid or subordinate the role of appearances. (Tietje & Cresap, 2005, p. 35)

So What: As the expression goes, "Beauty is in the mind of the beholder," but often what is in the beholder's mind reflects their society's constructed norms or standards of "beauty" and what that society determines will fall into the category of "unattractive" or "ugly," with a continuum between the poles. Based on these socially constructed standards, which often vary by cultures and historical time frames, people often make judgment about others based largely on physical appearance related to their intelligence, competence, employability, and romantic options. Like other forms of oppression, socially ascribed identities related to physical appearance place people into hierarchal positions granting or denying social power and privilege, domination and subordination. Lookism intersects with ageism and adultism, racism, sexism, cissexism, heterosexism, ethnocentrism, linguicism, and other forms of oppression.

Racism and White Supremacy

What: Bell (1980) of New York University Law School advanced the theory of "interest convergence," meaning that white people will support racial justice only when they understand and see something in it for *them*selves, when there is a "convergence" between the interests of white people and racial justice. Bell asserted that the United States Supreme Court ended the longstanding policy in 1954 of "separate but equal" in *Brown v. Board of Education* because it wanted to present to the world, and particularly to the Soviet Union during the height of the Cold War, a United States that supported civil and human rights.

Castañeda and Zúñiga (2013) define "racism" as: "the set of institutional, cultural, and interpersonal patterns and practices that create advantages for people legally defined and socially constructed as white, and the corollary disadvantages for people defined as belonging to racial groups that were not considered whites by the dominant power construct ..." (p. 58). Tatum (1999) understands racism intersectionally by emphasizing that "it is important to acknowledge that while all whites benefit from racism, they do not all benefit equally. Other factors, such as socioeconomic status, gender, age, religious affiliations, sexual orientation, mental and physical ability, also play a role in our social influence and power" (p. 12).

What: The philosophy and practice of white supremacy devalues all non-European-heritage lives and cultures. The institution of slavery in the "Americas" was built on a foundation of white supremacy. Primarily white people, backed by wealthy whites, invaded Africa, and then tracked, enticed, snared, and captured the proud people on the continent, chained and packed them like sardines into crowded ships' cargo holds, and transported them across vast oceans to foreign shores stripping those who survived of their dignity, languages, cultures, families, and humanity. The kidnappers as well as the residents of these lands viewed the "cargo" as cheap lives that *did not matter*, except to fulfill their needs for unpaid labor and to satisfy their sadistic ego and sexual gratification. If the enslaved had the "audacity" to misbehave or to escape the reserve called "the plantation," whites tracked, enticed, snared, captured and either returned them to the reserve where their so-called "masters" tortured them as examples to inhibit others from attempting escape, or they killed them.

Though whites did not need a rationalization for their terror, they justified their brutality on their interpretations of religious scriptures and, also, on the newly constructed "science" of "race." The "founding fathers" of the United States took Linneaus's constructions not only to reinscribe and revalidate the institution of slavery—many of these "founders" themselves enslaved large numbers of kidnapped Africans—but they also wrote into the U.S. Constitution the so-called "three-fifths clause" counting enslaved Africans as equivalent to three-fifths of a full human being for census purposes. As we can see, then, black lives certainly did not matter.

So What: Though the U.S. Congress passed on January 31, 1865 and the President signed into law on February 1, 1865 the 13th Amendment of the U.S. Constitution abolishing slavery, black and brown lives continued not to matter relative to white lives through Reconstruction, the Jim Crow South, into the 20th century CE, and beyond as we have clearly witnessed in the spate of murders of black people by police officers.

Now What: Black people in the United States coined in the 1960s the battle cries "Black is Beautiful" and "Black Power" as counter hegemonic narrative discourses in a nation that viewed skin with greater amounts of melanin as ugly and where white people fought ruthlessly to preserve supremacy over all people of color. More recently black people coined the rallying cry "Black Lives Matter" in a country where historically black lives have not mattered much relative to white lives.

What: The concept of "Social Reproduction" (originally proposed by Marx, 1867) asserts that social institutions, including schools, *reproduce* social inequities, especially in terms of socioeconomic class and race, which exist in the larger society.

So What: For example, the prison industrial complex within the United States (the country with the highest rate of 716 inmates per 100,000 of the population) *disproportionately* incarcerates and for longer terms (Nellis, 2016) people of color over white people for similar crimes. Though the U.S. represents 4.4% of the world's population, it houses 22% of the world prison inmates.

While most police officers enter law enforcement with good intentions to serve and assist the public and to support their own families, they bring with them their past socialization sometimes aided and abetted by members of their departments. Though usually subtle, the process by which systemic racism reproduces itself into law enforcement and other social institutions can also at times express itself quite blatantly. (See Immigration as Official U.S. "Racial" Policy: A Brief History, Liberatory Praxis Appendix F.)

Environmental Racism

What: Reverend Benjamin Chavis Jr., the former leader of the NAACP, introduced the term "environmental racism" in 1982 during a series of protests held at the proposed Warren County, North Carolina PCB landfill site. He explained it as

> … racial discrimination in environmental policy-making and enforcement of regulations and laws; the deliberate targeting of communities of color for toxic-waste facilities; the official sanctioning of the presence of life-threatening poisons and pollutants in communities of color; and the history of excluding people of color from leadership in the environmental movement.

So What: The case of an oil pipeline going through tribal lands in the United States demonstrates an example of "environmental racism" in North Dakota at the Oceti Sakowin encampment by thousands of protesters, including people from Standing Rock Sioux nation and from numerous other tribal communities in opposition to the Dakota Access Pipeline. Environmental racism is the disproportionate exposure to and impact on communities of color to environmental pollutants, toxins, and other contaminants depriving them of the ecological benefits of clean ground, water, and air. The project when designed would carry oil from the Bakken oil fields in North Dakota and Montana across the Plains to Illinois. Protestors argued that a completed pipeline would desecrate spiritual ancestral lands, endanger the water supply, and unfairly burden the Standing Rock Sioux nation, which would also gain nothing from any economic development resulting from the project.

Originally, the U.S. Army Corps of Engineers planned to cross the pipeline under the Missouri River north of Bismarck, North Dakota, but decided to reposition the route due to potential threats to the drinking water in the vastly majority-white municipality of Bismarck. The Corps decided, instead, to direct the pipeline under the river just upstream from the northern perimeter of the Standing Rock Sioux nation's land. The Corps made its decision after failing its federal mandate to consult with the people who would be most affected by the pipeline: The Standing Rock Sioux people—the "othered" abject bodies do not matter or matter far less than the white people around Bismarck. Onto these bodies, therefore, "law enforcement" officers justified dousing streaming torrents from giant water cannons in sub-freezing temperatures. They also justified evicting protestors from their lands, and incarcerating and prosecuting them.

The United States government set aside this land for the Sioux—lands it had previously stolen from native peoples—in the 1851 Treaty of Fort Laramie. The placement of the proposed pipeline stands as yet another incident in the long and brutal track record of the dominant group inflicting physical and cultural genocide on the abject bodies who get in the way or challenge a patriarchal hegemonic imperative.

"Colorblindness" Is Denial

What: With the ascendency of Barack Obama during the primaries and his election as the forty-fourth president of the United States in 2008, on numerous occasions the media have asserted that the United States can now be considered as a "post-racial" society, where the notion that "race" has lost its significance, and where that country's long history of racism is now at an end. For example, National Public Radio Senior News Analyst, Daniel Schorr, during the presidential primaries on January 28, 2008, on the program "All Things Considered," noted that with the emergence of Barack Obama, we have entered a new "post-racial" political era, and that Obama "transcends race" and is "race free."

And according to MSNBC Television political analyst, Chris Matthews, responding to Obama's State of the Union message on January 27, 2010:

> He is post-racial by all appearances. I forgot he was black tonight for an hour. You know, he's gone a long way to become a leader of this country, and past so much history, in just a year or two. I mean, it's something we don't even think about. (quoted in Phillips, 2010, n.p.)

So What: These commentators and others imply a number of claims in their statements: The first that the United States has become a "race-blind" or "colorblind" society—that race has become unimportant, that we don't see "race" anymore. The second implication states that racism (i.e., prejudice along with social power to enact oppression by white people over people of color) is a thing of the past. But is any contemporary Western country now a "colorblind" society? Or even more importantly, should these countries be "colorblind/race-blind" societies? The very notion of "race-blindness" is deeply problematic.

Though when we tell another that "I don't see your race; I just see you as a human being," may seem as a righteous statement, what are we really telling the person, and how may this come across: "I discount a part of you that I may not want to address," and "I will not see you in your multiple identities." This has the tendency of erasing the person's background and historical legacy, and hides the continuing hierarchical and systemic positionalities among white people and racially minoritized people. In addition, the assertion that we have fully addressed and finally concluded the long history of racism is simply unfounded.

In their book *Whitewashing Race: The Myth of a Color-Blind Society* (Brown et al., 2003), the authors show how the concept of "colorblindness/race-blindness" attempts to deny and further entrench hierarchical and deeply rooted systemic racial inequities and privileges accorded to white people that permeate throughout our society. We must as societies get beyond this false and counterproductive notion of "colorblindness/race-blindness" and confront head-on our past histories and current realities of racism and transcend, to use Mica Pollock's (2004) term, "colormuteness" by engaging in honest and open conversations on the impact and legacy of race relations in our countries.

Religious Oppression[2]

What: Religious Oppression relates to the ways dominant groups in countries systematically oppress, marginalize, and subordinate minoritized religions, spiritualities, non-believers and freethinkers on the individual/interpersonal, institutional, and social/cultural levels. It also involves the unearned privileges of members of the dominant religion and its adherents while simultaneously denying such privileges to other religious/spiritual traditions and non-believers. As in all the many forms of oppression, religious oppression is maintained by dominant hegemonic discourses normalizing dominant religious traditions and practices.

Examples of Christian Hegemony

In dominant-Christian nations, Christian hegemony is often not as apparent to Christian as it can be to non-Christians. Consider the example of the autumn season when seemingly earlier and earlier each year in October, merchants and media begin proclaiming "Happy Holidays" and "Merry Christmas." While many holidays, both religious and secular, occur around this time, "Happy Holidays" is in all actuality coded language for "Merry Christmas" and "Happy (Christian) New Year." In fact, most non-Christian major holidays do not come in December.

How many people who follow Christian faiths are familiar with non-Christian holidays and celebrations that come around this time of the year? What are these "Winter Parties," "Winter Concerts," "Winter School Breaks," and "Winter Vacations" really about? I would ask, how many Christians would even have heard of the Jewish commemoration of the historical holiday of Chanukah had it not usually fallen in December on the Gregorian calendar? In actuality, Chanukah is a relatively minor Jewish holiday.

What we are experiencing is a form of Christian cultural imperialism (hegemony): a promotion of the larger Christian culture, celebrations, values, and beliefs. I define Christian hegemony as the overarching system of advantages bestowed on Christians. It is the institutionalization of a Christian norm or standard, which establishes and perpetuates the notion that all people are or should be Christian, thereby privileging Christians and Christianity and excluding the needs, concerns, cultural practices, and life experiences of people who do not define themselves as Christian. Often overt though at times subtle, Christian hegemony is oppression by intent and design, as well as by neglect, omission, erasure and distortion.

While some of its religious significance has diminished over time as traditional Christian religious practice has entered the public square, on critical analysis, the clearly religious meanings, symbolism, positionality and antecedents of generalized holiday observances belie any claims that they have become fully secularized. The effect of the so-called "secularization of religion," in fact, not only fortifies but indeed strengthens Christian privilege by perpetuating Christian hegemony in such a way as to avoid its detection as religion or to circumvent any mandates for the separation of religion and government. Christian dominance, therefore, is maintained by its relative invisibility. When anyone poses a challenge or attempts to reveal its religious significance, those in the dominant group brand them as "ridiculous," "oversensitive," "subversive" or as "sacrilegious."

Examples of Christian cultural imperialism during the so-called Holiday Season are many:

- The constant and prolonged promotion of Christmas music in public spaces and on radio stations; Christmas specials on television throughout November and December each year, and often in "Christmas in July" sales.
- Christmas decorations (often hung at taxpayer expense) in the public square in cities and towns throughout Christian-dominated countries.
- The highly visible and widespread availability in retail stores of Christian holiday decorations, greeting cards, foods, and other items during Christian holiday seasons.
- In the United States, for example, the president and first woman lighting the "National Christmas Tree" on the Ellipse behind the White House.

Our society marks time through a Christian lens. Even the language we use about the calendar reflects Christian assumptions. Western and most other areas of the world refer to the current timeframe as the "twenty-first century," and the dawning of "the new millennium." Among the definitions of millennium in the Merriam-Webster's Eleventh New Collegiate Dictionary (2003), definition 2a is: "a period of 1000 years" (p. 789). Let us not forget, however, that the year 2000 was calculated with reference to the birth of Jesus, and it is therefore the beginning of the next *Christian* millennium. In fact, definition 1a in the same dictionary defines millennium as: "the thousand years mentioned in Revelation 20 during which holiness is to prevail and Christ is to reign on earth" (p. 789).

This fact is brought home each time we hear someone mention the date followed by "in the year of our Lord, Jesus Christ." The century markers BC (before Christ) and AD (anno Domini) are clearly Christian in origin. Therefore, the year 2000 is one important milepost, though for many religious traditions it also marks a heightening of their invisibility. An attempt to decenter Christian hegemony in terminology related to the marking of time is replacing BC with BCE (Before the Common Era) and AD with CE (Common Era), although the renaming does nothing to end the marking of time before and after a "common" (Christian) era. (See Religious Imperialism Case in Point, Liberatory Praxis Appendix F.)

Islamophobia

What: Islamophobia can be defined as prejudice and discrimination toward the religion of Islam and Muslims who follow its teachings and practices. Like racism and sexism, for example, Islamophobia is much more than a fear, for it is a taught and often learned attitude and behavior, and, therefore, falls under the category of oppression.

Two months following Japan's attack on Pearl Harbor, on February 19, 1942, President Franklin Delano Roosevelt signed Executive Order 9066 authorizing military officials to operate "military areas" as "exclusion zones," from which "any or all persons may be excluded." This order justified the exclusion and forced relocation of all people of Japanese ancestry from the entire Pacific coast into concentration campus in the interior U.S. Though the country was at war with Germany and Italy as well, and though no single case of suspected Japanese American espionage activity was ever proven, the government stripped an estimated 110,000 Japanese U.S.-American citizens of their constitutional protections and their property and transported them long distances.

It was not until 1988 when Congress passed legislation apologizing and providing monetary reparations to Japanese Americans for this tragic chapter in U.S. history. The legislation confirmed that the actions taken by our government were founded on "race prejudice, war hysteria, and a failure of political leadership."

So What: Fast forward to the horrendous events of September 11, 2001. A national poll found that 31% of U.S. residents asserted that our government should incarcerate Arab Americas in concentration camps as we did with Japanese Americans during World War II. Have we learned anything from history? To stereotype and scapegoat all followers of Islam for the events of 9/11 is as invalid as blaming all Christians for the despicable actions perpetrated by Timothy McVeigh, the Oklahoma City bomber who was a devout Christian.

The Council on American-Islamic Relations (CAIR) following 9/11 released its 2006 report finding that approximately 25% of U.S.-Americans consider Islam as a religion of hatred and violence, and that those with the most biased attitudes tend to be older, less educated, politically conservative, and are more often to belong to the Republican Party. Though two

U.S. Supreme Court cases (*Engel v. Vitale*, 1962, and *Abington School District v. Schempp*, 1963) ruled unconstitutional any *mandatory* prayers or Bible readings at public schools or the promotion of religion, subsequent rulings declared the constitutionality of many forms of personal religious expression on school campuses.

The physical education teacher of a Muslim elementary school student in Iowa, however, forbad her from wearing a traditional Muslim full-body swimming garment during instruction in the school pool, but ordered her, instead, to wear a western-style bathing suit, which would force the student to act against her faith. Her mother was compelled to educate the principal on Muslim religious practices. After much discussion, the principal agreed to permit the student to wear a swimming garment of her choice, though he warned the girl's parent that the child would most likely incur angry and mocking epithets from her classmates.

Muslim students, faculty, and staff, however, are routinely not accorded the opportunity to have a safe prayer space on campus to perform the *salat* (prayer), as required by the Five Pillars of Islam. A case in point involved a 17-year-old high school junior in Ohio, who was barred by school administrators from praying in an empty classroom at lunch and before and after class hours. In this case, CAIR stepped in on the student's behalf, and convinced the school district to reverse its policy.

Since September 11, 2001, we see growing numbers of violent acts directed against Muslims. During the single year, for example, CAIR listed a total of 1,522 civil rights violations against American Muslims, 114 of which were violent hate crimes. The report included incidents of violence, as well as harassment and discriminatory treatment, including "unreasonable arrests, detentions, and searches/seizures." The CAIR report included an incident in which a Muslim woman wearing a *hijab* (the garment many Muslim women wear in public) took her baby for a walk in a stroller, when a man driving a truck nearly ran them over. The woman cried out that, "You almost killed my baby!," and the man responded, "It wouldn't have been a big loss."

Nearly one-quarter of all reported civil rights violations against American Muslims involve unwarranted arrests and searches. Law enforcement agencies routinely "profile" Muslims of apparent Middle Eastern heritage in airports or simply while driving in their cars for interrogation and invasive and aggressive searches. In addition, governmental agencies, such as the IRS and FBI, continue to enter individuals' private homes and mosques and make unreasonable arrests and detentions.

Individuals have targeted Sikhs and Hindus as well. It is widely assumed that Sikhs are targeted because they wear turbans, which the public imagination equates with Muslims, which equates with "terrorism."

Sexism, Misogyny, Patriarchy

> Man for the field and woman for the hearth,
> Man for the sword and for the needle she,
> Man with the head and woman with the heart,
> Man to command and woman to obey,
> All else confusion.
> —Alfred Lord Tennyson, from "The Princess"

What: "Sexism" is oppression based on the sex we are assigned at birth, especially against females and intersex people, and is founded on a patriarchal structure of male dominance promoted through individual, institutional, social, and cultural systems.

What: Misogyny refers to the hatred, dislike, resentment of women and girls often resulting in prejudiced attitudes and discriminatory actions.

Oppression directed against all females, lesbians, gay males, bisexual females and males, transgender people, and intersexuals goes by many names and has several subdivisions and definitions. What connects these forms of oppression is the socially constructed and socially enforced binary systems that divide people along strictly demarcated boundaries and borders into either/or categories related to societal norms of self-presentation. The socially constructed notions of "sex," "gender," and "sexuality" are organized and maintained upon oppositional binary frames with their attendant meanings, social roles, values, stereotypes, and behavioral and attitudinal imperatives, expressions, and expectations for the purpose of maintaining power and domination: male versus and over female, heterosexual versus and over homosexual and bisexual, and gender normative versus and over people who challenge social gender norms and imperatives of gender self-expression.

So What: These socially constructed binary oppositions establish and maintain hierarchical borders of power and oppression privileging groups and individuals constructed as "dominant" while marginalizing and disempowering groups and individuals constructed as "subordinate." The borders establish a polarity of exclusion in various degrees on one side and inclusion on the other. The most extreme and overt forms of oppression are directed against those who most challenge, confound, or contest these binary frames established within societal norms in their presentation of self and in their attempts to obliterate the very boundaries from which hierarchies of domination and subordination stem. In the case of gender, the binary imperatives lock all people into rigid gender-based roles that inhibit creativity and self-expression, and therefore, we all have a vested interest in challenging and eventually obliterating the binaries.

Within a patriarchal system of male domination, cisgender heterosexual male bodies matter more, while "othered" bodies matter less. These "othered" bodies include female and intersex bodies, and bodies that violate the "rules" for the reproduction and maintenance of the dominant patriarchal system, such as trans, gender diverse, non-binary, and gay, lesbian, bisexual, pansexual bodies, and bodies with disabilities. In addition, within many Western societies, non-European-heritage bodies are regarded also as abject bodies.

Social customs and norms created and continually reinforce many shared preconceptions about the "sexes." Some of these may be inconsistent or even contradictory, but they share the common element that they prescribe rules of conduct for us all. When "males" and "females" assigned at birth both exhibit similar outward behaviors, the sex we are assigned at birth will often determine the societal meanings affixed to those behaviors. For example, what may be seen as "assertive" behavior in a man may be called "pushiness" in a woman. A man may be seen as being "enthusiastic" or "passionate," whereas a woman is accused of being "emotional" or "on the rag." Where a man is viewed as "confident" or "firm," a woman, on the other hand is considered "stubborn" or "bitchy." When a woman aims to serve as corporate executive, stepping outside the gender role assigned to her, she is sometimes accused of "trying to be like a man" and considered "too masculine."

Now What: Feminists, transgender, and intersex people have exposed the truth regarding this fabrication we call "gender roles" as a social construction, one which our society ascribes to each of us as it assigns us a sex at birth. As scripts are given to actors in a play, these binary gender scripts also were written long before any of us entered the stage of life. In fact, the roles in which we were cast have, very often, little connection to our natures, beliefs, interests, and values. These preconceived binary scripts become internalized standardized mental pictures that societies model and pass to future generations. What it is to be "male" or "female," "girl" or "boy," "woman" or "man," social actors pass on as theatrical actors memorize their scripts and pass to future actors.

Society and institutions on the macro level, and individuals and families on the micro, act as extreme and fanatical examples of directors in the coercive societal battalions bent on destroying all signs of gender diversity in young and old alike, and in the maintenance of gender scripts. Most of us function as conscious and unconscious co-directors in this drama each time we enforce binary gender-role conformity in others, and each time we relegate our critical consciousness by failing to rewrite or destroy the scripts in ways that operate integrally to us.

This conjures up images of the Hollywood movie "The Truman Show" starring Jim Carrey in the lead role as Truman Burbank. The film documents a man who for most of his life remains unaware that he lives within a human-made artificial set of a reality television show, broadcast 24 hours a day to billions of people around the world. The show's executive producer and director, Christof, placed Truman at birth in the fictitious town of Seahaven, and manipulates every aspect of his life. (I will leave it up to you to analyze why the director of this farce has the name "Christof.") To dissuade Truman from exploring past the limits of the constructed set, Christof pretends to kill Truman's father in a fabricated storm to teach him to fear the water. In addition, actors playing the part of TV news reporters warn of the dangers of travel and promote the benefits of staying home.

Stemming from some unforeseen glitches in the scenery and unexplained and habitual coincidences in the placement of the actors around him, however, Truman becomes suspicious until he discovers the truth about the artificiality, manipulation, and control Christof has perpetrated on him for the past 30 years. Truman eventually outwits Christof and escapes the fabricated set into the warmth and brightness of a true sun, and the coolness and wetness of natural rain.

Each time we rewrite the scripts so as to give an honest and true performance of life, each time we work toward lifting the ban against our transcending and obliterating the gender status quo by continually questioning and challenging standard conceptualization of gender and gender roles, each time we challenge definitious (and the very categories) of "Men," "Women," "Girls," "Boys," only then will we begin as individuals and as a society to experience true gender integrity.

Anyone who acts outside of their expected gender-role assignment, however, others very often target them with heterosexist and cissexist harassment and attacks, *regardless of their actual sexual identity* or *gender identity*. In this way, sexism, with its attendant gender-based roles, are maintained and even strengthened by sexism's tools (or as Pharr, 1988, calls homophobia "a weapon of sexism"). These features serve to maintain power and privilege for those who accord with these norms, while marginalizing and disempowering groups and individuals who violate them. (See Liberatory Praxis Appendix H: Investigating Gender Roles Classroom Exercise.)

Patriarchy

> What is patriarchy? A society is patriarchal to the degree that it promotes male privilege by being *male dominated*, *male identified*, and *male centered*. It is also organized around an obsession with control and involves as one of its aspects the oppression of women.
>
> —Johnson (1997, p. 5)

Friedrich Engels (1884) saw how economic developments encouraging the accumulation of private property required the fortification of the monogamous family to guarantee that men's property would be inherited by their biological heirs. Engels was the one of the first to argue that women's subordination was not the result of any biological dispositions, but rather, caused by "men's efforts to achieve their demands for control of women's labor and sexual faculties [which] have gradually solidified and become institutionalized in the nuclear family." (Holborn & Steel, 2012, n.p.)

So What: Marxist Feminists have expanded Engels and Marx's theoretical foundations to explain the subordination and exploitation of women within the family unit. While acknowledging the problematic nature of the capitalist system, Marxist Feminism emphasizes the hierarchal gendered structure socialized and enforced initially within the family and then by other social institutions. In addition, Collins (1998) states: "Predicated on assumptions of heterosexism, the invisibility of gay, lesbian, and bisexual sexualities in the traditional family ideal obscures these sexualities and keeps them hidden" (p. 65).

If a patriarchal social and economic system of male domination can keep women pregnant and taking care of children following birth, they can restrict their entry, or at least their level and time of entry, into the workplace, and ensure women's dependence upon men economically and emotionally. As women produce more and more children, expanding numbers of little consumers emerge to contribute to the Capitalist system ever increasing profits for owners of business and industry. The patriarchal system necessary to control women's bodies amounts to imperatives to control women's minds and life choices.

In addition, the family's incessant reification and promotion of hegemonic binary gender categories is now (partially) what drives families in the U.S.

to ex-communicate their LGBTQ children and provides fuel for the socially conservative capitalist class to spread sexism, cissexism, and heterosexism because of capitalists' direct benefit from traditional gender roles rooted in the family-household system. Thus, when a patriarchal family structure converges with a patriarchal religious system, which itself reinforces and intensifies the enforcement of strictly defined gendered hierarchies of male domination by restricting women's reproductive freedoms and decision making and ordaining requisite sexual and gender matrices, women's oppression and the oppression of those who transgress sexual- and gender-based boundaries became inevitable.

Throughout history, examples abound of male domination over the rights and lives of women and girls. Men denied women the vote until women fought hard and demanded the rights of political enfranchisement, though women in some countries today still are restricted from voting; strictly enforced gender-based social roles mandated without choice that women's only option was to remain in the home to undertake cleaning and childcare duties; women were and continue to be by far the primary target of harassment, abuse, physical assault, and rape by men; women were and remain locked out of many professions; rules required that women teachers relinquish their jobs after marriage in some countries; in fact, the institution of marriage itself was structured on a foundation of male domination with men serving as the so-called "head of the household" and taking on sole ownership of all property, thereby restricting these rights from women. In other words, women have been constructed as second-class and even third-class citizens, but through it all, women as a group have challenged the inequities and have pushed back against patriarchal constraints.

Though many people are fully aware of the continuing existence of sexism and male privilege, and they are working tirelessly for its eradication, many others, however, fail to perceive its harmful effects on themselves and others. This apparent invisibility of sexism and male privilege in many Western countries, in fact, not only fortifies but, indeed, strengthens this form of oppression and privilege by perpetuating patriarchal hegemony in such a way as to avoid detection. In other words, male dominance is maintained by its relative invisibility (though for many of us, it stands as blatantly obvious), and with this relative invisibility, privilege escapes analysis and scrutiny, interrogation and confrontation by many. Dominance is perceived as unremarkable or "normal," and when anyone poses a challenge or attempts to reveal its true impact and significance, those in the dominant group brand them as "subversive" or even "accuse" them of being "overly analytical." Possibly those who make these accusations are not themselves sufficiently analytical.

Toxic forms of hypermasculinity require the promotion and use of firearms to keep at bay the intensive psychosocial compulsive fear and dread of penetration from bullets, from homosexuals, from the female gaze since patriarchy promises males the right to the aggressive outward intrusive gaze, the right of penetration of "others." Laws are built upon and reflect the society in which they are meant to affect. Patriarchal individualistic societies oppress and inhibit women's reproductive freedoms, encourages the inequities in salaries between men and women, establishes and maintains the massive development of wealth for a very few while encouraging the enormous financial disparities between the very rich and everyone else, and many other issues.

Oppression Affects Everyone

So What: It is paradoxical that in our society, love of difference makes one the same, while love of sameness makes one different. In this regard by analogy, Frederick Douglass, who escaped enslavement and worked for the cause of liberation, once said when he described the dehumanizing effects of slavery not on those enslaved alone, but also on white slavers whose position to slavery corrupted their humanity. While the social conditions of Douglass's time were very different from today, nonetheless, Douglass's words hold meaning: "No [person] can put a chain about the ankle of [another person] without at last finding the other end fastened about [their] own neck" (Douglass, speech at a Civil Rights mass meeting, Washington, DC, 1883).

Though it cannot be denied that oppression serves the interests of dominant group members, eventually it will backfire, and the chain will take hold of them. Therefore, within the numerous forms of oppression, members of targeted (sometimes called "minoritized" or "subordinated") groups are *oppressed*, while on many levels, members of the dominant or agent groups are *hurt*. Although the effects of oppression differ qualitatively for specific targeted and agent groups, in the end everyone loses.

As an example, I investigated the ways that heterosexism not only oppresses lesbian, gay, and bisexual people, but on many levels, also hurts people who define as heterosexual (Blumenfeld, 1992).

First, heterosexist conditioning compromises the integrity of people by pressuring them to treat others badly, which are actions contrary to their basic humanity. It inhibits one's ability to form close, intimate relationships with members of one's own sex, generally restricts communication with a significant portion of the population, and, more specifically, limits family relationships.

Heterosexism locks all people into rigid gender-based roles, which inhibit creativity and self-expression. It often is used to stigmatize, silence, and, on occasion, target people who are perceived or defined by *others* as lesbian, gay, or bisexual but who are, in actuality, heterosexual.

In addition, heterosexism is one cause of premature sexual involvement, which increases the chances of teen pregnancy and the spread of sexually transmitted diseases. Young people, of *all* sexual identities, are often pressured to become *heterosexually* active to prove to themselves and others that they are "normal."

Societal heterosexism prevents some LGBT people from developing an authentic self-identity and adds to the pressure to marry someone of another sex, which in turn places undue stress and oftentimes trauma on themselves as well as their spouses and children.

Heterosexism, combined with sexphobia or erotophobia (fear and revulsion of sex) results in the elimination of discussions of the lives and sexuality of LGBT people as part of school-based sexuality education programs, keeping vital information from all students. Such a lack of information can kill people in the age of HIV/AIDS. And heterosexism (along with racism, sexism, classism, sexphobia) inhibits a unified and effective governmental and societal response the HIV/AIDS pandemic.

With all the truly important issues facing the world, heterosexism diverts energy and attention from more constructive endeavors. It also prevents heterosexuals from accepting the benefits and gifts offered by LGBT people, including theoretical insights, social and spiritual visions and options, contributions in the arts and culture, to religion, to education, to family life, indeed, to all facets of society. Ultimately, it inhibits appreciation of other types of diversity, making it unsafe for everyone because each person has unique traits not considered mainstream or dominant. Therefore, we are *all* diminished when any one of us is demeaned.

The meaning is quite clear: When any group of people is targeted for oppression, it is ultimately everyone's concern. We all, therefore, have a self-interest in actively working to dismantle all the many forms of oppression.

We are *all* born into an environment polluted by the many forms on the wheel of oppression, which fall upon us like acid rain. For some people, spirits are tarnished to the core, others are marred on the surface, and no one is completely protected. Therefore, we all have a responsibility, indeed an opportunity, to join together as allies to construct protective shelters from the corrosive effects of prejudice and discrimination while working to clean up the systemically oppressive environment in which we live. Once we take sufficient steps to reduce this pollution, we will all breathe a lot easier.

Notes

1. See Appendix E: Making Universities Welcoming for Students, Staff, Faculty, and Administrators of All Sexual Identities and Gender Identities and Expressions.
2. See Appendix D: Raising Issues of Religious Pluralism in Schools.

· 1 0 ·

BACKLASH

Backlash: A Case in Point

Now What: Demanding "Never Again" and "Enough Is Enough" to gun violence and shouting "We Call BS" to the arguments against changing gun laws, a new generation of young people has been sparked into activism as a shooter's bullets cut down their peers and teachers at Marjory Stoneman Douglas High School. Within a very short time, they have captured the imagination and admiration of those of us who have long hoped and fought for policy initiatives to bring an end to the senseless over-availability of firearms that kill an estimated 33,000 people annually in the United States.

But as with all social movements for progressive social change, a strong and powerful opposition stands in the way. Members of the conservative political Right, many who represent the interests of gun manufacturers and their lobbyists, have long engaged in and are continuing to wage war against gun safety advocates, even when, especially when, these advocates are young people.

During the conservative cultural moment within the context of declarations of "fake news," "conspiracy theories," "witch hunts," and verifiable distortions and lies in reaction to anything and everything reported that goes against their agendas and "values," the backlash to derail, by demeaning and impugning the integrity and motivation of these new youth advocates, was predictable in its speed and veracity.

People in the extreme crevices of the political and theocratic Right through many relative centrists accuse these young people of serving as pawns or coconspirators of the political Left's antigun agenda, that they are mere puppets who have been coached what to say and how to say it.

On his radio show, Rush Limbaugh called out the student activists: "Everything they're doing is right out of the Democrat Party's various playbooks. It has the same enemies: the N.R.A. and guns." Donald Trump Jr. took to twitter to attack 17-year-old David Hogg, one of the student leaders from Douglas High School, for criticizing the Trump administration to protect his father, a former F.B.I agent. Trump Jr. referred to a YouTube video calling David Hogg an "Outspoken Trump-Hating School Shooting Survivor is Son of FBI Agent; MSM Helps Prop Up Incompetent Bureau."

Donald Trump Jr. also admired a tweet connected to an article by the far-right website, True Pundit (in BuzzFeed News, 2018), which referred to David Hogg as "the kid who has been running his mouth about how Donald Trump and the GOP are teaming to help murder high school kids by upholding the Second Amendment." The Right also refers to David and the other student gun safety activists as "crisis actors." During an interview with CNN's Anderson Cooper, Hogg responded to the charge: "I'm not a crisis actor. I'm someone who had to witness this and live through this, and I continue to be having to do that. I'm not acting on anybody's behalf" (in Chavez, 2018).

With Douglas High School students observing from the balcony, Florida state legislators voted down, by a margin of nearly 2 to 1, a proposal to discuss the merits of banning AR-15 rifles in the state. And adding further insult to traumatic injury, Levi Patterson, the little league baseball team coach composed of 7- to 9-year-old 3rd graders in the town of Neosha, Missouri, has moved ahead in his planned raffle to fund his players despite growing criticism. The raffle winner will be awarded a new AR-15 rifle like the one used in the Florida tragedy.

In the General Electric TV Commercial (2014), "Ideas Are Scary," a newborn and ultimately abandoned idea appears close to death in hospital. Somehow, though, it survives infancy into adolescence. As it ventures unwashed and homeless through the town searching for basic sustenance, it finds only harsh judgments, scorn, abuse, and rejection from people everywhere it goes. Then one day, by chance it stumbles upon the GE building, where people help it inside, support, and nurture it. Sometime thereafter, it walks out upon the bright stage of life where it has grown healthy and vibrant, with its beautiful multicolored plumage raised in brilliance and pride to a hearty and resounding ovation.

Yes, new ideas and the movements they spark have usually, at least initially, appeared messy and scary because they do, indeed, "threaten what is known," because they truly "are the natural-born enemy to the way things are," the status quo. In terms of ideas that challenge entrenched systems of power, oppression, and privilege, forces for maintenance of the status quo often wage figurative and literal battles to exterminate counter-ideas and actions to prevent and turn back any gains progressive movements have fought so tirelessly to advance.

We see history replete with intense and often violent backlash from many factions against movements working to end, for example, the dehumanizing and oppressive institution of slavery, apartheid in South Africa, human sex trafficking worldwide, and so-called "ethnic cleansing"; to advance women's suffrage and movements for women to control their bodies; to workers' rights; to the right to quality education and health care for all; to civil and human rights for people of color, for women, for LGBTQ people, for intersex people, for people with disabilities, for young people and elders, for people of all religions and for atheists and agnostics, for people of all ethnicities and national backgrounds, for equality of opportunity for people of all socioeconomic classes; and the instances continue endlessly.

Faludi (1991), in her now-classic exposé, *Backlash: The Undeclared War against American Women*, details the intense resistance to feminist ideas and movements for gender equality. By shining a powerful illuminating spotlight on this backlash, Faludi reveals and debunks the myths and stereotypes perpetrated by social institutions, from business to the media, working to restrain women in all facets of their lives.

Sherry Watt's "Privilege Identity Exploration Model"

What: Educators within any content area, and particularly in social justice education, raise topics that often stir emotions and a certain amount of discomfort in students. Educators, therefore, must be prepared not only with subject content but also with attending to issues of interpersonal and group facilitation skills. Discussing and coming to an awareness of issues of social oppression and social privilege can be difficult. In her insightful book, *The Emperor Has No Clothes: Teaching about Race and Racism to People Who Don't Want to Know*, Okun (2010) talks about privileged resistance as "the enactment of defensiveness and denial on the part of those sitting in positions of privilege to any acknowledgement of that privilege and the oppression that creates it" (p. 34).

What: Sherry Watt studies forms of resistance and denial around issues of oppression and dominant group privilege and outlines several assumptions within her "Privileged Identity Exploration Model" (2007) to consider when discussing these types of difficult dialogues both within and outside a classroom context.

- Assumption #1—The exploration of privileged identity is an ongoing socialization process.
- Assumption #2—There is no ultimate level of consciousness that can be reached regarding one's privileged identities.
- Assumption #3—Engaging in difficult dialogue is a necessary part of unlearning social oppression.
- Assumption #4—Defense modes are normal human reactions to the uncertainty that one feels when exploring their privileged identities in more depth.
- Assumption #5—Defense modes are expressed in identifiable behaviors.
- Assumption #6—Expressions of defense modes may vary by situation.

Watt identifies and categorizes behaviors people tend to exhibit when recognizing, contemplating, or addressing their privileged identities. According to Watt, when raising and discussing issues of oppression and privilege, several forms of resistance may emerge:

- Denial: A rejection of the concept of dominant group privilege. ("It's not my dominant group privilege that aided me. I worked hard for what I have gained.")
- Deflection: The notion that majority rules and that the minority cannot expect the majority to accommodate or adhere to minority needs or standards. ("They can't expect the dominant culture to change for them. If someone is going to live in America, then they need to understand that we were founded by white Europeans, that our founding fathers were white males, and the majority rules.")

- Rationalization: The notion that the individual did not set the conditions for the inequities that may exist in the society currently or historically. ("My relatives arrived in the United States after slavery, and I had nothing to go with it.")
- Intellectualization: The assertion that the individual is not prejudiced and does not discriminate. (The "my best friend is a …" attitude. "I am opposed to hate groups." "Harvey Milk was one of my heroes. Besides, my best friend is a transgender woman.")
- Principium: A defensive reaction arising from a personal or political belief. Though the person may feel badly that a certain social identity group may not have achieved full equality and equity within society, this is the way it was *meant* to be. ("As I see it, white Christian people's culture has created some of the greatest civilizations in the world, and other cultures can learn a lot from these white Christian cultures.")
- False Envy: Sometimes manifesting a certain affection for a minoritized person or a group of people, it is an effort to deny the complexity of the social and political context. At times, it manifests itself in dominant groups' claiming victimhood at the hands of minoritized groups. ("Actually, white Christian men are the victims. We should be talking about reverse discrimination/oppression.")
- Minimalization: Reducing the effect that social identity has upon one's life chances, and that issues of oppression based on social identity are no longer a problem. ("People of color all have the same chances to succeed as white people do. It's not about race. It's about motivation. Besides, racism used to be a problem, but it's no longer a problem today. Remember, we even had a black president.")
- Benevolence: Projecting an excessively sensitive attitude toward a social and political issue or group based on a position of charity. ("I treat everyone with respect. I don't see race. I am color blind.")

· 1 1 ·

THE SOCIAL PRODUCTION OF "KNOWLEDGE(S)"

What: It is often said that the winners of wars and those in power write the history books. Well, throughout the history of the United States, for example, in their role as social institutions, schools have reproduced the cultural norms, often with the attendant range of social inequities and dominant group privileges found within the larger society.

This truism came to light again in the state of Michigan's May 2018 proposed social studies standards (Michigan Department of Education, 2018), the building block of the state's curriculum and guide for K–12 teachers, as it fabricates a clearly conservative political perspective. Much of the past curricular standards from 2007, plus several of the newly proposed standards written by veteran teachers and other educational leaders, were severely pared down or entirely eliminated by a group of political conservative reviewers. Led by state Senator Patrick Colbeck (R-Canton)—who was campaigning for governor—and others he invited to join the review panel, within sections where teachers were to discuss with students the accomplishments and setbacks of minority groups, the panel deleted, for example, references to the LGBTQ community, American Indians, Latinos, immigrants, and people with disabilities.

Instead, they added new wording emphasizing generic ways teachers should discuss how expanding rights of some groups can also serve to infringe the rights and freedoms of others. In addition, gone now are issues related to climate change from a section enumerating the expectations for a 6th-grade geography component. And showing their partisan political colors, they struck the term small "d" "democratic" from "core democratic values," changing it simply to "core values." Also now deleted are entire sections addressed to aid students in critical thinking skills development. The Michigan Department of Education invited Colbeck to join a focus group to review the state's proposed curriculum after he and 17 other conservative state legislators wrote a letter complaining how the proposals were not politically neutral as claimed.

Michigan follows the Texas model of curricular standards handed down in 2010. Then the Texas School Board clearly took a retrenchment position from the very modest gains made in curricular development of providing multiple perspectives, which could stimulate students' critical thinking skills, to a default monocultural position from a conservative Christian European heritage perspective. Basically, the Board confused education with indoctrination. Following closely on the heels of a bill passed by the Arizona legislature and signed into law by Governor Jan Brewer severely restricting ethnic studies courses and multicultural curricular inclusion in that state's schools, the Texas School Board voted in sweeping changing to its social studies curriculum. Considering 213 amendments for changes in the state's social studies standards, known as the Texas Standards for Knowledge and Skills for grades kindergarten through 12, social conservatives, who comprised most of the Board, voted strictly along party lines: 9 Republicans, 5 Democrats. Board member Cynthia Dunbar, R-Richmond, a high school anatomy and physiology teacher, made her position and the position of the other Christian social conservatives very clear in her opening prayer at the hearing, in which she asserted that U.S. laws and the government itself should be founded on the Christian Bible:

> I believe no one can read the history of our country without realizing that the Good Book and the spirit of the savior have from the beginning been our guiding geniuses. Whether we look to the first charter of Virginia, or the charter of New England ... the same objective is present—a Christian land governed by Christian principles. ... I like to believe we are living today in the spirit of the Christian religion. I like also to believe that as long as we do so, no great harm can come to our country. All this I say in the spirit of my Lord and Savior, Jesus Christ. Amen. (Dunbar quoted in Sutton & Dochuk, 2016, p. 166)

Dunbar authored the 2008 book, *One Nation Under God: How the Left Is Trying to Erase What Made Us Great*, arguing that the Founders created "an emphatically Christian government" (p. 18) and that government should be guided by a "biblical litmus test" (p. 47).

The extensive list of changes to the Texas social studies curriculum include information that presents Confederate President Jefferson Davis on par with Abraham Lincoln; deletion of Rev. Dr. Martin Luther King's "Letter from a Birmingham Jail"; addressing the Civil War as an issue of states' rights; giving more attention to conservative organizations like the Moral Majority, National Rifle Association, and the Heritage Foundation; replacing the term "Capitalism" with "free-enterprise system"; referring to the United States as a "constitutional republic" rather than as a "democracy"; questioning whether the United Nations imperils U.S. sovereignty; vindicating McCarthyism of the 1950s; teaching about the Christian influences on the Founders (and I would add even though many did not define themselves as Christians *per se*, and some considered themselves as secular); giving expanded information of a list of Confederate officials and conservative political leaders like Phyllis Schaffley; eliminating references to John Madison; refusing to update B.C. and A.D. to B.C.E. and C.E.; watering down and sometimes deleting sections of U.S. civil rights history; watering down and questioning the legal doctrine and rationale for the separation of religion ("church") and state. An amendment proposed but eventually voted down was a change in the term "Atlantic Slave Trade" to "Atlantic Triangular Trade."

So What: On a micro-level, what the Texas School Board and earlier the Arizona legislature show us are some of the ways in which those who hold power determine and define "knowledge" and how "knowledge" is consciously and very deliberately produced and disseminated. This dominant-group-controlled production of "knowledge" maintains the marginality of other groups, and it denies all students options in understanding multiple perspectives from which to construct meaning.

Though Texas grade school students comprise only approximately 8.5% (4.7 million) of the estimated 55.2 million students in the United States, Texas is the second largest textbook market for book publishers. The curricular changes in Texas, therefore, have implications for the content in textbooks nationwide.

In Colonial America, few regions, except for the larger New England towns, mandated by law the building of schools or the provision of childhood instruction. Schools that were constructed and teachers who were hired were done so only because local citizens decided to pool their resources. During this time, classroom lessons were tied directly to Protestant religions and the

Protestant Bible, which the early "settlers" brought with them from England. School lessons primarily centered on preaching, catechizing, and prayers, which called for freedom from influences of the Devil and attacks from the native populations. In addition, the most frequently used schoolbook was *The New England Primer* (first published in 1687) based on *The Protestant Tutor*, published earlier in England. The intent of both the *Tutor* and the *Primer* was to teach reading through the Protestant catechism. Several Catholic parishes in colonial America established parochial or parish schools partly due to the Protestant teachings that pervaded the public-school curriculum.

In their attempts to "civilize" and convert Indians to Christianity, the French, Spanish, as well as the English colonists established Indian schools, though most Indians refused to attend. Black people, however, generally were not accorded the right to an education, especially in the southern colonies, which passed laws enacting heavy fines and physical punishment against anyone found educating them.

Following the Revolutionary War, leaders such as Thomas Jefferson and others called for state-supported and -mandated public education, believing that the very survival of the new Republic depended on an educated populous. Jefferson, for example, advocated for a three-year publicly supported education for all white children—no such guarantees were to be extended to children of enslaved Africans—with advanced education provided to a select few males—not females—of poorer families whose families cannot afford to educate them. As Jefferson (1782) wrote, the schools will be raking a few geniuses from the "rubbish":

> Of the boys thus sent in any one year, trial is to be made at the grammar schools one or two years, and the best genius of the whole selected, and continued six years, and the residue dismissed. By this means twenty of the best geniuses will be raked from the rubbish annually, and be instructed at the public expense, so far as the grammar schools go. (p. 275)

The first statewide school system was established in Massachusetts in the 1820s largely due to the efforts of Horace Mann, the first secretary of education of any state in the United States. While traveling throughout Massachusetts, Mann found an unequal patchwork of local schools dependent on the tax base of each community. He proposed a new structure, which he called "common schools." These schools were to serve all children, of all income levels. He hoped these schools would help to end, or at least reduce, the financial inequities between citizens of the state. Mann and other political and community leaders also supported a homogeneity of opinion and belief. They proposed that the main purpose of public education was for the development of good character based on religion, which was itself based on the central teachings of the Protestant Bible.

During the 18th century, the public schools throughout the United States used extensively the *McGuffey Readers*. These were graded primary readers for grades 1 through 6. Edited by William Holmes McGuffey, these books were infused with texts preaching Protestant gospel, even though children of several faiths attended the schools. So, both during colonial times and the early years of public education following the Revolutionary War, a Protestant foundation permeated schooling.

As wisely and eloquently stated by English author Edward Bulwer-Lytton in his 1839 play, *Richelieu; Or the Conspiracy*, "the pen is mightier than the sword," this adage holds that the written word acts as a powerful tool in the transmission of ideas. Why else would oppressive regimes and other avid enforcers of the status quo engage in censorship and book burnings throughout the ages?

For example, Pope Gregory IX in 1239, in his quest to maintain the Catholic Church's economic and ideological stranglehold, ordered all copies of the Jewish holy book, the *Talmud*, confiscated, and one of his successors, Pope John XXI, commanded that the *Talmud* be burned on the eve of the Jewish Passover in 1322.

Protestant reformer Martin Luther, in his 1526 treatise *On the Jews and Their Lies*, argued that "First, their synagogues should be set on fire." Jewish prayer books should be destroyed, and rabbis forbidden to preach. The homes of Jews should likewise be "smashed and destroyed" and their residents "put under one roof or in a stable like gypsies, to teach them they are not master in our land. … These poisonous envenomed worms should be drafted into forced labor. The young and strong Jews and Jewesses should be given the flail, the ax, the hoe, the spade, the distaff, and the spindle and let them earn their bread by the sweat of their noses."

As Luther's dire pronouncements make perfectly clear, what begins as banning then torching of books and other property eventually results in the denial of civil liberties, torture, and eventually murder of people scapegoated by dominant social groups and by their government leaders.

This was certainly the case in Nazi Germany. Nazi storm troopers, in 1933, invaded, ransacked, and padlocked The Institute for Sexual Sciences in Berlin, founded by Dr. Magnus Hirschfeld, a gay Jewish sexuality researcher.

The Institute conducted early sexuality research, the precursor of the Indiana-based Kinsey Institute in the United States. Storm troopers carried away and torched thousands of volumes of books and research documents, calling the Institute "an international center of the white-slave trade" and "an unparalleled breading ground of dirt and filth."

Soon thereafter, Nazis and conservative university students throughout Germany invaded Jewish organizations and public and school libraries and confiscated books they deemed "un-German." The German Student Association, *Deutsche Studentenschaft*, declared a national "Action against the Un-German Spirit." On May 10, 1933, the students along with Nazi leaders set ablaze over 25,000 volumes in Berlin's Opernplatz. Joseph Goebbels, the Reich Minister of Propaganda, "fired" up the crowd of over 40,000 sympathizers by declaring "No to decadence and moral corruption. Yes to decency and morality in family and state."

More recently, Arizona state officials in 2010 stripped away the Mexican American Studies programs from Tucson public schools. Arizona Superintendent of Public Instruction, John Huppenthal, suspended the highly successful and student-empowering program. Students previously enrolled in the Mexican American Studies program achieved a 94% high school graduation rate, up significantly from around 50% of Latinx students not enrolled. The program has given students a sense of cultural pride, a passion and joy in the learning process, and a feeling of hope for their futures.

The then Arizona School Superintendent Tom Horne, in 2010 when the state legislature passed the measure, House Bill 2281, asserted that the law was necessary because, in particular, Tucson, Arizona's, Mexican American, African American, and Native American studies courses teach students that they are oppressed, encourage resentment toward white people, and promote "ethnic chauvinism" and "ethnic solidarity" instead of treating people as individuals.

Huppenthal released a list of books he banned from classrooms throughout the state, including *The Tempest* by Shakespeare; *Rethinking Columbus: The Next 500 Years* (1998) by Bigelow and Peterson; *The Latino Condition: A Critical Reader* (1998) by Delgado and Stefancic; *Critical Race Theory: An Introduction* (2001) by Delgado and Stefancic; *Pedagogy of the Oppressed* (1970) by Freire; *United States Government: Democracy in Action* (2007) by Remy; *Dictionary of Latino Civil Rights History* (2006) by Rosales; and *Declarations of Independence: Cross-Examining American Ideology* (1990) by Zinn.

In Part II of this book, we investigate the overall importance for and immediacy of social justice, especially in the field of education.

PART II

SOCIAL JUSTICE EDUCATION

· 1 2 ·

CONNECTIONS BETWEEN SOCIAL JUSTICE EDUCATION AND MULTICULTURAL EDUCATION

> Any situation in which some [people] prevent others from engaging in the process of inquiry is one of violence. The means used are not important; to alienate [people] from their own decision-making is to change them into objects.
> —Freire (1970, p. 85)

> When someone with the authority of a teacher describes the world and you are not in it, there is a moment of psychic disequilibrium, as if you looked into a mirror and saw nothing.
> —Rich (1994b, p. 217)

What: I have never forgotten one essential point my educational psychology professor related to my class back at San José State University when I was working toward my Secondary Education Teacher's Certification in 1970. His point crystallized for me the intent of true and meaningful learning. My professor explained that the term "education" is derived from two Latin roots: "*e*," meaning "out of," and "*ducere*," meaning "to lead" or "to draw." "Education," he said, "is the process of drawing knowledge out of the student or leading the student toward knowledge, rather than putting or depositing information into what some educators perceive as the students' waiting and docile mind"—what the Brazilian philosopher and educator Paolo Reglus Neves Freire (1970) termed "the banking system of education."

For genuine learning to occur, for it to be transformational, it must be student centered—grounded on the shared experiences of the learners—and composed of essential elements or domains: the "affective" (feelings) and the "cognitive" (informational). I design and implement my classes on a dialogic approach within a social justice framework in which students and educators cooperate in the process, whereby all are simultaneously the teacher and the learner. Educational psychologist Vygotsky (1962) referred to this process as *Obuchenie*.

Education, as I have gained from Freire, is a path toward permanent liberation in which people became aware (*conscientized*) of their multiple positionalities (identity intersectionality) and through praxis (reflection and action) transform the world. Educators, to be truly effective, must spend many years in self-reflection and must have a clear understanding of their motivations, strengths, limitations, "triggers," and fears. They must thoroughly come to terms with their positionalities in the world in terms of their social identities: both the ways in which they are privileged and how they have been the targets of systemic inequities. They are not afraid of showing vulnerability and admitting when they are wrong or when they "don't know." They have a firm grasp of the content area, and they work well with and are accessible to students and peer educators.

Realizing that students come from disparate backgrounds in terms of social identities, and that students learn in a variety of ways, educators must be "culturally competent" and practice "culturally relevant pedagogies," and they must be informed on the historical and cultural backgrounds of diverse student populations, pedagogical frameworks, theories of cognitive development, personality types, preferred sensory modes of learning, and others.

> To fulfill that mission, my teachers made sure they "knew" us. They knew our parents, our economic status, where we worshipped, what our homes were like, and how we were treated in the family.
>
> —hooks (1994, p. 3)

In the ideal classroom, the overriding climate is one of safety. This is not, however, the same as "comfort," for very often, comfortable situations might feel fine, but are not necessarily of pedagogic value. "Safety" in this case refers to an environment where educators facilitate a learning process: one in which people can share openly without fear of retribution or blame, where one can travel to the outer limits of one's "learning edges" in the knowledge that one will be supported and not left dangling.

The multicultural/social justice classroom poses exceptional challenges or, more importantly, opportunities to find creative solutions to address not only potential but also actual student resistance to course materials and concepts, for we touch upon some very personal and potentially triggering issues related to identity, social inequities, and critical histories that for many reasons may not receive as much space and time as necessary in the schools and in the greater society.

Robert Kegan

What: Within the constructivist framework, Kegan (1982) has developed a three-part method to bring students to a new level of awareness or to help them "unlearn" prior misinformation or knowledge that inhibits personal or academic growth.

In stage one—*Confirmation*—educators attempt to meet learners where they are, to draw them out, listening to them and legitimizing their beliefs without judgment, guilt, or blame. In stage two—*Contradiction*—educators "stretch" students' existing views by reframing the topic by offering additional information or new perspectives. They solicit alternative views from other students, draw out contradictions, and provide the opportunity for exchange. In stage three—*Continuity*—educators continue and extend the process begun in stage two, giving constructive feedback, offering praise for engaging in the process, and using humor if and when appropriate.

Emily Style

What: Educator and curriculum theorist Style (1988) emphasizes that to be effective, curriculum needs to bring in multiple perspectives on any given topic or multiple ways of viewing the world. It must "function both as window and as mirror": windows revealing outward the realities of others and the larger world, and mirrors reflected back and inward illuminating the students themselves. In this way, the curriculum creates an essential balance and affirmation of the "dialectic between the self and the world" (p. 1).

A foundational element in critical multiculturalism/social justice is social reconstructionist or transformational education in which the educator's role is to help prepare future citizens to reconstruct society to better serve the interests of all groups of people and to transform society toward greater equity for all.

> [There are] connections between multicultural social justice education, democracy, and education for democracy. Just as critical multicultural, social justice education does not simply involve examining the equal contributions of culture(s) to a society, *thick*[1] education for democracy does not seek to merely educate learners about electoral processes and representative government. These projects aim to address the realities of power imbalances that directly connect to cultures, identities, experiences and realities constructed by diverse groups and individuals in society.
> —Carr, Pluim, and Thésée (2017, p. 3)

So, what if any are the connections between the processes and goals of social justice and those of multicultural education in the schools? Below is the mission statement of multicultural education, in part, according to the U.S. National Association for Multicultural Education (NAME):

> Multicultural education is a philosophical concept built on the ideals of freedom, justice, equality, equity, and human dignity as acknowledged in various documents, such as the U.S. Declaration of Independence, constitutions of South Africa and the United States, and the Universal Declaration of Human Rights adopted by the United Nations. It affirms our need to prepare students for their responsibilities in an interdependent world. It recognizes the role schools can play in developing the attitudes and values necessary for a democratic society. It values cultural differences and affirms the pluralism that students, their communities, and teachers reflect. It challenges all forms of discrimination in schools and society through the promotion of democratic principles of social justice. (NAME website)

While NAME articulates and promotes what it understands as the clear links of multicultural education to social justice, theorists and practitioners imagine and practice multicultural education in several forms and on many levels. It does not exist as a monolith, but rather, as many multiculturalisms. According to Maurianne Adams,

> Social justice education pedagogy is based upon a set of principles and practices for teaching about oppression and social justice. SJE pedagogy aims to generate active engagement with social justice content through learning processes that are consistent with the goals of social justice. The priority of social justice educators is to affirm, model, and sustain socially just learning environments for all participants, and by so modeling to offer hope that equitable relations and social structures can be achieved in the broader society. (2016, p. 28)

Each semester for several years, I have taught at least one course centering on issues of social justice in education. I base the course on several key concepts and assumptions, including how issues of power, privilege, and domination within the United States connect to inequitable social divisions in terms of race, ethnicity, socioeconomic class, sex, gender identity and expression, sexual identity, religion, nationality, linguistic background, physical and mental ability/disability, age, and other variables. We address how issues related to social identities impact generally on life consequences, and specifically on educational outcomes. Virtually all students registered for my courses, which are mandatory for students registered in the teacher education program, are pre-service and in-service teachers.

I have discovered, however, that many if not most of students' other coursework in their university experiences and continuing into their eventual in-school careers project curriculum and pedagogy through the lens of monoculturalism, where school structures and climate represent primarily the dominant culture, which Kincheloe and Steinberg (1997) term the "Conservative" approach. This has its foundation in the belief in the superiority of a Western patriarchal cultural system based on the contributions of Western civilization promoted through the imposition of colonialism and the concept of Manifest Destiny. This approach is a reaction against civil rights and other liberation movements.

Note

1. A *thick* (or *thicker*) representation of democracy recognizes the role of power in society, acknowledges unequal access to formal political processes and institutions, and, instead, concentrates on issues of equity, social justice, political literacy, and transformative education (Carr, 2013; White & Cooper, 2015).

· 1 3 ·

DIMENSIONS AND CHARACTERISTICS OF MULTICULTURAL EDUCATION[1]

What: Several pioneers in the field of multicultural education have enumerated many primary tenets.

James A. Banks (2007), for example, discusses the "dimensions of multicultural education." In the arena of Content Integration, Banks explains this dimension as the extent to which educators employ examples and actual content from a variety of cultures and groups to illustrate major concepts, principles, generalizations, and theories within their subject area.

The Knowledge Construction Process dimension of multicultural education rests on the extent to which educational activities assist students critically to comprehend, investigate, and determine how implicit cultural assumptions, frames of references, perspectives, and possibly researcher biases and textbook writers influence how knowledge is constructed.

The dimension of Prejudice Reduction helps students develop positive and democratic beliefs and attitudes toward individuals and groups in the varieties and forms of social identities. In addition, the Multicultural Dimension of Equity Pedagogy emphasizes that educators adjust and maintain their teaching methods to facilitate the academic achievement of students from diverse learning styles, experiences, and backgrounds.

Banks' final dimension, Empowering School Culture and Social Structure, includes the restructuring of the schools' culture and organization so that all students from diverse background experience equality of opportunity to achieve and grow socially and academically to their potential.

Sonia Nieto and Patty Bode (2012) enumerate their "Seven Basic Characteristics of Multicultural Education." They discuss how multicultural education is Antioppression Education in that it is not merely the "heroes, holidays, foods, and festivals" approach, but goes further by attempting to combat and reduce all forms of oppression, including racism, ethnocentrism, sexism, heterosexism, cissexism (transgender oppression), ableism, classism, ageism, adultism, linguisism, lookism, religious oppression, and all the others.

They also discuss how multicultural education is Basic Education and how it is important for all students by promoting cultural literacy, which is as basic and necessary as reading, writing, mathematics, and computer literacy. Multicultural education is intended as a lens of perception through which learning is projected. It is a philosophy and a means of perceiving the world.

Multicultural education is Pervasive because it permeates everything including the school climate; physical environment; curriculum in every lesson and unit, curriculum guide, bulletin boards, activities and games, and letters sent to parents; in educational materials, technological aids, library acquisitions; cafeteria food; and relationships among students, teachers, administrators, school staff, and community members. It is also a process that is Dynamic and continually Ongoing. It involves relationships among people and often centers on the intangibles such as expectations of student achievement, learning environments, students' learning preferences, and other cultural variables.

And multicultural education is Education for Social Justice. On the level of the schools, it challenges, confronts, and disrupts misconceptions, untruths, and stereotypes that lead to structural inequality and discrimination based on social identities. It provides all students with the resources needed to learn to their fullest potential while drawing on the talents and strengths that students bring with them to the school. And it creates a learning environment that promotes Critical Pedagogy, which is a primary characteristic of multicultural education. It is meant to provide students with the skill of learning how to think and act in more expansive ways, reflecting on what they learn and applying that learning to real situations.

On a societal level, multiculturalism ensures that people are treated with fairness, respect, dignity, and generosity, and it affords each person the real opportunity to achieve their potential by providing them access to the goods, services, and social and cultural capital (Bourdieu, 1986) of a society. In addition, it affirms the cultures and talents of each individual and the group or group to which they identify.

Types of Multicultural Education

What: On the scale of "multicultural education," researchers Carl A. Grant and Christine E. Sleeter (2007), for example, enumerate several types. One focuses on what they refer to as "Teaching the Exceptional and the Culturally Different." This approach rests on the assumption that students in special education and those who are different in some way from the socially constructed national norm must acquire the cognitive skills, concepts, language, knowledge, and values traditionally required by their country of residence, which will ultimately enable them to gain employment and function within their nations' institutions and dominant culture.

This approach, the antithesis of social justice education, rests on the so-called "cultural deficiency" or "cultural deficit" model (see, e.g., Irizarry & Antrop-González, 2007) in which educators view these students as culturally deprived, disadvantaged, at risk for dropping out of school, and failing in life because of *their* cultural or socioeconomic background or disability. This ties in with the "culture of poverty" theory, which asserts that people of the working and poor classes focus solely on issues of survival in which they live for the moment without an orientation or concern in planning for the future, with such attributes for those who live in poverty as having psychological problems, lacking in positive role models leading to reduced moral and ethical standards and personal instability, language deficiencies even when using their native language by thinking only concretely with an inability to think in abstractions, and other alleged cultural deficits.

This approach, however, fails to consider the severely unlevel social playing field related to inequalities of opportunity within an overarching environment of systemic forms of oppression. This impacts how educators view and treat students, which in turn often affects students' educational outcomes and self-concept. It also adds to the "self-fulfilling prophecy," coined by preeminent sociologist, Robert K. Merton (1949), which proposes that a prediction (prophecy) directly or indirectly causes itself to become true because of the positive feedback between the belief and the behavior. For example, if a teacher expects little from a certain student, that student will perceive the teacher's low expectations and perform at that level. On the other hand, if a teacher expects high results from a student, the chances for that student's educational outcomes increase.

The "Human Relations Approach" (sometimes referred to as "Intergroup Relations") stands as Grant and Sleeter's second type of multicultural education. In the simplest of terms, sometimes this has been referred to as the "I'm Okay, You're Okay" approach. Kincheloe and Steinberg (1997) term this the "Liberal Approach" and discuss the "race-blind" focus in which the aim is to work toward a world with only one race, that of the human race. This form of multicultural education, however, avoids discussions and analysis of the asymmetries of societal power dynamics. It focuses on the attitudes and feelings students have about themselves and others to promote a sense of unity, tolerance, and acceptance among people. Here, the school curriculum addresses the individual differences and similarities among people, and the contributions of the groups in which students are members—including information about various ethnic, racial, disability, gender, or social class groups about whom students may hold certain stereotypes—as a pedagogic tool for prejudice reduction and friendships between students of differing groups.

Kincheloe and Steinberg (1997) term this the "Pluralist" approach, where the school values differences between cultures in a type of "cultural enrichment," sometimes referred to as the "Heroes, Holidays, Foods, and Festivals Approach." They emphasize that this is the primary or most practiced form of multiculturalism in the schools today. Societal power dynamics are not addressed, but rather, the approach can result in a certain "exoticism" of differences through what Kincheloe and Steinberg term as a virtual form of "cultural tourism." This approach has been employed in the mainstreaming of students with disabilities, and integration of refugee students who have fled war-torn and poverty-stricken countries into the public schools. It was also used following the attacks on September 11, 2001 to inform students about the cultural traditions and religion of Islam to reduce fears and prejudices (Islamophobia) against Muslims.

General strategies for best outcomes in this form of multicultural education include infusion in more than one subject area, especially when educators begin with the students' real-life experiences and when students experience social and academic success that are based on team-building models and cooperative learning activities not contingent on the failure of others. Educators stress the development of the personal skills of empathy and impulse control, as well as anger management.

Grant and Sleeter list the "Single-Group Studies Approach" as a third type of multicultural education. Examples include African American Studies, Asian American Studies, Latinx Studies, Women and Gender Studies, LGBTQ Studies, Disability Studies, and many others. Educators teach units or entire courses focusing on the culture of a specific group and the history of the victimization of and current issues facing this group *from the perspective of that group*, rather than from that of the socially dominant. This goes beyond simply studying the heroes, holidays, foods, and festivals, but deeper into addressing structural issues of societal marginalization and oppression. This type of multicultural education seeks to raise the social status of the *minoritized* group, while also underscoring its achievements even under (or because of) oppressive conditions.

This approach includes such strategies as designing the classroom with representations of the groups' cultural traditions; building on students' learning styles, and, when possible, on the learning styles of that group; bringing in speakers from that culture (but *not* placing students of that culture who are members of the class in the awkward and objectionable position of "speaking for" all people of their group); employing school faculty who are members of groups being studied, especially when these groups include people who are underrepresented in faculty and administrative school positions. This approach begins to *recenter* the school focus and curriculum from exclusively or primarily that of the dominant culture to a somewhat more inclusive and diverse center of gravity.

Kincheloe and Steinberg, calling this the "Left-Essentialist" form of multiculturalism, while acknowledging its many strengths, address the downsides as often its failures to highlight the historical situatedness (social construction) of these categories, but it, rather, proposes that a constellation of properties or traits (essences) define the construction of particular groups. This singular trait brings the group together into "Identity Politics," in which many groups focus on primarily one form of identity and oppression as being of prime importance. Currently, though, many individuals who have and still are practicing identity politics have turned somewhat more into "intersectional politics" or "ideology politics" where people of multiple forms of social identities are joining together into coalitions around certain ideologies to effect societal change.

The "Multicultural Education Approach," as discussed by Grant and Sleeter, further decenters the school focus and curriculum by organizing around the concept of "cultural pluralism." The Jewish immigrant to the

United States and sociologist of Polish and Latvian heritage, Horace M. Kallen (1915), coined the term "cultural pluralism" to challenge the view of the so-called "melting pot," which he considered inherently undemocratic. Kallen envisioned a country in the image of a great symphony orchestra, not sounding in unison ("monoculturalism" with its cultural homogeneity), but rather, one in which all the disparate cultures play in harmony and retain their unique and distinctive tones and timbres.

This Cultural Pluralism multicultural education approach promotes the value and strength of cultural diversity, works to reduce prejudice and discrimination against oppressed groups and promotes human rights for all, works toward equal opportunity and social justice for all groups to bring about a more equitable distribution of power among and between people of diverse cultural groups. The school curriculum continually introduces students to diverse perspectives in a total rather than fragmented manner, free from traditional biases and stereotypes. This approach seeks to reform the entire process of the educational environment. The ideological foundation rests on the concept and need for social change based on cultural pluralism and equality of opportunity.

And the final general type according to Grant and Sleeter is the "Multicultural and Social Reconstructionist Education Approach" (also referred to as the "Social Reconstructionist Approach," "Critical Teaching Approach," and "Critical Multiculturalism Approach"). Its goal is to prepare students to reconstruct their society to better serve the interests and needs of all groups of people. The four unique educational practices serving as the foundation of this approach are (1) the valued role of democracy as actively practiced in the schools in which all members of the educational community have some "voice" in the decision-making and implementation processes, (2) students learn to critically analyze institutional inequality in their own life circumstances on and off campus; (3) students learn, develop, and use skills of social action to effect positive social change, and (4) students develop skills to build bridges, alliances, and coalitions across various oppressed groups.

Terming this the "Critical Multicultural Education," Kincheloe and Steinberg add that this approach addresses larger issues of social justice education by investigating differentials in social power dynamics and social privilege, and how power shapes the human consciousness in the ways people make meaning of their different identity positions. It promotes and assists students in enhancing self-reflection and critical thinking skills, and it encourages students to take actions to promote positive social change. This approach also goes by the name of "Emancipatory Pedagogy," after renowned educational theorist and reformer Paolo Reglus Neves Freire (1970).

James A. Banks' "Approaches to Multicultural Curriculum Reform"

What: Banks (2007) developed an assessment tool for educators to rank qualitative levels of curricular integration regarding multicultural class materials, his Multicultural Curricular Content Integration scale.

Banks' first and most basic level he refers to as "The Contributions Approach." Here, educators discuss the heroes, holidays, foods, dances, music, artifacts, and other discrete elements of a given culture. Little emphasis is provided as to the meanings and importance of these cultural elements within the communities in which they exist, and the mainstream dominant culture, from whose perspective this cultural tour is based, remains unchanged.

"The Additive Approach" Banks presents as his second step or level upward on which content, concepts, themes, and perspectives are included onto the cultural elements of level one into the curriculum without changing its structure, purposes, and characteristics. Banks sees many disadvantages with this level of curricular integration. For one, it often views "ethnic" content from the perspective of the mainstream.

As an example of the problematic nature of this mainstream view, several years ago the Amherst (Massachusetts) Regional High School produced the Broadway musical, "West Side Story" (Mehren, 1999). As soon as plans for the production were announced, controversy ensued. Leading the opposition was Camille Sola, a 17-year-old student who spoke out at a student forum by reviling Leonard Bernstein and Stephen Sondheim's show, first performed in 1957, as racially and culturally insensitive and what she considered as its offensively stereotypical depiction of Puerto Rican males, its romanization of street gangs, its frequent use of racial and ethnic slurs, and overall negative portrayal of Puerto Rico.

Following Sola's petition drive signed by her peers, she was encouraged by the discussions at the school and within the Amherst community about issues of racism and cultural misappropriation. This resulted in the school administration changing its annual spring dramatic production from "West Side Story" to the breezy 1990s "Crazy for You," based on the 1930 George and Ira Gershwin musical "Girl Crazy." As this example and as Banks makes clear, this "additive" level of multicultural curricular content integration fails to provide students with a view of society from diverse perspectives or to truly comprehend the interconnections between cultures. It can and often does result in pedagogical problems for teachers, confusion for students, and community controversies.

Banks next discusses "The Transformation Approach," where we begin to see genuine multicultural curricular content. Here, the goals, structure, and perspectives are expanded with an infusion of various perspectives, frames of references, and content from diverse groups. This infusion has greater potential for expanding and enriching students' understandings of the nature, development, and complexity of their society and others throughout the world.

Banks' highest level, "The Social Action Approach," takes all the elements of the previous Transformation Approach and adds components that require students to make decisions and take actions related to the concept, issue, or problem studied in the curriculum unit. In this way, students make decisions on important social issues and take actions to help solve them. This approach provides education for social critique, decision making, and social change by developing critical thinking skills.

G. D. Borich and M. L. Tombari's "Educator Leadership and Power" Taxonomy

Borich and Tombari (1997) enumerate the various forms of educator power.

1. Expert Power: Certain individuals become leaders because others perceive them as experts. Successful teachers have expert power. Their students see them as both competent to explain and do certain things, and knowledgeable about topics. Such influence is earned, rather than conferred by having a title. Expert power is the legitimation of an individual's leadership because others perceive that individual as an expert.
2. Referent Power: Students often accept as leaders those teachers whom they like and respect. They view such teachers as trustworthy, fair, and concerned about them. The term "referent power" is used to describe leadership earned in this way.
3. Legitimate Power: Some roles by their very nature carry with them influence and authority. Police officers, presidents, and judges exert

social power and leadership by their very titles. This type of power has been referred to as legitimate power; unlike expert and referent power, it cannot be earned. Teachers possess a certain degree of legitimate power. Our society expects students to give teachers their attention, to respect them, and to do what they say.
4. Reward Power: Individuals in positions of authority can reward the people they lead. These rewards can take the form of privileges, approval, or more tangible compensation, such as money. To the extent that students desire the rewards conferred by teachers, teachers can exert a degree of leadership and authority. However, students who do not care much about good grades or teacher approval are difficult to lead solely by exerting reward power. Reward power, then, is leadership based on rewards or benefits that an individual can give to members of a group.
5. Coercive Power: By law, teachers and other school personnel can act *in loco parentis*, or with the same authority the parent has. Consequently, within limits, schools can punish students who defy the authority or leadership of the teacher by such techniques as suspension or expulsion, denial of privileges, or removal from the classroom. Teachers who rely on such techniques to maintain social power in the classroom are said to be using coercive power. The use of coercive power, however, may end misbehavior for a time, but at the cost of failing to develop trusting relationships or meeting students' needs for belonging.

Some Concluding Chapter Thoughts

On several occasions, students enrolled in my social justice education courses express their excitement over the content and in the possibility for real progressive social change in reducing the destructive and deadly forms of oppression, expanding peoples' options in their decision-making process, bringing people of disparate identities and nations together in a more peaceful and cooperative school environment and in the world. At the same time, though, they feel overwhelmed, daunted by the enormity of the process, and the ultimate span of time this overall project will take to come to fruition.

They also fear that with all their other professional obligations, including bureaucratic, they have or will have once they serve as teachers in their own classrooms, they simply will not have the time, energy, or support to project a social justice lens through their curricular materials and pedagogy. They also experience trepidation that a social-justice-oriented classroom will bring to the surface tensions and clashes arising within the larger society since, as we learn in my courses, the societal inequities related to social identities are reproduced, rather than originating, in educational environments from the society in which they are embedded.

Yes, the process toward social justice in a truly multicultural classroom, school, nation, and world is not always comfortable, not always neat, but the socially just classroom and society provide a space for everyone to be heard, to reflect, to engage in critical dialogue, and to enter a space of understanding, though not always in agreement of views and cultures different from one's own.

> We don't learn the importance of anything until it is snatched from our hands.
> —Malala Yousafzai ("The Daily Show," Comedy Channel, October 8, 2013)

Malala Yousafzai, the courageous and tireless champion for the rights of women and girls throughout the world to access quality education, has never swerved from her message even after the Taliban in her Pakistani town hijacked her school bus and pummeled bullets into her skull, critically wounding her at the early age of 14.

The "it" to which this remarkable young woman refers in her quote above denotes not her life, as one might expect, but rather, "education" in the formal as well as the informal sense. Today Malala's resolve shines ever brighter as she knows full well the consequences of fighting brutal patriarchal oppression. More importantly, though, she recognizes that women's equality and their very lives depend upon and demand educational access and equity.

The distinguished multicultural educator Nieto (2002) likens the socially just multicultural classroom and school to a great tapestry:

> A tapestry is a hand-woven textile. When examined from the back, it may simply appear to be a motley group of threads. But when reversed, the threads work together to depict a picture of structure and beauty. A tapestry also symbolizes, through its knots, broken threads and seeming jumble of colors and patterns on the back, the tensions, conflicts, and dilemmas that a society needs to work out. The spirit of both collaboration and struggle is evident in the school. (p. 18)

As the tapestry, social justice is a valuable, productive, beneficial, and a beautiful thing to construct and engage in as it becomes more and more a completed project.

Note

1 See Appendix B: Critical Consciousness: Reflecting, Thinking, Observing, Reading, Researching, and Writing Through a Critical Lens.

PART III

LIBERATORY PRAXIS

· 1 4 ·

LIBERATION

> [C]onsider a vision for social justice and liberation that values critical consciousness, participation, connectedness, passion, bridge building across divides through dialogue and action, and alliances and coalitions for change, as pathways to individual and collective empowerment, equity, safety, and security for all social groups in society. Such a vision requires an understanding of how various forms of privilege and oppression are connected at the psychological, interpersonal, intergroup, structural/institutional, and global levels.
> —Ximina Zúñiga (2013, p. 590)

Now What: It was a brilliantly sunny, though rather cool, mid-June afternoon. Banners flying, music blasting, people of all walks of life assembled, reuniting, greeting, kissing, embracing, catching up on lives lived in the space between. The signal was given with a contagious cheer rising from the crowd, and for the next few hours the streets would be theirs: Dykes on Bikes revving their engines; shirtless muscled young men dancing to a disco beat atop flatbed floats winding their way down the streets; dazzling drag queens in red and gold and silver; the Freedom Trail Marching Band trumpeting the call; a black-and-white cocker spaniel wearing a sign announcing "DON'T ASSUME I'M STRAIGHT"; lesbian moms and gay dads pushing strollers or walking beside youth of all ages; Gays for Patsy Klein decked out in their finest country duds, two-stepping down the boulevard; AIDS activists falling to the pavement of those same boulevards in simulated death to expose governmental and societal inaction, which is still killing so many; married same-sex couples walking hand in hand; Parents, Families, and Friends of Lesbians and Gays (PFLAG) proclaiming "We are proud of our lesbian, gay, bisexual, and transgender families," alongside political, social, and service organizations, business and religious caucuses of all stripes and denominations, and of course bystanders watching the procession, holding court from the sidelines.

And in the midst of this merriment and this protest, the humorous posters and angry placards, the enormous rainbow balloon sculptures arching overhead, and the colorful streamers and glistening "fairy dust" wafting from open windows, amid the shiny black leather and shimmering lamé, the multicolored T-shirts and the drab business suits, came the youth, their radiant young faces catching the rays of the sun, marching side-by-side, hand-in-hand, their middle school and high school Gay/Straight Alliance banners waving exaltedly in this storm of humanity, announcing their entry, their solidarity, their feisty outrage, and yes, their pride changing "Two, Four, Six, Eight, Queer is Just as Good as Straight, Three, Five, Seven, Nine, LGBTs are Mighty Fine"; then, gaining intensity, singing, "Hey Hey, Ho Ho, Homophobia Has Got to Go," and then, as if hit by an all-consuming revelation, shouting, "We're Here, We're Queer, We're Not Going Back, We're NOT Going Back, WE'RE NOT GOING BACK!"

And indeed, they will not go back into those dank closets of fear and denial that stifles the spirit and ruins so many lives. Oh, they will physically return to their schools and their homes. They will continue to study and play sports, to watch movies, listen to their iPods and Smart Phones, and write about their day on Facebook and Twitter. Some will most likely continue to serve as community organizers, and some will go on to become parents, teachers, political leaders once their school days are behind. The place they will go to, though, is nowhere that can be seen. It is a place of consciousness that teaches those who have entered that everyone is diminished when any one of us is demeaned; that heterosexism, sexism, biphobia, cissexism, racism, classism, ableism, ethnocentrism, jingoism, religious oppression, as well as all the other forms of oppression have no place in a just society.

From the sidelines of the parade, beginning as a whisper and ending as a mighty roar of support: "We are so glad you are here" came voices from the crowd. "We wish we could have done this when we were in high school," cried others too numerous to count. "Thank you so much for your courage!"

From where has this courage come, and how has this change actually come about? It seems that a great many factors have merged providing the conditions for liberatory social change. Researchers are continually unearthing our complex, extensive, and rich histories across millennia and cultures. Throughout this long history, young people have been on the front lines serving as energetic and inspirational pioneering change agents.

Throughout the world, on university and grade school campuses, in communities and homes, and in the media, issues of diversity and social justice are increasingly "coming out of the closet." We see young people developing positive social identities at earlier ages than ever before. Activists are gaining selective electoral and legislative victories. Primarily in academic milieus, greater emphasis and discussion is centering on topics of social justice education where writers, educators, and students analyze and challenge current notions and categories of socially constructed identities and issues of power and privilege.

Young people have been and continue to be at the heart of progressive social justice change movements. Researcher Catherine Corrigall-Brown (2005), in her study of youth participation in social movements, found that activism is directly related with higher levels of self-esteem and self-efficacy and also associated with verification and crystallization of identity development.

Youth are transforming and revolutionizing the society and its institutions by challenging overall power inequities related not only to racial, religious, ability, sexuality, and gender identity categorizations and hierarchies, but they are also making links in the various types of oppression, and they are forming coalitions with other marginalized groups. They are dreaming their dreams, sharing their ideas and visions, and organizing to ensure a world free from all the deadly forms of oppression, and along their journey, they are inventing new ways of relating and being in the world. Their stories, experiences, and activism have exciting potential to bring us to a future where people across identities categories will live freely, unencumbered by social taboos and oppressive cultural norms.

· 15 ·

#NEVERAGAIN YOUTH-LED FIREARMS SAFETY MOVEMENT

A Study in Activism

> The people in the government who were voted into power are lying to us. And us kids seem to be the only ones who notice and our parents to call BS. Companies trying to make caricatures of the teenagers these days, saying that all we are self-involved and trend-obsessed, and they hush us into submission when our message doesn't reach the ears of the nation, we are prepared to call BS.

Now What: Emma Gonzalez, a senior at Marjory Stoneman Douglas High School in Parkland, Florida, excited the crowd at a gun control rally in Fort Lauderdale just four days after a gunman plowed down students and faculty with an AR-15 semiautomatic assault rifle killing 17 and injuring another 15 precious souls. Through her voice, her passion, her outrage, and her deep commitment, Emma poured cleansing waters into an ever-increasing reservoir representing a movement that has long been filling in our country to wash away the deeply entrenched stain of gun violence.

It is a movement declaring that people are worth far more than corporate profits and political payoffs. It is a movement demanding that common-sense measures be taken to finally begin to end the scourge that is gun violence in the United States of America. It is a movement proclaiming clearly and forcefully that condolences and prayers are simply not enough, and most importantly that ENOUGH *IS* ENOUGH!

Emma continued:

> Politicians who sit in their gilded House and Senate seats funded by the NRA telling us nothing could have been done to prevent this, we call BS. They say tougher gun laws do not decrease gun violence. We call BS. They say a good guy with a gun stops a bad guy with a gun. We call BS. They say guns are just tools like knives and are as dangerous as cars. We call BS.

The United States stands at the cusp of great social change, led by strong and articulate young people who are cutting through the BS of longtime and large-scale entrenchment holding in place a system catering to the rich and the well positioned.

Black Lives Matter and professional athletes sparked by the courageous actions of NFL star Colin Kaepernick are challenging institutional racism; women are pouring out into the streets and onto the ballots to break the logjam blocking their entry into the ranks of key policy makers; the #MeToo and #TimesUp Movements are standing up by demanding an end to sexual harassment and gender inequality.

Disability Rights activists are sitting in and acting up to ensure quality health care for all and the security of benefits for all who require them to maintain a high quality of life; LGBTQ people and their allies continue to push for full equality and the freedom to enter public facilities most closely aligning with people's gender identities; labor activists are demanding a realignment of the nation's economic priorities overwhelmingly and increasingly separating the haves from the rest of us.

It takes courage to speak out and counter the violence, the scapegoating, the fear and resistance to change, and the ignorance, and yes, the hatred surrounding our lives. Fortunately, young people are developing positive identities at earlier ages than ever before. Activists of all ages are gaining selective electoral, legislative, and judicial victories.

Emma said: "They say no laws could have prevented the hundreds of senseless tragedies that have occurred. We call BS. That us kids don't know what we're talking about, that we're too young to understand how the government works. We call BS."

Young people have been integral in the development and success of social movements from the very beginning, and today, they are shaking up norms and traditions as have youth from the past.

Civil Disobedience

Now What: A new generation of young social and political activists poured out of their schools around the country on Wednesday, March 14, 2018, to mourn and to protest the senseless loss of 17 innocent beautiful souls cut down by a shooter exactly one month earlier at Marjory Stoneham Douglas High School.

Like those of us chronicled by then 23-year-old poet laureate Bob Dylan of an earlier generation during another defining historical moment, these new social warriors too gathered 'round people to give testimony on the tragedy of firearms violence by demanding that legislators and others in positions of power start swimmin' or they'll sink like a stone.

At 10:00 in the morning, the call was given for 17 minutes of silent meditation in remembrance of the 17 murdered comrades. Speakers then contributed their voices in demanding the right to safe schools and safe streets free from the plague of violence long overtaking our nation.

Following some rallies, students and their supporters marched to local parks to join with community members or to government houses to meet with legislators. Demonstrators in Washington, DC sat with turned backs on the White House in silence, before marching in solidarity to the U.S. Capitol to lobby lawmakers.

Many school administrators viewed these rallies as learning opportunities for students actively to engage in the civil project of our democracy by adding their voices and their talents for constructive social change. Others, however, did not heed the call by figuratively standing in the doorway and blocking the hall.

Administrators at Saint Pius X Catholic High School in Atlanta, Georgia, for example, launched e-mail messages and warned students over the intercom system that any student who engaged in the walkout faced severe disciplinary action, including school suspension as ordered by the Catholic Arch Diocese. Three female students from Saint Pius X High School spoke on camera with a reporter for MSNBC during the rally at a local Atlanta public school giving reasons why they defied their administrators and placed themselves at risk to add their voices of support in demanding their right to safe schools.

The young women had attempted to organize a similar rally at their Catholic school. When administrators rejected their request, they all agreed that they had to stand up and speak out with their voices and their bodies. Stated one: "This is a day I will remember for the rest of my life." All three acknowledged that they were taking risks by showing up, but these were risks they were certainly willing to take.

As an undergraduate student, I attended San José State University from 1966 to 1969, and 1970 as a graduate student. San José State at that time had a relatively progressive administration. We had freedom of political speech, we organized and staffed informational tables throughout the campus, we had access to university facilities to hold our meetings and rallies. (See Appendix I: A Civics Course on the Second Amendment.) In fact, I was a chief organizer of a rally in support of our university president against criticism coming from some of the more conservative members of the state university board who considered our president too "tolerant" of campus antiwar and antiracism protests and protesters.

Nonetheless, during the fall of 1967 and then again in 1968, we called for a student strike of classes. The purpose of the boycott was not to demonstrate against or criticize our professors, or even our university. It was, rather, to send a message to our leaders in government—state and national—that the war we were waging in Vietnam was wrong, that it was misguided, that it was illegal according to international law.

I will never forget sitting in Botany class the week prior to the first planned strike, when Professor Thaw forthrightly threatened to give an in-class quiz on the day of the strike, and anyone absent that day would receive an automatic "F" on the quiz with no possibility of a makeup. To this day, I do not know where my courage came from as I raised my hand and stated that "This is one 'F' I would be proud to 'earn.'" To my utter amazement, other students cheered, and eventually Professor Thaw rescinded his threat.

By boycotting classes, students take a risk—however small at the time—but a risk nonetheless. And this is one of the, if not *the*, major points in the philosophy of civil disobedience. For it to be truly meaningful, for it to be a truly beneficial, life-changing experience for the individual, there must be some aspect of risk and sacrifice; one must give something, pay something, in order to keep and to strengthen one's principles and one's sense of personal integrity.

My questions are thus: Will a person gain more, learn more, commit more to an idea or a cause if it is given freely to them or, rather, if they must risk something for it? Will the experience be more meaningful if one attends a rally between classes or if one puts one's principles on the line—and be willing to accept the consequences—to walk out or strike classes?

Schools are microcosms of the larger society. By students saying that "we will collectively take a stand," they are, at least symbolically, lodging their vote against what they believe to be an unjustifiable stand on the part of their government or by other leaders. They are declaring their opposition to politics and policies as usual.

Let us remember that three young people helped to set the stage for the relative political freedoms youth enjoy today.

Tinker v. Des Moines Independent Community School District

Now What: The Supreme Court of the United States handed down a landmark freedom of speech case for students on February 24, 1969. It involved two Des Moines, Iowa, high school students, John Tinker, 15, and Christopher Eckhardt, 16, and John's 13-year-old sister, Mary Beth Tinker, a Des Moines junior high school student.

In December 1965, John, Christopher, and Mary Beth attended a meeting with a group of adults and other students in Des Moines at the Eckhardt home. The purpose of the meeting was to come up with strategies whereby they could publicize their objections to the hostilities in Vietnam. They came up with an idea to express their support for a truce between the warring parties by wearing black armbands during the holiday season and by fasting on December 16 and New Year's Eve.

Meeting participants had previously engaged in nonviolent activities to work toward ending the war, and they decided to join the program. When Des Moines school district officials learned of the proposed activity, on December 14 they adopted and distributed a policy stating that any student found wearing a black armband, and failing to remove it on request, would be suspended from school and allowed to return only without the armband.

John, Christopher, and Mary Beth wore black armbands to school in violation of the stated policy, and school officials sent them home. Parents of the students petitioned the U.S. District Court to issue an injunction to school officials from disciplining the students, though the court dismissed the complaint on grounds that the school district had the right to take its actions to prevent breaches of school discipline.

On appeal to the U.S. Supreme Court, the justices ruled in favor of the students and against the school district in that the wearing of armbands for the purpose of expressing views is considered as a symbolic action, according to the court, "closely akin to 'pure speech'," and well within the Free Speech clause of the 1st Amendment and the Due Process Clause of the 14th Amendment. In addition, the Court found school officials failed to prove that the wearing of the armbands would substantially disrupt school discipline.

Speaking for the 7 to 2 majority in the case, Justice Abe Fortes wrote:

> ... In the absence of a specific showing of constitutionally valid reasons to regulate their speech, students are entitled to freedom of expression of their views.

This case would have implications for numerous cases that followed.

Our society is constructed in such a way as to deny voice to young people in the decision-making process in the affairs of state. Young people do not hold powerful positions in the executive suites in business and industry, in the media outlets, in the halls of Congress. Their strength, however, exists when they take collective action. Government leaders then begin to listen.

In their collective strength, they can and have changed the world for the betterment of all.

· 16 ·

VISIONING SOCIAL JUSTICE AND LIBERATION

> When we are committed to liberatory praxis, we must engage in a process of *conscientization* that includes deconstructing the multiple layers of colonization in our internal and external spaces and practices in order to chart a new territory for ourselves, our fields of study, and our communities. The process of *concientization* is a group process, a community process, and a political process.
> —Maria Scharron-del Rio (2018)

Now What: As stated previously, we can visualize "oppression," and its attendant dominant group privileges, as comprising a metaphorical wheel, with the numerous spokes each representing the various systemic forms that oppression takes. These include ableism, adultism, ageism, biphobia, chauvinism, cissexism, classism, environmental degradation and exploitation (ecoism), ethnocentrism, heterosexism, jingoism, linguicism, lookism, religious oppression, sexism, xenophobia, and more.

In the university courses I teach on topics of social justice in education, I ask students to imagine a world free from all the deadly forms of oppression. What would such a world be like? How might that world affect you as an individual and as a member of a group? As I ask these questions, some students' faces brighten, some seem stunned and surprised, while other students tend to outright reject the notion that humanity can or will ever attain a liberated oppression-free world.

Following a lively and engaging class discussion, I present the case study of a specific form of oppression that once gripped Christian- (primarily Catholic-) majority-dominated nations like a steel vice, but the pressure of that religious vice has greatly (though certainly *not* completely) eased in its impact on sociopolitical policy implications and on the lives of individuals most at risk for this specific form of oppression. I gave the example of how people and groups have worked throughout the expanses of time to reduce the oppression toward left-handed people.

While theorists, educators, and activists may envision social justice and liberation in a variety of terms and aspects, several underlying tenets connect most together in imaging a community, a nation, and a world free from all the deadly forms of oppression, where all inhabitants of the international community maintain equality of opportunity to achieve their potential and function free from constraints based on their identities and backgrounds. Since these forms of constraints and oppression are rooted in socially constructed systemic patterns of power and privilege, likewise, we in the current and in future generations have the capacity to socially *de*construct these in unity and coalition.

From the second we float out from the womb until our final swim, our socialization pushes us steadily down the mainstream until we pour into the polluted ocean of conformity to hierarchal patterns and systems of power and privilege, which a lack of critical awareness helps to reproduce and replenish. As social justice-conscious people, however, we commit to the task of constructing impermanent dams along the mainstream to slow the current just long enough for ourselves and others to critically and mindfully reflect upon the waters so that when we approach and finally merge into the mighty ocean one by one, thousands by thousands, generations by generations, we and they forever change its contours and substance-filtering contaminants deposited by previous generations.

As our socialization process assigns us the scripts we are to play (collude in) on the stage in the drama of hierarchal systems of oppression, the contemporary production need not maintain its seeming inevitability and to self-perpetuate. For true liberation to occur, or "critical transformation" in the terms of Paolo Freire, individuals and members of groups all along the scale of oppression, from the oppressed to the advantaged, need first to come to a critical understanding of the roles they play. Social justice theorists enter the process of liberation from several, and often overlapping, perspectives.

> When I dare to be powerful, to use my strength in the service of my vision, then it becomes less important whether or not I am afraid.
>
> —Audre Lorde (1997, p. 13)

Some key terms to consider in our discussion of liberation include:

Ally (Upstander) and a Conceptual Model

What: "Ally" in social justice work includes a few meanings, the most inclusive being someone who joins with another or others for a shared purpose or goal. "Ally" sometimes refers to a person from a socially dominant group, with the privileges granted to members of these groups, and who uses these privileges to ensure a freer, more equitable, and less oppressive society for all. Another way of viewing an ally is as one who figuratively stands up (an "upstander") to social inequity and who promotes social justice.

An ally, though, does not represent people whose motivation to engage in this important work stems from a goal of achieving personal fame, attention, or reward. A true ally's inspiration comes from a perspective of social justice, from freeing oneself and others from constraints established in the past and in the promotion of a vibrant and progressively moving society within a genuinely democratic process.

What: A "coalition" develops when we join with others of similar and, also, diverse backgrounds and social identities to work toward common goals. Coalitions may at times be rather difficult to form and can also be uncomfortable for its participants. But, if we are doing good work with overriding positive goals, the discomfort is worth the challenge.

> Under the Hitler regime … the most important thing that I learned … was that bigotry and hatred are not the most urgent problems. The most urgent, the most disgraceful, the most shameful, and the most tragic problem is silence.
> —Joachim Prinz, Rabbi of Berlin, exiled in 1937 to the United States
> From his speech August 28, 1963, Washington, DC

Nancy J. Evans and Jamie Washington's "Steps Toward Becoming an Ally"

Now What: Several researchers have charted the processes reflecting trajectories for human physical, emotional, mental, personality, identity, and moral development, and many others. Evens and Washington (2013), with their qualitative model, investigate ally development. Although it focuses on allies to LGBTQ persons, topics, and communities, its contours can represent ally development routes more generally.

1. Awareness: of self and the similarities and differences with the person or community to which you are to be an ally.
2. Knowledge/Education: about the people, issues, identities, and cultures to which you are to be an ally.
3. Skills: "This area is the one in which people often fall short because of fear, or lack of resources or supports." "Skills" needed here include communication and social organizing, which can be learned "by attending workshops, role-playing certain situations with friends, developing support connections, or practicing interventions or awareness raising in safe settings—for example, a restaurant or hotel out of your hometown" (p. 417).
4. Action: the most important stage, which can be "the most frightening step" (p. 417). Action is a requirement for initiating change.

Empathy and "Empathic Listening"

So What: Shortly following their high school graduation in Southern California, two 18-year-old young men, best friends since childhood, drove to a casino just crossing the Nevada line where they intended to play video games before returning home the next day.

After engaging in the games for a while, one of the friends, Jeremy Strohmeyer, walked toward the restrooms. Seeing that he entered the women's room, the other young man, David Cash, walked in to see what Jeremy was doing. He noticed that Jeremy was playfully throwing wadded paper towels at a young black girl, who seemed at first to have enjoyed the attention.

But then the scene turned violent. Strohmeyer grabbed 7-year-old Sherrice Iverson, placed his hand over her mouth, and spirited her into a toilet stall as Cash watched by the sinks. He entered an adjacent stall and mounted the toilet edge allowing him to peer down as he saw Jeremy continuing to muffle the girl's screams and hearing as he warned Sherrice to keep quiet or he would kill her.

Not wanting to get involved, Cash returned to playing video games. He did not attempt to stop his friend from attacking the young girl. He did not seek help or call law enforcement officials. He calmly played games and waited the 20 minutes it took for Jeremy to return. David asked Jeremy what had happened. "I killed her," Jeremy asserted with a certain serenity in his tone on that summer evening in 1997. Soon thereafter, the two friends coolly entered nearby casinos where they enjoyed mechanical rides and continued to play video games until it was time for them to return home.

With the assistance of the video security system implanted at the casino, Strohmeyer was eventually caught, tried, and convicted to life imprisonment for rape and murder. Cash, on the other hand, was never indicted because inaction was not a crime in Nevada at the time. In reaction to the case and the lack of charges against Cash, Richard Perkins, Speaker of the Nevada Assembly, sponsored the Sherrice Iverson bill requiring Nevadans to notify law enforcement if they witness violent acts committed against a child. The law took effect in 1999, and a similar measure passed in California one year later.

Questioned on a CBS "60 Minutes" segment, "The Bad Samaritan," in 1999 that if given a chance, would he do things differently, Cash said, "I don't feel there is much I could have done differently." Asked a similar question during an interview on a Los Angeles radio station, Cash gave a similar reply and added:

> How much am I supposed to sit down and cry about this ... The simple fact remains that I did not know this little girl. I do not know starving children in Panama. I do not know people dying of disease in Egypt.

The *Las Vegas Sun* reported Cash as saying that he wanted to sell his story to the media. One movie company already had offered him $21,000, he added. "I'm no idiot," he declared. "I'll [expletive] get my money out of this" (quoted in Scott, 1997, n.p.).

Though I have studied the Holocaust and other genocides, until I discovered this case, I always had the gnawing and seemingly unanswerable question pulling at me, "How could these incidents have taken place throughout the ages"? David Cash taught me that mass murders happen on the macro level when people on the individual and collective levels let them happen, when witnesses—so-called "bystanders"—do little or nothing to intervene. When people either allow their fear or reluctance to "get involved" supersede their empathy.

Empathy, that special and majestic human quality, has always been a vital life force of our humanness. As we understand in psychology, unless there is developmental delay, infants demonstrate the rudimentary beginnings of empathy whenever they recognize that another is upset, and they show signs of being upset themselves. Very early in their lives, infants develop the capacity to crawl in the diapers of others even though their own diapers don't need changing.

Though empathy is a part of the human condition, through the process of socialization, others often teach us to inhibit our empathetic natures with messages like "Don't cry," "You're too sensitive," "Mind your own business," "It's not your concern." We learn the stereotypes of the individuals and groups our society has "minoritized" and "othered." We learn who to scapegoat for the problems within our neighborhoods, states, nations, and world. Through it all, that precious life-affirming flame of empathy can wither and flicker. For some, it dies entirely. And as the blaze recedes, the bullies, the demagogues, the tyrants take over filling the void where our humanness once prevailed. And then we have lost something very precious.

David Cash represents the termination of empathy on the individual micro level, resulting not only in the possibly preventable rape and murder of a young girl, but the death of his own soul. And when the demise of empathy comes to powerful leaders, the consequences, on the macro level, become exponentially deeper, toxic, and tragic.

I have learned many lessons in my studies of genocides perpetrated throughout the ages. Strong leaders whip up sentiments by employing dehumanizing stereotyping and scapegoating entire groups, while other citizens or entire nations often refuse to intervene. Everyone, not only the direct perpetrators of oppression, plays a key role in the genocidal dramas. Also, on a micro level, this is also apparent, for example, in episodes of schoolyard, community-based, as well as electronic forms of bullying.

Olweus (1993), international researcher and bullying-prevention specialist, enumerates the distinctive and often overlapping roles enacted in these episodes: the person or persons who perpetrate bullying; the active followers; those who passively support, condone, or collude in the aggression; the onlookers (sometimes referred to as "bystanders"); the possible defenders; those who actually defend the targets of aggression; and those who are exposed and attacked.

Now What: Burley-Allen (1995) offers these guidelines for Empathic Listening:

1. Be attentive. Be interested. Be alert and not distracted. Create a positive atmosphere through nonverbal behavior.
2. Be a sounding board—allow the speaker to bounce ideas and feelings off you while you assume a nonjudgmental, noncritical manner.

3. Don't ask a lot of questions. They can give the impression you are "grilling" the speaker.
4. Act like a mirror—reflect back what you think the speaker is saying and feeling.
5. Don't discount the speaker's feelings by using stock phrases like "It's not that bad," or "You'll feel better tomorrow."
6. Don't let the speaker "hook" you. This can happen if you get angry or upset, allow yourself to get involved in an argument, or pass judgment on the other person.
7. Indicate you are listening by
    o Providing brief, noncommittal acknowledging responses, e.g., "Uh-huh," "I see."
    o Giving nonverbal acknowledgements, e.g., head nodding, facial expressions matching the speaker, open and relaxed body expression, eye contact.
    o Invitations to say more, e.g., "Tell me about it," "I'd like to hear about that."
8. Follow good listening "ground rules":
    - Don't interrupt.
    - Don't change the subject or move in a new direction.
    - Don't rehearse in your own head.
    - Don't interrogate.
    - Don't teach.
    - Don't give advice.
    - *Do* reflect back to the speaker what you understand and how you think the speaker feels.

Bobbie Harro's "Cycle of Liberation"

Now What: On her "Cycle of Socialization," Harro (2013a) charts the process by which we internalize our socialization. She envisions liberation, though, as "critical transformation" with her "Cycle of Liberation" (2013b).

The cycle, or model, comprises several points, any of which individuals can enter depending on their degree of awareness. Harro emphasizes that travelers as they process along the pathways "will repeat or recycle many times," since "[t]here is no specific beginning or end point, just as one is never 'done' working to end oppression" (p. 619). She emphasizes that the Cycle is held

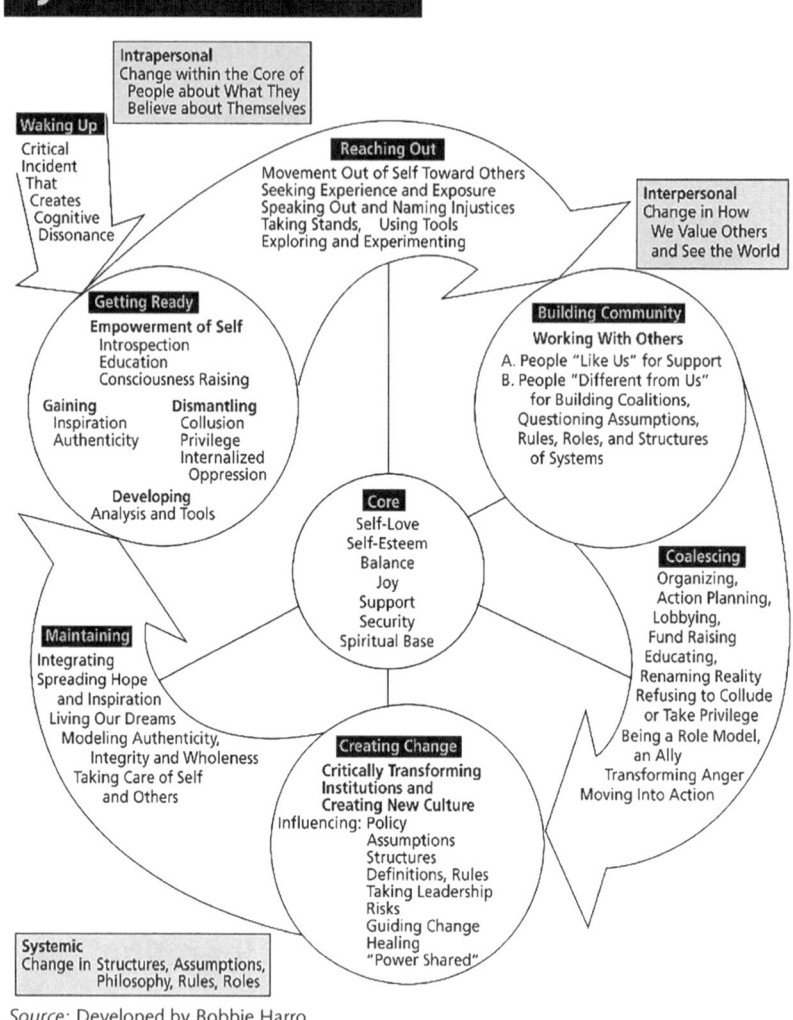

Figure 16.1. "Cycle of Liberation" by Bobbie Harro. Reproduced with permission.

together by a "core" set of factors: "qualities or states of being," some which are exhibited on the individual and collective levels all along the path toward liberation.

The points along the Cycle comprise the following:

- Waking Up
- Getting Ready
- Reaching Out
- Building Community
- Coalescing
- Creating Change
- Maintaining

Waking Up

Often this entry point onto the Cycle begins when we feel somehow differently than we had previously, evidenced by an *intra*personal shift at the center of how we felt or believed about ourselves. This might have been sparked by a critical incident of incidents or may have come about through a slow evolutionary process whereby we experience a sense "of cognitive dissonance, where something that used to make sense to us (or that we never questioned), ceases to make sense" any longer (p. 619).

Getting Ready

Though we may progress from a general sense of unease onto the Cycle at differing rates depending on who we may be, this point "involves consciously dismantling and building aspects of ourselves and our worldviews based on our new perspectives" (p. 620). Crucial factors involved in our initial part of our liberation include "introspection, education, and consciousness raising." We reflect on our thoughts and behaviors, the language we use that may indicate possible inconsistencies with our newly developing perceptions. We read, talk with people, and in other ways educate ourselves as we begin to make connections between our changing worldview and how we live our lives.

Reaching Out

Eventually, as we do our work toward liberation, we begin "to seek experiences outside ourselves to check our reality and to expose ourselves to a wider range of difference than we had before" (p. 621). We engage in dialogue and sometimes in debate with others, and we may disagree with others where we previously remained silent. As we begin to challenge the status quo, we may find resistance from some who would rather we stay quiet. On the other hand, we also may experience from others encouragement to continue speaking out.

Building Community

This *inter*personal phase of the Cycle involves two steps: "dialoguing with *people who are like us* for support (people who have the same social identities as we do, with regard to this issue of oppression), and dialoguing with *people who are different from us* for gaining understanding and building coalitions" (italics in original, p. 622). We engage in ongoing dialogues, learn from others' experiences, and come to a better and more integral understanding of ourselves.

Coalescing

Now that we have reduced some of our defenses to change, have joined with others, and strengthen our commitment, we are now at a point to challenge systems of oppression. In coalition, we may organize, shape actions, lobby key stakeholders, engage in fund-raising activities, and educate others. We may express our views more overtly, take public stands, and rally others to join the coalitions. We now understand ourselves differently and refuse to collude any longer in systems of oppression. "We are refusing to accept privileges, and we are acting as role models and allies for others" (p. 623).

Creating Change

According to Harro (2013b), "The parameters of this phase of the cycle of liberation include using our critical analysis of the assumptions, structures, rules, and roles of the existing system of oppression, and our coalition power, to begin transforming the system" (p. 623). This involves imagining new ways of living and being, a new culture reflecting changing assumptions and social structures concerning the rules we enact and roles we perform that align closely with our philosophy of a socially just, diverse, and equitable society and world.

Maintaining

We must remain ever vigilant each day to maintain, enhance, strengthen, and modify when needed our changed self-awareness and social consciousness.

Along with this daily maintenance, we need also to celebrate our successful efforts at changing the system, no matter how small, no matter how large. "This process says to the larger world, 'Look, this can work. You can change things by dialoguing and working together'" (p. 624).

Barbara Love's "Liberatory Consciousness"

Now What: As highlighted in Harro's (2013a) "Cycle of Socialization," people are born into their societies, which teach them the established rules, the values, beliefs, behaviors, and roles the individual must play in the maintenance of hierarchal systems of power and privilege. And due to this socialization, according to Love (2013):

> All humans now living have internalized the attitudes, understandings, and patterns of thoughts that allow them to function in and collaborate with these systems of oppression, whether they benefit from them or are placed at a disadvantage by them. (p. 601)

While we had no input in constructing the systems of oppression, by coming to a deeper understanding of ourselves and of these systems, we can function integrally as "liberation workers" by developing with mindful intentionality, in Love's terms, a "liberatory consciousness" (p. 601) free from the self-guilt one may experience and the blaming of others for its continuance. Barbara Love discusses her four elements of liberatory consciousness.

1. Awareness

As the term denotes, "awareness" involves developing the critical facility to perceive fully the depth and substance of our cultural and political environments, to attend to the details, the overt and covert meanings in language, in our and other people's behaviors and thoughts. As Love states, "It means making the decision to live our lives from a waking position" (p. 602).

2. Analysis

With the awareness, the information we gather from our "waking position," we have the means to reflect, examine, and posit what is happening as we make meaning from our perceptions. This analysis will provide us with practical options for actions we may need to take whenever what we perceive stands counter to our values of social justice.

3. Action

Following our awareness and analysis of our perceptions, we can now determine if any action is required, either by us as an individual, collectively by coalescing in unity with others, or by supporting and encouraging others to engage in action. The action component of a liberatory consciousness includes deciding what needs to be done, and then seeing to it that action is taken.

4. Accountable/Ally-Ship

While acknowledging and accepting the axiom that it is not the responsibility of minoritized peoples to teach people of dominant groups about systems of oppression and to dismantle social oppression all on their own, Love believes that when members of subordinated and dominant groups join as allies "across and between 'role' groups," a synergism derived from these unions can result in the furtherance of a liberatory consciousness for all involved.

> People raised on one end of patterns of gender, race, and class subordination or domination can provide a different perspective for people raised on the other. (Love, 2013, p. 604)

Serving as liberation workers can certainly be uplifting and empowering, whether acting individually and within coalition. It also can be challenging and often frustrating. Along with us giving credit for our successes, we need also to take responsibility, to be accountable, for the times we make mistakes. And yes, we *will* make mistakes. This work is certainly not easy, for if it were, we would have cured long ago the plagues of oppression that have infected our planet. Love provides some helpful advice.

> Rather than self-condemnation or blame from others, it will be important to have the opportunity and the openness to hear an analysis from others that allows us to reevaluate problematic behaviors or positions. (p. 604)

Each time we accept accountability, when we understand that sometimes our best intentions impact others in harmful ways, our liberatory consciousness expands.

Suzanne Pharr's "Liberation Politics"

Now What: Pharr (1996) understands liberation as an ongoing political project with continually renewed dialogue and a struggle against all the types of oppression, all the barriers preventing large sectors of the population from attaining access to economic resources and social justice. Pharr includes several factors as essential in liberation politics:

- Helping individuals to fulfill their greatest potential by providing truthful information along with the tools and skills for using it, supporting their autonomy and self-government, and connecting them to life in community with others;
- Fostering both individual freedom and mutual responsibility for others;
- Recognizing that freedom demands people always be able to make their own choices about their lives;
- Creating a politic of shared power [power with] rather than power-over;
- Learning the non-violent skills of compromise and mediation in the sometimes-difficult collective lives of family and community—in organizations, the workplace, and governing bodies;
- Developing integrity in relationships through understanding that the same communal values—generosity and fairness, responsibility and freedom, forgiveness and atonement—must be maintained not just in personal relationships but in the workplace, social groups, and governing bodies;
- Treating everyone as a valued whole person, not as someone to be used or controlled;
- Maintaining civility in our relationships and being accountable for our behavior;
- Seeing cultural differences as life-enhancing, as expanding possibilities;
- Placing a broad definition of human rights at the center of our values: ensuring that every person has food, shelter, clothing, safety, education, health care, and a livable income.

Pharr believes that this liberatory politics will come about as a society: "When we grasp the value and interconnectedness of our liberation issues, then we will at last be able to make true coalition and begin building a common agenda that eliminates oppression and brings forth a vision of diversity that shares both power and resources" (pp. 600–601).

Pat Griffin and Bobbie Harro's "Action Continuum"

Now What: In our social justice work for liberation, we have a full spectrum of options for our consideration, from supporting oppression to changing systems of power and privilege. Griffin and Harro (2016) constructed a convenient graphic organizer representing this spectrum. I include it here as they fashioned it.

Actively Participating	Denying, Ignoring	Recognizing, No Action	Recognizing, Action	Educating Self	Educating Others	Supporting, Encouraging	Initiating, Preventing

Supporting Oppression >>>>>>>>>>>>>>>>>>>>>>>>>>>>>>>>>>>Confronting Oppression

Actively Participating: Telling oppressive jokes, putting down people from target groups, intentionally avoiding target group members, discriminating against target group members, verbally or physically harassing target group members.

Denying: Enabling oppression by denying target group members are oppressed. Does not actively oppress, but by denying that oppression exists, colludes with oppression.

Recognizing, No Action: Is aware of oppressive actions by self or others and their harmful effects but takes no action to stop this behavior. This inaction is the result of fear, lack of information, confusion about what to do. Experiences discomfort at the contradiction between awareness and action.

Recognizing, Action: Is aware of oppression, recognizes oppressive actions of self and others and takes action to stop it.

Educating Self: Taking actions to learn more about oppression and the experiences and heritage of target group members by reading, attending workshops, seminars, cultural events, participating in discussions, joining organizations or groups that oppose oppression, attending social action and change events.

Educating Others: Moving beyond only educating self to questions and dialogue with others too. Rather than only stopping oppressive comments or behaviors, also engaging people in discussion to share why you object to a comment or action.

Supporting, Encouraging: Supporting others who speak out against oppression or who are working to be more inclusive of target group members by backing up others who speak out, forming an allies group, joining a coalition group.

Initiating, Preventing: Working to change individual and institutional actions and policies that discriminate against target group members, planning educational programs or other events, working for passage of legislation that protects target group members from discrimination, being explicit about making sure target group members are full participants in organizations or groups.

Some Additional Social Justice Action Strategies

Now What: I am often asked to suggest social justice action strategies. While I always open with the caveat that it is impossible and certainly not my intention to give a comprehensive narrative how to bring about social justice in any given situation because what might work effectively in one school or workplace or region of a country may not function in another, I do, nonetheless, offer some foundational guidelines for consideration.

Even in effective coalitions, it may be rough in the work people perform because this work often goes against a tide of obstruction and resistance. For this and many other reasons, we must understand that our work needs to be long-term by taking on a small amount at any given time. We cannot reverse the pendulum of oppression and privilege overnight. I have learned from experience that "burnout" can often be caused by having unrealistic expectations. Thousands of years of bias and discrimination will not end in one day, one week, one year, one decade, or one lifetime.

It is better not to work alone for social change. Work first with others who may be potential allies. Talk with them about their beliefs, stereotypes, and impressions. Talk with them without blame, shame, or guilt. Allow people to speak about their concerns, issues, and impressions. It is not about trying to avoid making mistakes. It is about learning from mistakes and about being honest, truthful, and able to build a movement for progressive social change.

If you are working to promote social justice within a community, in your workplace, a school, or in another organization or institution, you might want to begin by assessing the "institutional climate" (the "inner workings," social relations, belief systems, norms, values) of that institution or community. You can manage this informally, or hold public hearings, conduct interviews, or distribute research surveys. Also, investigate the official and unofficial policies that either inhibit or promote social understanding and dominant group privilege: that restrict and advance social inclusion and equity. Find out what if any workplace and community training sessions are conducted in your location focusing on social inclusion and dominant group privilege. Bring in professional trainers and investigate resources that you can use to initiate these training sessions.

Institutions and communities are encouraged to develop support groups for social justice advocates to form networks and learning experiences, and to learn successful strategies from one another.

School and community libraries are encouraged to develop and maintain up-to-date and age-appropriate collections of books, videos, CDs, DVDs, journals, magazines, posters, internet websites, and other information on the experiences and histories of diverse people and communities.

Organizations within your community are encouraged to establish and sponsor community-wide forums to discuss issues related to social justice and inclusion.

Schools are encouraged to include accurate, honest, up-to-date, and age-appropriate information on topics of diversity and social justice at *every* grade level, across the curriculum, and in other school programs and assemblies. Also, announce issues and events related to social justice in your school, workplace, and in local community newspapers and other forms of media.

Schools and other community institutions are encouraged to select and hire people who advocate for issues of social justice, inclusion, and diversity to serve as supportive role models for all people.

For minoritized people to join existing groups and institution, be certain that policies and major decision-making procedures are inclusive and democratic. Do not expect minoritized people to automatically join existing groups and organizations.

On the personal level, continue to educate yourself about the histories, needs, and experiences of diverse peoples and systems of oppression. When in the company of someone different from yourself, stop talking for a few minutes and listen, truly listen to them without having the expectation that it is their responsibility to teach you. Listen to, and truly hear their voices when they do relate their experiences to you.

Attempt not to become defensive, argumentative, and do not downplay or minimize their stories. These are their experiences, their perceptions, and the meanings they make, and, therefore, it is not open for debate. Do not argue or attempt to change their positions about their experiences. Also, do not minimize their experience, their feelings, their beliefs, and their stories of bias and oppression. And do not talk *for* other people: "But my Latina friend said. ..." Rather, speak only for yourself and your experiences. Never ask people about their hair, their skin color, their noses, their style of clothing unless and until they open the discussion in these areas of discussion.

Attend cultural and community events focusing on diverse experiences. Interrupt and stop oppressive "jokes" and bigoted speech when you hear them. To sensitize yourself to the concept of dominant group privileges in all forms, attempt to place yourself in the shoes of a member of a subordinated group as you travel through your day. What do you notice and often take for granted that might be interpreted differently by someone in that subordinated group?

Monitor politicians, the media, and organizations to ensure accurate coverage of issues of social power and privilege. Call or write the media complimenting them when they have presented accurate and informative coverage and notify them of your concerns when you perceive inaccuracies or biased coverage. Also, write articles and letters to your local and national newspapers and websites for publication on issues and events related to social justice and inclusion. Work and vote for candidates (including school board members) taking social justice positions. Talk with young people age-appropriately about social justice topics.

Working for social justice offers innumerable rewards for all who engage in the process for the right reasons. It increases our pride of self and an increased sense of personal integrity that comes when we know we are making the world a better place.

Rheua Stakely's "Action Strategy Planning Sheet"

Now What: I structure the courses I teach and workshops I facilitate on the "The What?, The So What?, and The Now What?" model. During the "Now What?" phase, as we discuss strategies for liberatory social justice change, I offer each student or participant my friend Rheua Stakely's "Action Strategy Planning Sheet" (unpublished) to mindfully consider the range of actions they can take after the course or workshop terminates to effect change in their lives. I allow students and workshop participants time alone to fill in as many of the boxes they wish to within a given amount of time. Then, people join in small groups to share their strategies. Finally, we reform as a large group, and some individuals can choose to share one or a few of their strategies.

I include the sheet here for consideration. The labels on the top and left side can be changed to meet individual needs.

Table 16.1. Action Strategy Planning Sheet.
By Rheua Stakely

	I as an INDIVIDUAL	MY GROUP or DEPARTMENT	MY INSTITUTION
WITHIN ONE MONTH			
WITHIN SIX MONTHS			
WITHIN TWO YEARS			

"Dialogues on Diversity" and a Conceptual Model

> Intergroup dialogue is a face-to-face facilitated conversation between members of two or more social identity groups that strives to create new levels of understanding, relating, and action. ... Intergroup dialogues encourage direct encounter and exchange about contentious issues, especially those associated with issues of social identity and social stratification.
> —Zúñiga (2013, p. 635)

Now What: While engaging in my doctoral studies at the University of Massachusetts-Amherst in the Social Justice Education Program, I and Lisa D. Robinson, another student in the program, interviewed several undergraduate students of African heritage and Jewish European heritage at the university to accumulate information focusing on the question, "What is the relationship on campus between African American heritage and Jewish European heritage students?"

The results from this sample showed that there was tension, conflict, and misunderstanding on campus between the two groups, which were particularly heightened when outside speakers are brought to campus, and a number of African American speakers whose talks focused on their interpretations that Jews were largely responsible for the slave trade during previous centuries. Another main theme was that many of the students did not know much about the others' culture and history, and they expressed a desire to learn more.

Stemming from our initial research, Lisa and I designed and facilitated a general education, two-credit, full-weekend course at an off-campus conference site, bringing together undergraduate students of African and Jewish European heritage. We based the course on an intergroup dialogic model, including several exercises, and formalized and informal discussions, recreational activities, intergroup sleeping arrangements, and, of course, great food. In addition to the full weekend, we required students to attend a "debriefing session" at the university one month later.

The participants suggested a variety of strategies to improve intergroup relations and reduce conflict between African American and Jewish American students of European descent. These included inviting progressive African American and Jewish American speakers to campus; instituting an African American and Jewish American relations course taught by African Americans and Jewish Americans; developing more opportunities for dialogue and interaction, including more formalized dialogue courses; continuing the Black/Jewish/Other Student Video Project then underway on campus; developing workshops emphasizing African American and Jewish history and culture; and generally offering opportunities for discussions highlighting similarities between the groups while acknowledging their differing cultural and historical perspectives.

From Lisa and my observations, in addition to students' confidential written and verbal assessments to us, the course fulfilled our goal of reducing some of the misunderstanding and tensions between these groups. The ripple effect (spheres of influence) developed as student participants talked with and educated their peers.

Before and since Lisa and I initiated our "Intergroup Dialogues Weekend," on our campus and throughout the nation, workshops and full courses focus on bringing together identity group that may have a history of misunderstanding and conflict for participants to get to know one another more intimately and reducing some stereotyping between groups. For example, I brought the dialogic model with me when I served as an associate professor in the School of Education at Iowa State University in Ames, Iowa, where evident heightened and continuing tensions that existed between LGBTQ students and conservative Christian Evangelical students sometimes erupted.

The model functions best when an equal number of students from the specific groups come into the space as equals, and when the co-facilitators include the social identities represented in the groups: for example, in our dialogue group, one identified as lesbian, gay, bisexual, transgender, or queer, and the other facilitator as Christian Evangelical.

Zúñiga, Naagda, and Sevig (2010) formulated an intergroup dialogue model to encourage members of groups with a history of misunderstanding and conflict to engage in an educational process that promotes conversation, inquiry, critical thinking, active listening, conflict exploration and an exploration of common ground, alliance and coalition building, and action strategies that contribute to socially just communities.

The intergroup dialogue model includes a four-stage design that integrates personal experiences with human relations and antioppression education content, and an experiential and sequential approach to group work, which attends to communication, consciousness-raising, and bridging of differences.

Stage I: Group Beginnings

- Getting acquainted,
- Forming and building relationships,
- Developing norms/guidelines,
- Distinguishing between dialogue, discussion, and debate

Stage II: Differences and Commonalities

- Exploring differences and commonalities of experience in terms of social identities.
- Exploring the advantages/disadvantages that people in social groups face in society.
- Investigating the role people play in systems of power and privilege.
- Looking at how these impact the relationship between the groups.

Stage III: Exploring and Dialoguing about Hot Topics

- Talking about difficult issues.
- Examining personal, interpersonal, sociocultural, and institutional factors shaping participants' experiences and perspectives.
- Practicing active listening, asking questions, perspective taking, and critical reflection.

Stage IV: Alliance Building and Social Action

- Visioning and ally development
- Action planning and skill building
- Affirmation and closure
- Evaluation

Bullying, Cyberbullying, and Social Norms Theory

Now What: Several strategies have been suggested to reduce instances of bullying and harassment within institutions, though it must be pointed out that what might be successful in one location might not be efficacious in another. No simple one-size-fits-all methods exist, specifically when we look at bullying prevention strategies. Numerous factors must be considered in developing a program of action: factors such as the environmental "climate" of the educational institution, workplace, community, or country, plus demographic variable in terms of age, gender, culture, and others. For example, what might work effectively in one school might fall far short within another educational setting.

The theoretical foundation known as "Social Norms (or Norming) Theory" has proven success in some environments. First suggested by Perkins and Berkowitz (1986), they base their work on the premise that behavior is often influenced by *erroneous* perceptions of how other members of a social group think and act. What an individual believes, others think and do (in social norms theory called a "perceived norm") and what in fact are others' real attitudes and actions (an "actual norm") are often at odds. The distance between a perceived and an actual norm is referred to as "misperception."

Social norms theory involves interventions intended to correct misperceived social norms. A critical element in this approach is to correct misperceptions of norms by focusing on the positive and healthy attitudes and behaviors of the majority to increase these behaviors. This element should be developed in consort with the use of information regarding these positive norms, to direct interventions with abusers. Fabiano (1999) enumerates six stages in the social norms intervention process: (1) assessment to collect data; (2) selection of the normative message; (3) testing the message with the target group; (4) selecting the normative delivery strategy; (5) determining the "dosage" (amount, form) of the message; and (6) evaluation of the effectiveness of the message.

Focusing on peer influences, social norms interventions have shown promise, especially when combined with other strategies—for example, with detailed policy changes—in addressing issues related to changing unhealthy behavioral patterns, such as the frequency of alcohol consumption and the use of tobacco, prevention of sexual assault, improvement of overall academic climate in an educational institution, and reducing discriminatory behaviors.

From this perspective, social norms theory can be an effective strategy in the reduction of bullying behaviors in general, and specifically, cyberbullying, cyberharassment, and cyberstalking. In one study (Salmivalli, Lagerspetz, Björkqvist, Österman, & Kaukiainen, 1996), researchers found that between 80% and 90% of young people expressed aversion to bullying behavior and disapproved of people who bully others, though this proportion decreased somewhat during adolescence. The same study showed, however, that merely 10% to 20% of those surveyed actively intervened on behalf of those who were victimized by the bullying behaviors of a peer or peers. In addition, Bigsby (2002) examined perceptions of bullying behaviors in an elementary school and found that students and their parents *over*estimated (misperceived) the degree and amount of bullying behaviors that occurred. This indicates that while bullying behaviors—and aggression in general—may be (mis)perceived as being an accepted norm by a considerable number of people in a given environment, in reality, the vast majority find these behaviors distasteful at best. Social norms theory in many contexts has proven effective in empowering those who oppose an unhealthy or abusive behavior, as well as empowering "by-standers" who are aware of negative behaviors, but who feel powerless to intervene.

Whichever strategy one employs needs to take into consideration the unique characteristics and traits found within each specific environment. What has become consistently clear, however, is that bullying is a persistent and pervasive problem, and that policies and educational efforts need to be implemented for the benefit of all.

Along with strategies addressing ways to reduce or eliminate aggressive behaviors between individuals on campus, one needs to investigate the ways in which bullying prevention efforts identify and address the cultural systems. The identification of the cultural systems is critical since they can be reproduced on a campus from the larger society, which authorize or endorse these aggressive actions.

Empowering the Bystander to Act as an Upstander

Now What: There are some recommendations for schools to apply the social norms theory into practice. Administrators and practitioners can:

- Develop peer mediation and employee leadership training that empowers and assists faculty and staff in developing ways to successfully reduce bullying incidents;
- Include in anti-bullying policies the language that protects upstanders from retaliation for taking action;
- Include ongoing support from family members, other faculty and staff, and community members;
- Look into developing an ongoing social justice type study or discussion group; and include faculty and staff in campus climate policy decisions.

Furthermore, in addition to learning the 3 Rs (reading, writing, and arithmetic), faculty, staff, and administrators need to "read" the self, in other words, to develop self-awareness, which helps people "solve" social, emotional, and ethical problems that arise in their lives, what Cohen (2006) refers to as undergoing social, emotional, ethical, and academic education (SEEAE) to develop social, emotional, and ethical competencies. In a school context, we can learn from Townsend (2009) to advance preventive policy regarding workplace bullying:

> My overall point is that the organizational climate for women and minorities will not improve until we embody in our own discourse, including its tacit assumptions, the perspective that women and minorities are not deficit because they do not fit the norms of White middle- and upper-class males. When we overtly move to discourse that claims minorities and women are different than White males, we must be careful that these differences are still not viewed as deficiencies. (p. 742)

Townsend (2009) recommends that to improve the institutional climate for all, the organization must ensure: (1) parity in terms of salary, whereby women and men earn equal pay for equal work and position; (2) equal and equitable access to higher-level positions; (3) support for affirmative action in hiring, establishment, maintenance, and enforcement of sexual harassment procedures; (4) access to child care services, paid maternity, paternity, and other family leave policies; and (5) the development and use of a gender-inclusive or gender-neutral language policies (Townsend, 2009, pp. 737–738).

* * *

> Liberation is the *belief that we can succeed*, a sense of confidence in ourselves and in our collective efforts. Liberation is *joy* at our collective efficacy and at surviving in a world that sometimes tries to kill us. Liberation is the knowledge that *we are not alone ... commitment* to the effort of critical transformation ... [and] *passion and compassion*, those strong and motivating feelings that we must live by our hearts as well as our minds. Liberation is based in something far bigger than me ... or us as a coalition. ... It's about that force that connects us all to one another as living beings ..., the vision that there can be a better world and we can help to create it.
>
> —Harro (2013b, pp. 624–625)

Not on Our Campus! "Principles of Community"

Now What: Over the July 4th weekend 2006, an individual or group scribbled hate-filled graffiti throughout the campus and the surroundings of Iowa State University in Ames, Iowa. The perpetrator or perpetrators of these criminal acts, in their own distorted way, linked the various forms of oppression by expressing misogynist, racist, heterosexist, cissexist, Islamophobic, and anti-Jewish epithets and symbols. The timing of these actions around the 4th of July, Independence Day, highlighted the continuing attempt by some to exclude groups of people from participating in the freedom and justice promised in our founding documents but still not yet attained.

A committed and concerned group of student leaders organized a committee to confront the hate. They gave me the honor or serving as a faculty advisor. At one of the initial meetings, they agreed by consensus to create a group statement, which they ultimately titled their "Principles of Community," listing their vision for a safe and inclusive campus community. They arrived at these principles by engaging in a sizable number of one-on-one interviews with their student peers throughout the campus. This is what they developed.

Principles of Community

Diversity is a journey that is continually evolving where different challenges are faced and solutions are sought. At Iowa State University, our journey is mapped by six Principles of Community. By using the *Principles of Community* as the compass, we show how we have begun our journey.

Respect

We seek to foster an open-minded understanding among individuals, organizations, and groups. We support this understanding through outreach, increasing opportunities for collaboration, formal education programs, and strategies for resolving disagreement.

Purpose

We are encouraged to be engaged in the university community. Thus, we strive to build a genuine community that promotes the advancement of knowledge, cooperation, and leadership.

Cooperation

We recognize that the mission of the university is enhanced when we work together to achieve the goals of the university. Therefore, we value each member of the Iowa State University community for his or her insights and efforts, collective and individual, to enhance the quality of campus life.

Richness of Diversity

We recognize and cherish the richness of diversity in our university experience. Furthermore, we strive to increase the diversity of ideas, cultures, and experiences throughout the university community.

> *Freedom from Discrimination*
>
> We acknowledge that we must strive to overcome historical and divisive biases in our society. Therefore, we must commit ourselves to create and maintain a community in which all students, staff, faculty, and administrators can work together in an atmosphere free from discrimination, and to respond appropriately to all acts of discrimination.
>
> *Honest and Respectful Expression of Ideas*
>
> We affirm the right to and the importance of a free exchange of ideas at Iowa State University within the bounds of courtesy, sensitivity, and respect. We work together to promote awareness of various ideas through education and constructive strategies to consider and engage in honest disagreements.

* * *

It is my hope that we can all join as allies to defeat all the many forms of oppression and make the world a more nurturing, perfect, welcoming, and socially just place for people of all social identities and backgrounds. Let us transform the world!

LIBERATORY PRAXIS APPENDICES

APPENDIX A

MULTIPLE IDENTITIES ESSAY

Developed by Warren J. Blumenfeld, Ed.D.

Most of us hold concurrent "social identities" (consciously or unconsciously) based on "socially constructed" categories: for example, on our personal and physical characteristics, our moral beliefs and values, on our ages, abilities, socioeconomic class backgrounds, and on our cultural, racial, ethnic, national, linguistic, sex, gender, sexual and affectional, and religious identifications. Sometimes these identities are *ascribed* to us by others (sometimes at our birth), and/or sometimes we self-identify, or these identities are *achieved* (throughout our lives).

Description of the Assignment: This assignment requires you to use yourself as a "text" to describe and analyze yourself from at least *four* specific vantage points. (NOTE: please include those layers of yourself that you feel comfortable sharing. *Also, somewhere in your paper, include your Myers-Briggs Personality types and analyze whether you feel this personality inventory represents who you believe you are.*)

Myers-Briggs website: http://www.humanmetrics.com/cgi-win/jtypes2.asp

1. *Body Identity*: identify your physical description. How do you see YOURSELF physically?
2. *Social Identities*: identify the external cultural norms/social meanings associated with yourself in terms of physical description, skin color,

"race," ethnicity, nationality, religion, linguistic background, sex assigned at birth, gender identity and expression, sexual identity/orientation, ability/disability, socioeconomic class background, age, and any other aspect of your identity for which you identify and would like to share. Include here your Myers-Briggs Personality Profile. *Chart the trajectory of your coming to consciousness* of your and other's "race," and other social identities like sex assigned at birth and gender, ethnicity, religion, sexual identity, socioeconomic class, linguistic background, nationality, ability/disability, religion, and other identities. Myers-Briggs website for Multiple Identity Analysis Project: http://www.humanmetrics.com/cgi-win/jtypes2.asp.
3. *Moral/Attitudinal/Affective Identity*: identify your internal personal values and beliefs, the elements that comprise your personality and your character, and articulate how they do or do not align with your social identities. (Do others truly see YOU when they see you, or do they see something/someone else?)
4. Incorporate a description of your experiences as a student in P–12 schools (discuss what school was like for you generally). Then suggest how your *social identities* may have affected *your* understanding of cultural and individual diversity in schools.

Objective: Students will develop insight about the relationship between their collective (group memberships/identities) and individual identities. It will assist students in addressing Dr. Stephen Brookfield's first phase of critical thinking, specifically to discover the assumptions that guide their decisions, actions, choices. (See "Appendix B: Critical Consciousness").

Methods: To complete this assignment, you will need to step away from yourself and think about *how others see you, how you see yourself,* and *critically evaluate the dis/connection(s) between the two.* You will convert the information learned into an effective paper. How you present your "reading" of yourself is up to you. You must, however, project a clear message regarding *each of the four vantage points* described above, and you must demonstrate evidence of genuine thoughtfulness and *critical analysis.* Make the project your own and be creative and playful. (NOTE: You may wish to talk with/interview family members to enrich your understanding of your family history, which may have a significant influence on your identity and your understanding of your schooling experiences.) References in APA format. The Multiple Identities Assignment is due by ... and is worth a possible 30 points. This assignment will be evaluated according to the following criteria:

POINTS	CRITERIA
27–30	Outstanding degree of clarity, thoughtfulness, critical analysis, and writing style put into assignment.
24–26	The assignment shows above-average clarity, thoughtfulness, critical analysis, and writing style.
21–23	The assignment shows some weakness in the area of clarity, thoughtfulness, critical analysis, or writing style.
18–20	Below-average effort was put into the assignment. It lacks clarity and does not illustrate much thoughtfulness, low critical analysis, or writing style.
0–17	Minimal effort given, not completed, or completed too late.

Multicultural Teaching Applications: This assignment is intended to emphasize the distinction between *collective* and *individual* identities, and it highlights how misperceptions could get in the way of seeing the full person. Gaining an understanding of the lenses through which we are seen (though not *fully* seen) helps us to understand our relationships with others, particularly our students in terms of their cultural, ethnic, national, religious, racial, gender, sexual identity, socioeconomic class, linguistic, religious, age, and ability or disability diversity/backgrounds.

APPENDIX B

CRITICAL CONSCIOUSNESS

Reflecting, Thinking, Observing, Reading, Researching, and Writing Through a Critical Lens

by Warren J. Blumenfeld, Ed.D.

In this class, you are expected to think critically/reflectively/creatively to the concepts, topics, issues presented, and to class discussions, readings, videos, and written assignments. This class, therefore, may be calling on you to think or respond somewhat differently than in some of your other courses. I will, therefore, require that you *justify* and *backup* your thoughts and "opinions." Opinions without justification are just that—opinions—and you can expect to have points deducted without providing critical thinking (which includes rationale/justification). In this course, you will be expected to think "outside of the box."

According to Dr. Stephen Brookfield,[1] critical thinking involves *four interrelated phases*:

1. Discover the assumptions that guide your decisions, actions, and choices. (What do I think and why do I think of it the way I do?).
2. Check the accuracy of these assumptions by exploring as many different perspectives, viewpoints, and sources as possible (pose questions, talk with others, take courses, read, research, etc.).
3. Use abstract ideas to interpret the information effectively.
4. Take informed decisions that are based on these researched assumptions. (Informed decisions are based on evidence we can trust, can be

explained to others, and have a good chance of achieving the effects we want.)

Some questions you may want to ask yourself during course discussions, when reading course assignments, when watching course videos, and when researching and writing your papers:

- You might want to first consider the "larger picture" by extracting the overarching theme(s) and subtheme(s) of the materials *as a group* (the macro level) and of each *individual* piece of the materials (the micro level). This will place the materials into a fuller context with one another.
- Consider the person(s) choice of words.
- What are the points being made, and what is the overall message?
- What are behind the points and behind the message?
- What is in the mind of the writer of the piece or the character(s) in the video? To know this, you must *suspend, for a time, your reactions to the person(s)*. You must attempt to walk in *their* shoes, to perceive the world and the people around them as they would perceive—in other words, you must be able to develop *empathy*. From where comes *their* motivations, *their* behaviors, *their* actions?
- What underlying assumptions are made by the person(s) delivering the message?
- What is the person(s) underlying philosophical/political/behavioral perspective?
- What are the person(s) social identities, and do these impact their perspective(s)?
- Pull out each point, analyze it from various perspectives, determine how each point fits with other points being presented, put the individual points back together into the whole, determine whether the points are consistent or contradictory, unified or disjointed, etc.
- What are the words the person(s) set off in quotations/underlining/bolding? What is the overall effect?
- What is the impact of the message on the receiver? What impression does the message have on you? Again, justify your answer.
- What are the possible repercussions of this message?
- What was one or more points that either you did not know previously or that particularly surprised you?

- Give your commentary on the author(s) ideas, assumptions, conclusions. Do not simply summarize the author(s) article(s).
- Have you read or heard something like this elsewhere? Connect it to previous readings, author(s), video(s), or theory(ies). *Compare* and *contrast* this reading with readings of similar themes (from the same week's materials, from previous week's materials, or with outside-of-course readings), or with readings that may appear on the surface different but connect in some way.
- Virtually ask the author(s) questions for clarification, critical questions, questions that may challenge some of their assumptions or conclusions.
- Construct a virtual discussion between and among authors of different articles, where they seem to agree and to disagree.
- What was left out or questions you have that were not answered? Ask "critical questions!"
- Are there any points with which you take issue or with which you disagree? Why? Fully justify your critique! Are there any outside sources you can reference to back you up? If so, refer to them.
- What ideas, concepts, issues, and/or theories that were covered connected in some way(s) to your personal experiences? How? In what way(s)? Explain and fully analyze.

Note

1. Distinguished professor, University of St. Thomas, Minneapolis, MN.

APPENDIX C

MERITOCRACY ACTIVITIES

Developed by Warren J. Blumenfeld, Ed.D.[1]

In-Class Meritocracy Debate[2]

Within the educational system and the larger U.S. society, there is a debate over whether this country is a Meritocracy.

The class will randomly divide into two teams. Each side will argue either yes or no on the following question:

"Is the United States a Meritocracy?"[3]

Definition

According to *The Oxford Dictionary*, a Meritocracy is: "1. Government by persons selected competitively according to merit, 2. A group of persons selected in this way, 3. A society governed by meritocracy." Basically, it is advancement based on individual ability, motivation, and achievement.

Debate Format and Roles[4]

Debate Facilitator (1), Jury (3)

Two Teams (approximately ½ of class on each team)

1. Each team will have up to 6 minutes to make an *opening statement*.
2. Each team will then have up to 4 minutes to provide a *rebuttal* to the other teams' opening statement.
3. Teams will alternate posing *questions* to the other side. Each team should prepare at least four questions. The responding team will have up to 2 minutes to deliver a *response* to the question.
4. Each team will have up to 3 minutes to make a *closing statement*.
5. Members of the jury will then prepare a written summary that identifies their vote on the debate as well as the points made during the debate that convinced them to take that stance.
6. *Each team member must make at least one point or answer a question.*

Meritocracy Essay

Developed by Warren J. Blumenfeld, Ed.D.
Each student will write a paper, minimum 5 pages: The paper will include:

1. A written discussion of the points you have researched for the class debate, and the points you would like to make during the debate. This could include, if this is your role in the debate, your side's opening statement, rebuttal of the other side's opening statement, your side's closing statement, how you would address the questions the other side may pose to your side, any additional information you find relevant to advance your side's argument.
2. A critical analysis of how you *actually* stand on the issue. Please see next few pages for Critical Analysis guidelines. Reference your points. Do not give only your opinion! *This is a RESEARCH assignment, and not an opinion piece!*

The Meritocracy Debate will be conducted in class on (date) and the essays are due on (date) and are worth a possible total of 25 points.

POINTS	CRITERIA
23–25	Made outstanding points. Was clear and thoughtful. Obvious high degree of effort was given in the research preparation. Outstanding critical analysis.
20–22	Made above-average points in terms of clarity and thoughtfulness. Good effort was given in the research and execution in their debate preparation. Above-average critical analysis.

POINTS	CRITERIA
18–19	Made a few points. Showed average clarity and thoughtful. Not obvious high degree of effort given in the research preparation. Average critical analysis.
15–17	Made some points but lacked clarity or thoughtfulness. Did not convey that much effort was given to the research participation. Low critical analysis.
0–14	Made few if any points and lacked clarity or thoughtfulness. Little or no perceivable effort given in the research preparation. Lacked critical analysis.

Meritocracy Essay (for online courses or in-class without the debate)
Developed by Warren J. Blumenfeld, Ed.D.

Within the educational system and the larger U.S. society, there is a debate over whether this country is a Meritocracy.

You will write a paper on where you stand and why on the following question:

"Is the United States a Meritocracy?"

Definition

According to *The Oxford Dictionary*, a Meritocracy is: "1. Government by persons selected competitively according to merit, 2. A group of persons selected in this way, 3. A society governed by meritocracy." Basically, it is advancement based on individual ability, motivation, or achievement.

Also, what relevance does this topic have for this course and education in general in the United States?

Consider this as a *research paper* in the largest sense of the word. You are not simply to present your opinions or personal experiences, but rather, you *must* back up your points of view using reputable references.

Each student will write a paper, minimum 5 pages.

The Meritocracy Paper is due by (date) and is worth a possible 30 points.

POINTS	CRITERIA
27–30	Made outstanding points. Was clear and thoughtful. Obvious high degree of effort was given in the research preparation. Outstanding critical analysis and writing style.
24–26	Made above-average points in terms of clarity and thoughtfulness. Good effort was given in the research and execution in their debate preparation. Above-average critical analysis and writing style.

(Continued)

(Continued)

POINTS	CRITERIA
21–23	Made a few points. Showed average clarity and thoughtful. Not obvious high degree of effort given in the research preparation. Average critical analysis and writing style.
18–20	Made some points but lacked clarity or thoughtfulness. Did not convey that much effort was given to the research participation. Low critical analysis and writing style.
0–17	Made few if any points and lacked clarity or thoughtfulness. Little or no perceivable effort given in the research preparation. Lacked critical analysis or poor writing style evident.

Notes

1. warrenblumenfeld@gmail.com
2. This activity can be changed to raise other issues, for example, reproductive issues, marriage for same-sex couples, firearms regulations, immigration policy, equal pay for equal work, and many more.
3. Please use references from our course readings *and* from outside readings when appropriate. *This is a RESEARCH assignment, not a debate based only on opinion and beliefs!* See "Critical Consciousness" sheet at end of this assignment.
4. You will have time at the end of a class period to arrange who will be taking which parts. You will have one week to do your research for the debate.

APPENDIX D

RAISING ISSUES OF RELIGIOUS PLURALISM IN SCHOOLS

By Warren J. Blumenfeld, Ed.D.

Over the years, the Supreme Court has clarified the ways in which the First Amendment relates to public schools in the cases of *Engel v. Vitale*, 1962 and *Abington v. Schempp*, 1963. The court ruled that schools may not *sponsor* religious practices, though they may *teach* about religion as an academic topic. In addition, while not ruling directly on the matter of religious holidays in the school, the Supreme Court let stand a lower federal court decision (*Florey v. Sioux Falls School District*, 8th Circuit, 1980) declaring that recognition of religious holidays may be constitutional when the purpose is to give secular *instruction* about religion or religious traditions rather than to *promote* any specific religious doctrine or practice.

While it is not the intention here to give a comprehensive narrative on how to bring religious equity in the public schools—for what might work effectively in one school might not function in another—some foundational guidelines can be considered:

- Assessment: Hold public hearing, and/or conduct interviews, or distribute research surveys in your school, community, and/or your state to access the needs, concerns, and life experiences of members of different faith communities and of nonbelievers.

- Policies: Schools are encouraged to develop policies protecting students, faculty, staff, and administrators of every faith and nonbelievers from harassment, violence, and discrimination, and to provide equality of treatment.
- Personnel Trainings: Schools are encouraged to offer training to *all* school personnel, including guidance counselors and social workers, in religious diversity and bullying prevention, and specifically to address the religious accommodation needs of students and school personnel.
- Library Collections: School and community libraries are encouraged to develop and maintain an up-to-date and age-appropriate collection of books, videos/DVDs, and other academic materials pertaining to world religions and nonbelievers.
- Educational Forums: Schools can organize and sponsor community-wide forums to discuss issues related to religious diversity and religious pluralism.
- Curriculum and School Programs:[1] Schools are encouraged to include accurate, honest, up-to-date, and age-appropriate information regarding religious issues presented uniformly and without bias or judgment. In this regard, when introducing a controversial topic, such as Christian privilege and religious oppression, it is often effective to bring to the classroom a panel of outside speakers, composed of, for example, individuals who identify as Christian who have come far on their journey in understanding the benefits they are accorded simply based on their religious identity. Often students, particularly those who follow primarily Christian faiths, will be more inclined to "hear" those who are most like themselves. Also on the panel could be members of other faith communities as well as nonbelievers.
- Adult Role Models: Schools are encouraged to recruit faculty and staff from disparate religious and spiritual background, as well as nonbelievers, to serve as supportive role models for all youth.
- Teacher Certification: Include information and training on issues pertaining to religious diversity, religious oppression, and Christian privilege in college and university teacher education programs.
- Continuing Education:
  - Educate yourself about world religions and the history of religion and religious oppression in the United States and other countries throughout the world.

- Educate yourself on the needs and experiences of people from many religious and spiritual backgrounds. Without having the expectation that it is their responsibility to teach you, listen to and truly hear the voices of religious minorities and nonbelievers when they do relate their experiences to you. Attempt not to become defensive, argumentative, and do not try to change their minds. These are their experiences, their perceptions, and the meanings they make, and, therefore, not up for debate.
- Put yourself in the shoes of religious minorities and nonbelievers, especially during major Christian holiday seasons. Attempt to experience those seasons from their perspectives. What do you perceive? Ask yourself next time you automatically wish someone a Merry Christmas or Happy Easter, or when you are about to send someone a Christmas or even a Season's Greeting card, whether the person on the other end would truly welcome the gesture, or whether you might be imposing your traditions and values on that person.
- Attend cultural events of religions other than your own.
- Be aware of the generalizations you make. If you are Christian, do not assume that all people you meet are Christian as well. Assume there of people of other faiths and nonbelievers in your school, workplace, and community.
- To sensitize yourself on the topic of Christian privilege, if you are Christian, notice the times you explicitly or implicitly disclose this during the course of your day.
- Monitor politicians, the media, and organizations to assess their level of sensitivity to issues around religious pluralism.
- Work and vote for candidates (including school board members) taking positions in support of religious pluralism.

Note

1. While the First Amendment of the U.S. Constitution and a number of subsequent court decisions have make it clear that the *promotion* or *celebration* of religion is not appropriate in public schools, they have likewise asserted that the teaching of religions as an academic topic is within legal guidelines.

APPENDIX E

MAKING UNIVERSITIES WELCOMING FOR STUDENTS, STAFF, FACULTY, AND ADMINISTRATORS OF ALL SEXUAL IDENTITIES AND GENDER IDENTITIES AND EXPRESSIONS

By Warren J. Blumenfeld, Ed.D.

I. Assessment

Hold public hearings, and/or conduct interviews, and/or distribute research surveys in your school, community, and/or your state to access the needs, concerns, and life experiences of people of all sexual identities and gender identities and expressions on your campus.

II. Policies[1]

Enact nondiscrimination policies based on sexual and gender identity and gender expression in matters of hiring, tenure, promotion, admissions, financial aid, housing, physical and mental health and counseling, and public accommodations and facilities. Make reporting procedures of incidents of discrimination clear.

Have policies and procedures for dealing with homophobic/heterosexist, biphobic, and cisgender violence and harassment. Procedures for reporting incidents need to be clear and visible.

Have a written, inclusive, and affirming definition of "couples" that is nondiscriminatory toward same-sex and trans couples in a way that is appropriate for each institution.

Ensure equal access and equality of all benefits and privileges granted to all employees and students.

Have policies of active outreach in hiring openly lesbian, gay, bisexual, pansexual, asexual, trans, agender, intersex, questioning, queer, and/or LGBPATAIQQ-sensitive faculty, staff, and administrators in all segments of the campus community. Also, partners of potential hires should be assisted in acquiring campus job positions.

Actively recruit openly LGBPATAIQQ prospective students.

Develop and publicize an inclusive sorority and fraternity policy related to identity intersectionalities, including sexual identities and gender identities and expressions.

On your school's website, explain policies for changing names, gender markers, and for housing policies related to sexual identity and gender identity.

Develop a policy for trans students to compete in sports activities and on sports teams. According to the University of Massachusetts at Amherst policy, for example, "When an activity makes a gender designation, an individual who has transitioned to a different gender can participate in the division of the individual's current gender. If an individual is in the process of transitioning to a different gender, participation in a particular gender designated activity will be handled on a case by case basis."

National Collegiate Athletic Association (NCAA) Inclusion of Transgender Athletes Policies, September 13, 2011:

The following policies clarify participation of transgender student-athletes undergoing hormonal treatment for gender transition:
1. A trans male (FTM) student-athlete who has received a medical exception for treatment with testosterone for diagnosed Gender Identity Disorder or gender dysphoria and/or Transsexualism, for purposes of NCAA competition may compete on a men's team but is no longer eligible to compete on a women's team without changing that team status to a mixed team.
2. A trans female (MTF) student-athlete being treated with testosterone suppression medication for Gender Identity Disorder or gender dysphoria and/or Transsexualism, for the purposes of NCAA

competition may continue to compete on a men's team but may not compete on a women's team without changing it to a mixed team status until completing one calendar year of testosterone suppression treatment.

Any transgender student-athlete who is not taking hormone treatment related to gender transition may participate in sex-separated sports activities in accordance with his or her assigned birth gender.

- A trans male (FTM) student-athlete who is not taking testosterone related to gender transition may participate on a men's or women's team.
- A trans female (MTF) transgender student-athlete who is not taking hormone treatments related to gender transition may not compete on a women's team. (https://www.ncaa.org/sites/default/files/Transgender_Handbook_2011_Final.pdf)

III. Training and Development

Implement workshops for the entire campus community to sensitize and educate staff, faculty, and administrators on violence prevention, suicide prevention, and specifically to the social and academic needs and experiences of people based on sexuality identity and gender identity and expression.

IV. Services

Colleges and universities provide official recognition, support, use of campus facilities, and funding of campus student organizations founded on topics of sexual identity and gender identity and expression.

Physically safe, secure, and appropriate space with a welcoming, emotionally safe atmosphere should be available to organizations for meetings, social events, coffee houses, lectures, fora, workshops, and other events founded on topics of sexual identity and gender identity and expression.

Legal and fund-raising support services should be available to students on topics concerning sexual identity and gender identity and expression.

Campus housing should include living options for LGBPATAIQQ students, including all-gender and single-occupancy living options, and all-gender and single-occupancy restroom facilities throughout the campus.

Include a gender-inclusive housing option, including gender-inclusive bathroom and shower options, that is separate from sexual identity housing options.

University leadership should make strong, clear, and public statements on a regular basis that state the college's commitment to ending discrimination, conviction that violence and harassment are entirely unacceptable, and appreciation of the value of diversity on campus, including diversity of sexual and gender identity and expression.

Colleges and universities hire "out" LGBPATAIQQ and LGBPATAIQQ-sensitive therapists, counselors, faculty, staff, and administrators.

Peer counselors and/or campus crisis hotline volunteers should be adequately trained in sensitivity to topics of sexuality, sexual and gender identity and expression, and identity development.

Effective safer sex, birth control, and family planning education, imperative for all people of all sexual and gender identities, must be available and widespread on the campus and within the local campus community.

Social activities through residence halls, Offices of Student Activities, and other organizations must be not only inclusive of all sexual and gender identities, without pressures toward heterosexuality, but actively welcoming of LGBPATAIQQ people as well as same-sex and trans couples and individuals.

College and university presidents have a standing advisory committee, panel, or board, appointed or elected in consultation with LGBPATAIQQ students, staff, and faculty members.

Topics of campus climate should be assessed regularly, by the above-mentioned panel or in some other manner, to gauge the current status and the effectiveness of implemented changes in order to improve campus climate for all members of the campus community, including LGBPATAIQQ people.

Campus publications should strive to provide adequate and fair coverage of LGBPATAIQQ events and topics, both on- and off-campus.

Colleges and universities should aid students in alumni outreach, including LGBPATAIQQ outreach.

Student internship and mentorship opportunities may also be cultivated among local LGBPATAIQQ-owned businesses and LGBPTAIAQQ activist and community service organizations.

The diversity/intersectionality—in terms of race, ethnicity, religious background, nationality, ability, socioeconomic class, gender identity, sexual identity, linguistic background, age, physical appearance—within LGBPATAIQQ communities should be recognized and affirmed.

The location and availability of resources of value to LGBPATAIQQ people should be published in materials distributed to all students, faculty, staff, and alumni, and in student recruitment materials.

Personnel at the Career Planning/Placement Center, like personnel in every college area, should be knowledgeable of LGBPATAIQQ topics and be aware of employment opportunities in LGBPATAIQQ-owned or LGBPATAIQQ-friendly businesses and community service organizations. Furthermore, they should be knowledgeable about the laws in every state that pertain to legal discrimination based on sexual identity and gender identity and expression, and which states protect various identity groups and which do not.

While needs differ greatly at each of the thousands of institutions of higher education, it seems clear that for many, if not most, the most critically important and invaluable resource is an LGBPATAIQQ campus resource center with paid full-time administrators, staff, student interns, and a full array of resources, including a library, study spaces with current technology, speakers bureaus, funding for programming and resources, student financial and institutional support to attend conferences, and other vital services.

Hire and support Ombuds officers to negotiate and protect students when conflicts on campus arise.

Purchase and maintain computer software that allows students to use a name other than the name and gender designation on their school records: course and grade rosters, listings in school directories, and other documents, campus ID cards, e-mail, diplomas.

Allow students, staff, faculty, administrators to indicate the pronouns they use that will appear on all and any campus documents and lists. Options include: she, he, ze, and they.

Allow all members of the campus community to self-identify their gender on all forms and for housing options, including fraternity and sorority applications:

Examples:

Open ended: Gender Identity _____

or: Gender Identity (choose all that apply)

__ woman

__ man

__ trans or transgender (please specify): _____

__ another identity (please specify): _____

All schools are encouraged to mandate lockable and single-user changing and shower room facilities that are easily accessible to trans and intersex members of the campus community in recreational and athletic facilities.

Also, overall, schools are encouraged to create more privacy options in women's and in men's locker rooms: install private showers and changing-room cubicles.

Hire staff and physicians at the campus health center AND the campus counseling center who have extensive backgrounds in the needs and concerns of students in terms of their sexuality, sexual identities, and gender identities and expressions.

Develop lists that identify physicians and counselors who specialize in trans health and counseling for members of the campus community to choose if they desire.

Campus health centers need to cover in their insurance policies hormones and gender-affirming surgeries for transitioning students.

Designate patient advocates for LGBPATAIQQ students to report any concerns they may have regarding the quality of care they are receiving in the campus health center and the campus counseling center.

V. Curriculum/Educational Materials/ Programs/Academic Affairs

Topics relating to people of all sexual identities and gender identities and expressions should be formally and permanently integrated into existing courses across the curricular disciplines.

Speakers on LGBPATAIQQ topics, and particularly those who present scholarly research on LGBPATAIQQ topics, should be invited regularly to campus.

Courses dealing specifically with topics of sexual identity and gender identity and expression in the humanities, natural sciences, education, social sciences, and other disciplines should be established.

A visiting scholar position in Queer or Sexuality & Gender Studies should be created and supported on a continuing basis.

College and university libraries should increase their holdings of books, periodicals, and computer networking systems related to sexual identity and gender identity and expression.

Campus facilities should be available for regional Queer or Sexuality & Gender Studies conferences, with administrative support provided.

Fellowship opportunities should be created and funded for teaching and research on LGBPATAIQQ topics.

Scholarship and research into LGBPATAIQQ history, culture, and theory should be encouraged and supported in faculty and students.

All multicultural education should be inclusive of the topics, history, culture, and experiences of LGBPATAIQQ people in the United States and worldwide. Multicultural awareness (social diversity) courses should be mandatory for all students at some point during the undergraduate years.

An archive and history of LGBPATAIQQ organizations on campus should be created.

Develop, support, and sustain LGBPATAIQQ Studies, Queer Studies, or Sexuality & Gender Studies programs (preferably departments) with degree-granting (Certification, AA, BA, Masters, Doctorate, Post-Doctorate) capabilities.

VI. Employee Concerns

Policies regarding equal benefits and nondiscrimination should be made clear in recruiting brochures, informational materials, campus publications, and orientation sessions.

The university should aid, support, and fund the creation of LGBPTAIAQQ faculty and staff discussion, support, and networking groups.

Trade unions and professional organizations should have inclusive policies and supportive services available to their members.

There should be equality in all benefits, including, for example, child care, bereavement leave, insurance coverage, library privileges, access to gym and other recreational facilities, listings in directories if spouses are customarily listed, housing for LGBPTAIAQQ couples where the qualifications are analogous to the qualifying basis for heterosexuals, "couple" rates must be made available to LGBPTAIAQQ couples, access to any and all other privileges and benefits by LGBPTAIAQQ partners if access is available to different-sex and cisgender spouses.

There should be ongoing staff development trainings on LGBPTAIAQQ topics for all employees.

Colleges and universities should cover the expenses of employees attending conferences on LGBPTAIAQQ topics.

VII. Community/Off-Campus Concerns

Community LGBPTAIAQQ groups should be invited to attend campus events as participants, guests, and event leaders and facilitators.

Information regarding affirming social, religious, and other community resources should be made easily accessible to all students, staff, faculty, and administrators.

Counselors, administrators, and faculty should be available to parents or other community members to alleviate any concern that may arise out of the implementation of any of the above recommendations, as well as any concerns arising during their students' coming out process, if that is the case.

Representatives of LGBPTAIAQQ student groups from other schools should meet regularly to keep each other appraised of upcoming events, plan events together, and strengthen networking and LGBPTAIAQQ communities.

Publications, fund-raising materials, and all other publications distributed to parents and alumni should include relevant and appropriate stories, essays, and news regarding LGBPTAIAQQ topics, organizations, and events.

Corporations, public agencies, and government, religious, and community agencies and institutions that do not have official written policies against discrimination based on sexual identity and gender identity and expression should be strongly discouraged or prohibited from on-campus employment or enlistment recruiting.

Note

1. These should be written, clear, and accessible.

APPENDIX F

IMMIGRATION AS OFFICIAL U.S. "RACIAL" POLICY

A Brief History

"Race" as Social Construction

Looking back to the historical emergence of the concept of "race," critical race theorists remind us that this *concept* arose concurrently with the advent of European exploration as a justification and rationale for conquest and domination of the globe beginning in the 15th century of the Common Era (CE) and reaching its apex in the early 20th century CE. (see, for example, Ladson-Billings, 1998).

Meanwhile, geneticists tell us there is often more variability *within* a given so-called "race" of humans than between human "races," and that there are no essential *genetic* markers linked specifically to "race." They assert, therefore, that "race" is socially constructed—a historical, "scientific," and biological myth. Thus, any of these socially-conceived physical "racial" markers are fictional and are not related with what is beyond or below the surface of the body (see, for example, Cameron & Wycoff, 1998).

Though biologists and social scientists have proven unequivocally that the *concept* of "race" is socially constructed, however, as Sefa Dei (2000) asserts, "the knowledge that race is an ideological, social/material construct does not take away the consequences when one is faced with actual racist incidents or practices."

Carl Linnaeus (1707–1778), born Carl Linné (also known as the "Father of Scientific Racism"), a Swedish botanist, physician, and zoologist, developed a system of scientific hierarchical classification (Linnaeus, 1735/1758). Within this taxonomy under the label *Homo sapiens*, ("Man"), he enumerated five categories based initially on place of origin and later on skin color: Europeanus, Asiaticus, Americanus, Monstrosus, and Africanus. Linnaeus asserted that each category was ruled by a different bodily fluid (Humors: "moistures"), represented by Blood (optimistic), Phlegm (sluggish), Cholor (yellow bile: prone to anger), Melancholy (black bile: prone to sadness).

Linnaeus connected each human category to a respective Humor, thereby constructing the Linnaeus Taxonomy in descending order: Europeanus: sanguine (blood), pale, muscular, swift, clever, inventive, governed by laws; Asiaticus: melancholic, yellow, inflexible, severe, avaricious, dark-eyed, governed by opinions; Americanus (indigenous peoples in the Americas): choleric, copper-colored, straightforward, eager, combative, governed by customs; Monstrosus (dwarfs of the Alps, the Patagonian giant, the monorchid Hottentot): agile, fainthearted; Africanus: phlegmatic, black, slow, relaxed, negligent, governed by impulse.

Immigration as Official U.S. "Racial" Policy

In many countries, their official immigration policies represent their understandings of "race." Take, for example, the policies of the United States, where the "American" colonies followed European perceptions of "race." A 1705 Virginia statute, the "Act Concerning Servants and Slaves," read: "[N]o negroes, mulattos or Indians, Jew, Moor, Mahometan [Muslims], or other infidel, or such as are declared slaves by this act, shall, notwithstanding, purchase any christian (*sic*) white servant. ..." We see here a clear indication which groups were not considered "white."

In 1790, the newly constituted U.S. Congress passed the Naturalization Act, which excluded all nonwhites from citizenship, including Asians, enslaved Africans, and Native Americans, the later whom they defined in oxymoronic terms as "domestic foreigners," even though they had inhabited this land for an estimated 12,000 years. The Congress did not grant Native Americans rights of citizenship until 1924 with the passage of the Indian Citizenship Act, though Asians continued to be denied naturalized citizenship status.

They employed scriptural justification to support the institution of slavery, for example:

> Ephesians 6:5–6: Slaves, obey your earthly masters with fear and trembling, in singleness of heart, as you obey Christ; not only while being watched, and in order to please them, but as slaves of Christ, doing the will of God from the heart.

And

> Luke 12:47: That servant who knows his master's will and does not get ready or does not do what his master wants will be beaten with many blows.

Later, Jefferson Davis, President of the Confederate states, asserted:

> [Slavery] was established by decree of Almighty God ... it is sanctioned in the Bible, in both Testaments, from Genesis to Revelation ... it has existed in all ages, has been found among the people of the highest civilization, and in nations of the highest proficiency in the arts. (Davis, in Clifton & Van De Mieroop, 2016, p. 16)

Many slaving ships had on board a Christian minister to oversee and bless the passage. Slaving ships included the names: "Jesus," "Grace of God," "Angel," "Liberty," and "Justice."

The U.S. Supreme Court, in *Dred Scott v. Sandford* (1857), decided a case on U.S. labor and constitutional law. It judged that "a negro, whose ancestors were imported into [the U.S.], and sold as slaves," whether enslaved or free, could not be an American citizen and therefore, could not sue in federal court; and the federal government had no power to regulate slavery in federal territories acquired after the creation of the United States.

Dred Scott, an enslaved man of "the negro African race" had been taken by his slave masters to free states and territories. He tried to sue for his freedom. In 7–2 decision written by Chief Justice Roger B. Taney, the Supreme Court denied Scott's request, and Scott remained enslaved.

Central to the European-American conquest of territory was the concept of "Manifest Destiny": Providence destined U.S. expansion from the Atlantic to the Pacific ("from sea to shining sea") by the so-called "Anglo-Saxon race." This justified in the mind of the European the theft of Indigenous people's territories and a war with Mexico.

In reaction to increasing numbers of European immigrants into the country in the 1850s, a movement calling itself "The American Party" (also known as "The Know-Nothings") formed to "purify" the country by limiting or ending Irish Catholic immigrants and others, and also ending the naturalization of those already here.

The American Party established itself as a "Nativist" anti-Irish Catholic movement by instigating fear among the larger population that the U.S. will soon be dominated by Irish and German Catholics unless their immigration were ended. The movement perpetuated the illusion that the Pope had been plotting to control and dominate the U.S. While a small movement in relative numbers, its primary supporters were European-heritage Protestant men.

To "civilize" Native peoples and make them "productive" members of European-American society, between 1879 and 1905, white Christian teachers operated 25 Indian boarding schools for the U.S. government throughout the U.S. This system was organized by Lieutenant Richard Henry Pratt, who founded and personally supervised the Carlisle Indian School in Pennsylvania.

As Pratt related to a Baptist audience regarding his theory of education:

> [We must immerse] Indians in our civilization, and when we get them under, [hold] them there until they are thoroughly soaked." And, "We must kill the Indian in him to save the man. (Pratt, in Bosworth, 2011)

Pratt and the white teachers stripped Indian children of their cultures: they cut short males' hair, they forced them to wear Western-style clothing to take a Western name, they prohibited students from conversing in their native languages and English was compulsory, they confiscated and destroyed all their cultural and spiritual symbols, and they imposed and mandated the learning and adoption of Christianity.

In 1883, Sir Francis Galton of England, a cousin of Charles Darwin, coined the term "eugenics," from Greek meaning "well born," "of good origins and breeding." He established a new branch of science to "improve" qualities of a "race" by controlling human breeding.

Harry Hamilton Laughlin (1880–1943), U.S. Eugenicist, became superintendent of the Eugenics Record Office from 1910 until 1939. He advocated for mandatory sterilization of "the unfit," and he crafted his "model sterilization law" for the "uprooting of inborn defectiveness" (Laughlin, 1914, p. 13). His law included involuntary sterilization for "the feeble minded, the insane, criminals, epileptics, alcoholics, blind persons, deaf persons, deformed persons, and indigent persons." Most U.S. states passed sterilization laws, and as late as 1992, 22 states still had these on their books.

Germany passed its sterilization law in 1927, and in 1933, Adolph Hitler made it compulsory by passing the *Law for the Prevention of Hereditarily Diseased Offspring*. Hitler loosely based the German law on Laughlin's model. Nazi Germany involuntarily sterilized approximately 350,000 of its citizens. Laughlin was awarded an honorary degree by the University of Heidelberg in 1936 for his work on behalf of the "science of racial cleansing."

Congress passed the first law specifically restricting or excluding immigrants based on "race" and nationality in 1882. In their attempts to eliminate entry of Chinese (and other Asian) workers who often competed for jobs with U.S. citizens, especially in the western United States, Congress passed the Chinese Exclusion Act to restrict their entry into the United States for a 10-year period, while denying citizenship to Chinese people already on these shores. The Act also made it illegal for Chinese people to marry white or black U.S.-Americans. The Immigration Act of 1917 further prohibited immigration from Asian countries, in the terms of the law, the "barred zone," including parts of China, India, Siam, Burma, Asiatic Russia, the Polynesian Islands, and parts of Afghanistan. The so-called "Gentlemen's Agreement" between the United States and the Emperor of Japan of 1907, to reduce tensions between the two countries, passed expressly to decrease immigration of Japanese workers into the United States.

The U.S. Supreme Court decided the 1896 case of *Plessy v. Ferguson*, against the plaintiff, Homer Plessy, who on June 7, 1892 was forced off a "Whites Only" car of the East Louisiana Railroad and onto a "Colored" car because he was 1/8 black and 7/8 white, according to Jim Crow laws following the "one drop" rule in which "one drop" of "black blood," makes one black. This case set the precedent of "Separate but Equal" until the Supreme Court overturned it in its 1954 *Brown v. Board of Education* decision that "separate is inherently unequal.

Between 1880 and 1920, in the range of 30–40 million immigrants from Eastern and Southern Europe migrated to the United States, more than doubling the population.

Madison Grant, a U.S. lawyer and Eugenicist who lived between 1865 and 1937, co-founded the Galton Society for the Study of the Origin and Evolution of Man in 1918, and wrote his book, *The Passing of the Great Race* (Grant, 1916), detailing the so-called "racial" history of Europe (a work that has come to be considered as a treatise of scientific racism, but one that had great influence on restrictions in U.S. immigration and anti-miscegenation policies and laws.) Grant divided European "races" into four distinct and separate categories in his racial hierarchy.

On top as the superior of all the races, he placed the "Nordics" of Northwestern Europe: the natural rulers and administrators, which accounted for England's "extraordinary ability to govern justly and firmly the lower races."

Next down the hierarchy he placed the "Alpines" of Central Europe who were somewhat inferior: "… always and everywhere a race of peasants" with a tendency toward "democracy" although submissive to authority.

Then came the "Mediterraneans" of Southern and Eastern Europe who Grant claimed were inferior to both the Nordics and the Alpines in "bodily stamina," but superior in "the field of art." They were also superior to the Alpines in "intellectual attainments," but far behind the Nordics "in literature and in scientific research and discovery."

On the very bottom as the most inferior of all were "the Jews" from anywhere. According to Grant: "… the Polish Jew, whose dwarf stature, peculiar mentality and ruthless concentration on self-interest" (p. 16), present themselves in "swarms" (p. 63).

> The result of the mixture of two races, in the long run, gives us a race reverting to the more ancient generalization and lower type. The cross between a white man and an Indian is an Indian, the cross between a white man and a Negro is a Negro, the cross between a white man and a Hindu is a Hindu, and the cross between any of the three European races and a Jew is a Jew. (Grant, 1916, p. 18)

Former President Theodore Roosevelt said of Grant's book:

> The book is a capital book; in purpose, in vision, in the grasp of the facts our people need to know. It shows an extradentary wide range of reading and a wide scholarship … It is the work of an American scholar and gentleman; and all Americans should be sincerely grateful to you for writing it. (Roosevelt in *Schribner's Magazine* to promote Grant's book)

The book was translated into German and provided added justification to Adolph Hitler in writing *Mein Kampf*. Hitler wrote to Grant and referred to Grant's book as his "Bible." The book not only influenced Adolph Hitler, but impacted U.S. immigration legislation of 1924.

Fearing a continued influx of immigrants, legislators in the U.S. Congress in 1924 enacted the Johnson-Reed [anti-] Immigration Act ("Origins Quota Act," or "National Origins Act"), setting restrictive quotas of immigrants from Asia and Eastern Europe, including those of the so-called "Hebrew race."

(the law placed restrictive quotes on Jews, Poles, Italians, Greeks, and Slaves (the acronym (J-PIGS). The law, however, increased immigration from Great Britain and Germany.

Jews continued to be, even in the United States during the 1920s, constructed as nonwhite. It is interesting to note that during this time, Jewish ethno-racial assignment was constructed as "Asian." According to Gilman (1991) "Jews were called Asiatic and Mongoloid, as well as primitive, tribal, Oriental." Immigration laws were changed in 1924 in response to the influx of these undesirable "Asiatic elements." The law, on the other hand, permitted large allotments of immigrants from Great Britain, Ireland, and Germany. This law, in addition to previous statutes (1882 against the Chinese, 1907 against the Japanese) halted further immigration from Asia and excluded blacks of African descent from entering the United States.

In the Supreme Court case, *Takao Ozawa v. United States*, a Japanese man, Takao Ozawa filed for citizenship under the Naturalization Act of 1906, which allowed white persons and persons of African descent or African nativity to achieve naturalization status. Asians, however, were classified as an "unassimilateable race" and, therefore, not entitled to U.S. citizenship. Ozawa attempted to have Japanese people classified as "white" since he claimed he had the requisite white skin. The Supreme Court, in 1922, however, denied his claim and, therefore, his U.S. citizenship.

President Herbert Hoover at the end of the 1920s promised to cut immigration from Mexico by 90%, what became known as the "Mexican Repatriation" efforts of the late 1920s and early 1930s. He authorized a wave of illegal and unconstitutional raids and deportation of as many as 1.8 million Mexicans.

With the imminent outbreak of war on the European continent, by 1939 two legislators in the U.S. Congress, Senator Robert F. Wagner (D-NY) and Representative Edith Rogers (R-MA) proposed an emergency bill, which, if passed, would have increased the immigration quoted by allowing an additional 20,000 Jewish children under the age of 14 (10,000 in 1939, and another 10,000 in 1940) from Nazi Germany to come to the United States. Though the bill was roundly supported by religious and labor organizations, conservative and nativist isolationist groups mounted wide-scale campaigns to prevent its passage.

Public opinion polls (Wagner-Rogers Act) at the time showed that 83% of U.S. residents opposed any increases in immigration. Though First Lady Eleanor Roosevelt implored her husband to advance the bill, President Franklin

Delano Roosevelt failed to publicly support it. In fact, Laura Delano Houghteling, the president's cousin and wife of the U.S. Commissioner of Immigration, James L. Houghteling, sternly warned: "20,000 charming children would all too soon, grow into 20,000 ugly adults" (Houghteling, in Medoff, 2003). The bill never came up for a full vote in the Congress, and it died, like the children it could have saved.

Also, in 1939, on May 13, 1937 Germans and other citizens from Eastern European nations, mostly all Jews fleeing Nazis brutality, booked passage on the German transatlantic ocean liner *St. Louis* from the port of Hamburg bound for Havana, Cuba. Most passengers had applied for U.S. visas, and they planned to wait in Cuba on their previously-approved landing permits and temporary transit visas until U.S. officials accepted them into the U.S.

Even before embarking from Germany, the passengers became the source of bitter political cross-partisan rivalries in Cuba as several conservative politicians and newspapers demanded the immediate cessation of its policy of admitting Jewish refugees on its land. The Cuban government, therefore, reneged on its offer to honor the passengers' landing permits when the *St. Louis* entered Cuban waters.

Faced with this unforeseen development, the ship's captain, Gustav Schroeder, turned the *St. Louis* toward the Florida coast of the United States in hopes that U.S. government officials would allow passengers entry on refugee status by processing their visa applications. Unfortunately, though, the political wars transpiring in Cuba on the plight of Jewish refugees were even more intense in the United States. Within the United States, President Roosevelt succumbed to conservative political pressure by following his immigration officials' decision to deny safe-haven to the ship's passengers.

The captain had no other choice than to turn his ship around back toward Europe. On route, knowing that returning to Germany meant certain death for his passengers, he negotiated with several governments, whereby Great Britain allowed entry of 288, the Netherlands admitted 181, Belgium took 214, and France took 224. The U.S. Holocaust Memorial Museum estimates that by the end of the war, all but one in Great Britain survived, approximately half of the remainder on the continent, 278, survived the Holocaust, and 254 died: 84 who had been in Belgium; 84 in Holland, and 86 who had been admitted to France.

Following U.S. entry into World War II at the end of 1942, reflecting the tenuous status of Japanese Americans, some born in the United States, military officials uprooted and transported approximately 110,000 Japanese

Americans to Internment (Concentration) Camps within several interior states far from the shores.

In *Korematsu v. United States*, 323 U.S. 214 (1944), the landmark United States Supreme Court decision ruled 6–3 that Executive Order 9066 was constitutional "as a matter of military urgency," ordering Japanese Americans into internment camps during World War II *regardless* of citizenship. Not until Ronald Reagan's administration did the U.S. officially apologize to Japanese Americans and paid reparations amounting to $20,000 to each survivor as part of the 1988 Civil Liberties Act.

Finally, in 1952, the McCarran-Walters Act overturned the "racially" discriminatory quotas of the 1924 Johnson-Reed Act. Framed as an amendment to the McCarran-Walters Act, the Immigration and Nationalization Act of 1965 removed "natural origins" as the basis of U.S. immigration legislation.

In the summer of 1954, though, President Dwight Eisenhower approved a policy drafted by U.S. Attorney General Herbert Brownell Jr. for the immigration service to enforce a campaign of mass deportation of approximately 1.1 million Mexican nationals.

The 1965 law increased immigration from Asian and Latin American countries and religious backgrounds, permitted 170,000 immigrants from the Eastern Hemisphere (20,000 per each country), 120,000 from the Western Hemisphere, and accepted a total of 300,000 visas for entry into the country. The 1965 Immigration Law, however, was certainly not the last we saw "race" used as a qualifying factor. The Arizona legislature passed, and Governor Jan Brewer signed, SB 1070, which mandated that police officers stop and question people about their immigration status if police even suspect that they may be in this country illegally, and the law criminalized undocumented workers who do not possess an "alien registration document." Other provisions allowed citizens to file suits against government agencies that do not enforce the law, and it criminalizes employers who knowingly transport or hire undocumented workers. The court placed the law on hold as it traveled through the judicial process challenging its constitutionality.

Prior to 1967, several states within the United States prevented consenting adults from engaging in sexual activities, let along marriage, with anyone from another so-called race. White adults could have consensual sex with and marry other white people, but they could not have sex with or marry people of any other so-called race. Black adults could have consensual sex with and marry other black people, but they could not have sex with or marry people of any other race, and so on.

In the case of *Loving v. Virginia*, 388 U.S. 1 (1967), the Supreme Court of the United States, however, disagreed with the above scenarios codified in law, ruling against equality and in favor of equity. They declared the state of Virginia's anti-miscengenation statute, the Racial Integrity Act of 1924, unconstitutional, thereby overturning *Pace v. Alabama* (1883) and ending all race-based legal restrictions on adult consensual sexual activity and marriage throughout the United States.

The plaintiffs in the case were Mildred Loving (born Mildred Deloris Jetter, a woman of African descent) and Richard Perry Loving (a man of white European descent), both residents of Virginia who married in June 1958 in the District of Columbia to evade Virginia's Racial Integrity Act. Upon returning to Virginia, they were arrested and charged with violating the act. Police entered their home and arrested them while they slept in their bed. At their trial, they were convicted and sentenced to one-year imprisonment with a suspended sentence on the condition that the couple leave the state of Virginia for a period of 25 years.

At the trial, the judge, Leon Bazile, used Biblical justifications to convict the couple:

> Almighty God created the races white, black, yellow, Malay and red, and He placed them on separate continents. And but for the interference with His arrangement there would be no cause for such marriages. The fact that He separated the races shows that He did not intend for the races to mix (Legal Information Institute, n.d.)

More recently, the day Donald Trump descended the escalator in his tower of gold, with head raised forward as he held court at his press conference announcing his run for the presidency on June 16, 2015, he tossed down the bodies of Mexican people as if they were red Trump steaks as his initial stepping stones on his march to the White House.

> [Mexico is] sending people that have lots of problems, and they are bringing those problems to us. They are bringing drugs, and bringing crime, and they're rapists.

Then Donald Trump declared war on Islam at a campaign stop on December 7, 2015:

> Donald J. Trump is calling for a total and complete shutdown of Muslims entering the United States until our country's representatives can figure out what the hell is going on.

Trump attempted to appease his base of supporters, especially conservative Christian Evangelicals, with his continuing attacks on Muslims in its various incarnations of executive orders. After two of President Trump's travel bans from majority Muslim countries were struck down in the courts, on June 26, 2018, the Supreme Court approved Trump's September 2017 travel ban into the U.S. from 5 majority Muslim countries: Somalia, Iran, Libya, Yemen, & Syria, plus North Korea and senior government officials from Venezuela.

In *Trump, President of the United States, et al. v. Hawaii, et al.*, by a narrow 5–4 decision, the Supreme Court ruled that "The [Trump] Proclamation is squarely within the scope of Presidential authority," on national security grounds.

In a blistering dissent by Justice Sonia Sotomayor,

> The majority here completely sets aside the President's charged statements about Muslims as irrelevant. That holding erodes the foundational principles of religious tolerance that the court elsewhere has so emphatically protected, and it tells members of minority religions in our country "that they are outsiders, not full members of the political community." (Burke, 2018)

In an Oval Office meeting, Jan. 11, 2018, Trump became frustrated with legislators when they proposed restoring protections for immigrants from Haiti, El Salvador, and African countries as part of a bipartisan immigration plan. "Why are we having all these people from shithole countries come here?" Trump said, referring to African countries and Haiti. He then suggested that the United States should instead bring more people from countries like Norway.

Attorney General Jefferson Beauregard Sessions quoted scripture to justify the Trump administration's choice to follow a government policy (not law) – never-before enacted – to physically separate thousands of children of undocumented migrants seeking sanctuary as they flee oppression in their native countries into detention centers.

> Romans 13: Orderly and lawful processes are good in themselves. Consistent and fair application of the law is in itself a good and moral thing, and that protects the weak and protects the lawful.

Ruthless Americanization

Immigrants who enter the United States are pressured to assimilate into a monocultural Anglo-centric culture (thinly disguised as "the melting pot"), and to give up their native cultural identities. Referring to the newcomers at the beginning of the 20th century CE, one New York City teacher remarked:

> [They] must be made to realize that in forsaking the land of their birth, they were also forsaking the customs and traditions of that land. ... (Richman, in Tyack, 1974)

An "Americanist" (assimilationist) movement was in full force with the concept of the so-called "melting pot" in which everyone was expected to conform to an Anglo-centric cultural standard with an obliteration of other cultural identities. President Theodore Roosevelt (1907) was an outspoken proponent of this concept:

> If the immigrant who comes here in good faith becomes an American and assimilates himself (sic) to us he shall be treated on an exact equality with everyone else. ... But this [equality] is predicated on the man's (sic) becoming in very fact an American and nothing but an American. ... There can be no divided allegiance here. Any man who says he is an American but something else also, isn't an American at all. ... We have room for but one language here, and that is the English language, for we want to see that the crucible turns our people out as Americans, of American nationality, and not as dwellers in a polyglot boarding house. (Roosevelt, 1907)

Many members of immigrant groups oppose assimilation and embrace the concept of *pluralism*: the philosophy whereby one adheres to a prevailing monocultural norm in public while recognizing, retaining, and celebrating one's distinctive and unique cultural traditions and practices in the private realm.

The Jewish immigrant and sociologist of Polish and Latvian heritage, Horace Kallen in 1915 coined the term "cultural pluralism" to challenge the image of the so-called "melting pot," which he considered inherently undemocratic. Kallen envisioned a United States in the image of a great symphony orchestra, not sounding in unison (the "melting pot"), but rather, one in which all the disparate cultures play in harmony and retain their unique and distinctive tones and timbres.

Social theorist Gunnar Myrdal traveled throughout the United States during the late 1940s examining U.S. society following World War II, and he discovered a grave contradiction or inconsistency, which he termed "an American dilemma" (Myrdal, 1944). He found a country founded on an overriding commitment to democracy, liberty, freedom, human dignity, and egalitarian values, coexisting alongside deep-seated patterns of racial discrimination, privileging white people, while subordinating peoples of color.

The human rights organization, Amnesty International, states that

> Racial profiling occurs when race is used by law enforcement or private security officials, to any degree, as a basis for criminal suspicion in non-suspect specific investigations. Racial profiling constitutes a form of discrimination, based on race, ethnicity, religion, nationality, and other identities, which, Amnesty International declares "undermines the basic human rights and freedoms to which every person is entitled. (National Institute of Justice, 2013)

If we learn anything from our immigration legislative history, we can view the current debates as providing a great opportunity to pass comprehensive federal reform based not on "race," nationality, ethnicity, religion, or other social identity categories, but rather, on humane principles of fairness, compassion, and equity.

Today, the United States stands as the most culturally and religiously diverse country in the world. This diversity poses great challenges and great opportunities. The way we meet these challenges will determine whether we remain on the abyss of our history or whether we can truly achieve our promise of becoming a shining beacon to the world.

APPENDIX G

RELIGIOUS IMPERIALISM

A Case in Point

I gave a lecture on the topic of heterosexism at Pace University in New York City several years ago. I talked about my own experiences as the target of harassment and abuse growing up gay and gender diverse, and I addressed my book, *Homophobia: How We All Pay the Price* (1992). In the book I argue that everyone, regardless of their actual sexuality identity, is hurt by heterosexism and, therefore, it is in everyone's self-interest ("interest convergence") to work to reduce and ultimately eliminate this very real and insidious form of oppression.

Following my presentation, two students came up to me—one woman and one man—to continue the discussion. The young woman began by telling me: "I'm really sad to hear about the abuse that you and others have received because you are gay or lesbian. I am here to tell you that I have a way to prevent that from ever happening to you again. I believe that Jesus Christ can help you. If you ask Jesus and pray hard, Jesus will save you from your homosexual feelings and help you to achieve the life that is meant for you, in his service, as a happy and healthy heterosexual. This will save you from the abuse you have suffered, and eventually grant you entry in Heaven."

My response: "So, let me see if I understand you: If I accept Jesus in my life and ask him to help me become heterosexual, then I won't suffer from heterosexism any longer? So, to be supported in society, I must change who

I am and conform to the dominant standards of society? So, for people like yourself to truly support me, I must become *like* you? While I understand that you are offering me, in your mind, a gift, do you not see how this attitude is itself a form of heterosexism, a form of oppression? Do you not see how this perpetuates oppression?"

She responded with surprise and claimed that she knew the "truth," and that if I accepted her "truth," it would grant me salvation and happiness, but if I rejected this, it would result in continued earthly and eventual eternal torment.

We continued our dialogue for more than one hour, and we ended cordially, and then she walked away. All the while, the young man had been closely looking on and listening to the young woman's and my discussion. Then the young man spoke to me. He asked: "Professor Blumenfeld, you stated that you are a writer, and that you have published a number of articles and books. Is this correct?"

"Yes," I responded.

"Okay, then," he continued. "You know that in the writing process, the first draft is never really complete or isn't any good."

"Yes, that's often the case," I agreed.

"Okay, then after you have had some time for reflection and you write your second draft, this is an improvement over the first draft, but still, it can be further improved. So, after more reflection and writing, your third version is great. Now you can send it to your publisher."

I said to him, "Oh no, please don't tell me that this is a metaphor for religious texts."

"Yes, indeed," he uttered. "The first draft is the Hebrew Bible—not so good. The second draft is the Christian scriptures—somewhat better, but not much. But the best version, the third, is the Quran. The real truth. The ultimate truth. The only truth."

My response to this young man: "As we speak, we are standing literally a few short blocks from the former World Trade Center towers. Utterances and understandings like yours and like the young woman I just spoke with, and by people of any faith, that there is one and only one ultimate religious truth results in people taking it upon themselves, for example, to crash airplanes into buildings. It gives people justification to march into the Middle East under the auspices of 'The Crusades' and mindlessly murder and kill thousands of people. Utterances like yours of people of any faith give people justification to kill in the name of their interpretation of the Devine."

"Why," I argued, "can't the young woman I just spoke with realize that her understanding of God, while valid and reliable for her, may simply not be valid and reliable for me or for you, too? And why can't you realize that your understanding may be great for you, but not necessarily for me and for the Christian woman? How many deaths must occur before we realize that there are many ways toward the truth, not one way for everyone when it comes to religion and spirituality?"

That was then, and though it occurred several years ago, this discussion comes back to my memory giving me an insight: That "truth" is what the dominant group at any given location and timeframe declares to be "true." "Knowledge" is anything the dominant group defines as "knowledge," though "knowledge" itself is socially constructed and produced. How many wars are we going to justify in the name of "God," our "God" versus their so-called "false gods?" Someone said to me once that throughout the ages more people have been killed in the name of religion than all the people who have ever died of all diseases combined. I don't know whether this is actually the case, but I do think it highlights a vital point in that we continually kill others and are killed by others, that we hate and oppress others over concepts that *can never be empirically proven.*

Throughout history, Jews and Muslims have killed each other, Christians and Muslims have killed each other, Christians and Jews have killed each other, Hindus and Muslims have killed each other, Catholics and Protestants have killed each other, Sunni Muslims and Shiite Muslims have killed each other, many faith communities have killed Atheists and Agnostics, and on and on and on. Individuals, nations, and religious denominations continue to believe that their reality fits all, and that it is proper and right to force their beliefs onto others "with God on our side."

APPENDIX H

INVESTIGATING GENDER ROLES CLASSROOM EXERCISE

What is usually the first question people ask parents on the birth of a child? Probably not "How much does the baby weight?" No, that question usually comes further down the line. What about, "Is the baby healthy?" Sometimes, but typically not first. Usually, people ask, "Is it a boy or a girl?" On the surface, this may seem as an innocuous question. In reality, though, it is rife with underlying social and even ethical assumptions and consequences.

Even before the infant's assigned sex is inscribed on the birth certificate, individuals, institutions, and society at large have made assumptions regarding that person's life course, assumptions based on a highly sophisticated and complex network of gender-based role expectations in terms of behaviors and attitudes. To unearth those assumptions and make them visible, in my university courses, I facilitate an interactive class exercise I learned titled "What is a man? What is a lady?" (I state "Lady" rather than "Woman" because the Feminist Women's Movement has expanded options somewhat for females, and for this exercise, I hope to have students think back to earlier constructions of "femaleness.")

On the board, I draw a male symbol and a female symbol separated by a vertical line. I then ask students to call out characteristics attributed to men. When they have concluded, I ask students to call out characteristics attributed to ladies. For the "Men" side, some common responses include:

tough, independent, nonemotional, protective, strong, competitive, competent, goal oriented, makers and fixers of things, sexually active, and others.

On the "Lady" side, some common responses include: caring, nurturing, emotional, sensitive, expressive, caretakers of others while often disregarding their own needs, good cooks, concerned with physical appearance. I then ask students to engage in a "Nature/Nurture" discussion by first imagining the following scenario:

> Imagine what it would be like if after you were born, you were immediately placed in a starkly bare and silent room where you had no contact with any other human beings, though your basic bodily needs for food and elimination of waste were met.

What if this situation continued for years? What kind of a person do you think you might be? What would your personality, your values, your emotions, your attitudes in general be like? What can we learn about what it means to be "human" from these questions? What can we learn about what it means to be "men" and "women" from these questions?

Then, going back to the list of characteristics for "Man" and "Lady" we wrote earlier on the board, I ask students either to add or delete items we might see from people who had undergone this extreme isolation process. Invariably, students begin to see how our socialization (nurture) may impose the greatest variable in the ways we express, present, perform, and *define* the sex we were assigned at our birth.

APPENDIX I

A CIVICS COURSE ON THE SECOND AMENDMENT

> A well-regulated militia being necessary to the security of a free State, the right of the People to keep and bear arms shall not be infringed.
> —Second Amendment, U.S. Constitution

As we learned in junior high school civics class, laws undergo various processes to become enacted and enforced. Through our system of federalism, legislative bodies on the national, state, and local levels write and pass laws, which are then signed and enforced by the executive branches and judged as falling within constitutional guidelines by the justices in the judicial branches.

Throughout the process in the development of the Constitution and ever since, people have engaged in often heated debates over what even the smallest word and concept should and does mean. Though the framers of the Constitution imposed "the right of the People to keep and bear arms," as with all laws, our legislators and, more specifically, our judiciary defines its parameters.

To engage in a reasoned discussion from the same vantage point, we must study not only the precise or strict text of a law or regulation, but also investigate the supporting or modifying laws and rulings related to it.

For example, the U.S. Supreme Court has expanded (clarified) the definition of "A well-regulated militia." The Court, in its 2008 ruling in *District of Columbia v. Heller*, extended the right to individuals. From the ruling:

"The Second Amendment guarantees an individual right to possess a firearm unconnected with service in a militia, and to use that arm for traditionally lawful purposes, such as self-defense within the home." That right, however, "is not unlimited."

Though the types of firearms at the writing of the Constitution appear rather primitive compared with the technologically evolved weapons of today, in 2016, the Court ruled on this point in *Caetano v. Massachusetts*:

> The Court has held that the Second Amendment extends, *prima facie*, to all instruments that constitute bearable arms, even those that were not in existence at the time of the founding, and that this Second Amendment right is fully applicable to the States.

So, does this mean that all firearms, even the military-style semiautomatic or so-called "assault" weapons, must be available for sale to individuals under constitutional law?

In four separate cases in different federal Circuit Courts of Appeals, judges ruled that states placing bans on semiautomatic weapons are, in fact, constitutional, and that the *Heller* decision excluded these types of weapons. Therefore, individual state laws were upheld.

1. Washington, DC, Circuit, 2011: Assault weapons and large capacity magazines are "too dangerous for self-defense reasons."
2. 7th Circuit, Chicago, 2015: Upheld a ban on "any semiautomatic gun that can accept a large-capacity magazine." Also, the concept of Federalism allows local municipalities to enact gun safety restrictions.
3. 2nd Circuit, New York & Connecticut, 2015: Unanimous ban: "semiautomatic assault weapons have been understood to pose unusual risks," resulting in "more numerous wounds, more serious wounds, and more victims. These weapons are disproportionately used in crime, and particularly in criminal mass shootings like the attack in Newtown. They are also disproportionately used to kill law enforcement officers."
4. 4th Circuit, Richmond, 2017: Maryland's ban on 45 kinds of assault weapons and its 10-round limit on gun magazines were upheld as constitutional.

To date, the U.S. Supreme Court has decided not to review these lower court rulings.

In addition, the federal ban on assault weapons, The Public Safety and Recreational Firearms Use Protection Act, was enacted by Congress in

September 1994. The ban, which also included barring high-capacity magazines, expired in September 2004 as required in its 10-year sunset provision. The measure has not since been reauthorized by Congress.

As a provision inserted as a rider into the 1996 federal government omnibus spending bill, the Dickey Amendment, named after Arkansas Republican Representative Jay Dickey and lobbied heavily by the National Rifle Association, passed the Congress into law. It mandated that "none of the funds made available for injury prevention and control at the Centers for Disease Control and Prevention (CDC) may be used to advocate or promote gun control."

So, what other limits, on the national, state, and local levels, should we as a nation consider and enact on the sale and ownership of firearms? Many people within the larger Gun Safety Movement have proposed "common-sense" solutions. Unfortunately, what one person determines as "common sense," another personal considers as "freedom killing."

How free, though, are any of us as an estimated 11,000 people are murdered annually, and another 22,000 lose their lives by guns through accident or suicide? How free are we as the guns lobby purchases our politicians in the service of firearms manufacturers in their quest to acquire even more power and profits?

Short of repealing the Second Amendment in its entirety (which remains an option but has no chance of succeeding in the current political climate), I propose what I consider as common-sense firearms safety measures:

- We must ban and criminalize the possession of semiautomatic and so-called "assault" weapons!
- We must close loopholes such as buying a weapon at a gun show!
- We must ban the purchase of firearms from those on the federal "no-fly" list, anyone convicted of domestic violence, and anyone who has a restraining order against them!
- We must repeal the Dickey Amendment!
- We must continue and extend the ban on the purchase of firearms and ammunition on the internet!
- We must ban so-called "Bump Stocks" and other technologies that increase the speed or force of semiautomatic weapons!
- We must increase the waiting period and make background checks universal and more rigorous and effective in the purchasing of firearms!
- In addition, we must initiate background checks each time an individual purchases ammunition!
- We must limit the number of firearms any individual can own!

- We must limit the number of bullets any firearm magazine can hold!
- We must ban and criminalize the purchase and possession of "armor piercing" bullets and hollow-tip bullets!
- We must ban so-called "ghost guns," which are kits that include gun parts the owner assembles into a completed firearm!
- We must hold gun shop owners liable when selling firearms and ammunition to anyone who is not legally eligible to own, such as minors, felons, or people with a history of mental illness!
- We must initiate an anonymous reporting system for persons wanting to report suspicious behaviors of those who own firearms!
- We must limit the purchase of any firearm to those ages 21 and above!
- All firearms owners must take and pass a course in the proper use and safety of their weapons!
- All firearms must contain a safety device designed to prevent the discharge of the weapon by unauthorized users!
- We must rethink the "logic" of permitting concealed weapons, especially in places like houses of worship, colleges, bars, restaurants, and political rallies!
- The U.S. government must increase funding for research investigating the causes and solutions of gun violence!
- We must interface all databases monitoring firearm ownership to assess the firearm-owning population more accurately and effectively!

And we must stand with the courageous, intelligent, and articulate young people of the #NeverAgain movement for gun safety who are poised to save our country from itself!

BIBLIOGRAPHY

Adams, M. (2016). Pedagogical foundations for social justice education. In M. Adams & L. A. Bell (Eds.), *Teaching for diversity and social justice* (3rd ed., pp. 27–53). New York, NY: Routledge.
Adorno, T. W., Frenkel-Brunswik, E., Levinson, D. J., & Sanford, R. N. (1950). *The authoritarian personality*. New York, NY: Harper.
Allport, G. W. (1954). *The nature of prejudice*. Cambridge, MA: Addison-Wesley.
American Association of University Women Educational Foundation. (2001). *Hostile hallways: Bullying, teasing, and sexual harassment in school*. Washington, DC: Author.
American Civil Liberties Union. Retrieved from http://www.aclu.org/lgbt/youth/11947res20040106.html
American Psychological Association. (1975, January 24–26). Resolution: Discrimination against homosexuals. APA Council of Representatives.
American Psychological Association. (2004, July). APA resolution on bullying among children and youth.
Anderson, M., Kaufman, J., Simon, T., Barrios, L., Paulozzi, L., Ryan, G., … School-Associated Violent Deaths Study Group. (2001). School-associated violent deaths in the United States, 1994–1999. *JAMA: Journal of the American Medical Association, 286*(21), 2695–2702.
Anzaldúa, G. E. (1987). *Borderlands/La frontera: The new Mestiza*. San Francisco, CA: Aunt Lute Books.

Azar, E. E., & Burton, R. W. (Eds.). (1986). *International conflict resolution: Theory and practice*. Boulder, CO: Lynne Reiner Publishers.

Bandura, A. (1965). Influence of models' reinforcement contingencies on the acquisition of imitative responses. *Journal of Personality and Social Psychology, 1*, 589–595.

Bandura, A., Ross, D., & Ross, S. A. (1961). Transmission of aggressions through imitation of aggressive models. *Journal of Abnormal and Social Psychology, 63*, 575–582.

Banks, J. M. (2007). Levels of multicultural curricular inclusion. In J. M. Banks & C. A. M. Banks (Eds.), *Multicultural perspectives* (6th ed.). Hoboken, NJ: John Wiley & Sons. Inc.

Barry, H., Chold, I., & Bacon, M. K. (1959). Relation of child training to subsistence economy. *American Anthropologist, 61*, 51–63.

Batts, V. A. (1989). *Modern racism: New melody for the same old tunes*. Rocky Mount, NC: Visions Publication.

Becker, A. (2008). *The chosen: The history of an idea, the anatomy of an obsession*. New York, NY: Springer.

Bell, D. A. Jr. (1980). Brown v. Board of Education and the interest-convergence dilemma. *Harvard Law Review, 93*(3), 518–533.

Bell, J. (2003). *Understanding adultism: A key to developing positive youth-adult relationships*. Olympia, WA: The Freechild Project.

Bell, L. A. (2007). Theoretical foundations for social justice education. In M. Adams, L. A. Bell, & P. Griffin (Eds.), *Teaching for diversity and social justice* (2nd ed., pp. 1–14). New York, NY: Routledge.

Berkhofer, R. F. (1972). *Salvation and the savage: An analysis of Protestant mission and American Indian response, 1787–1862*. Lexington, KY: University of Kentucky Press.

Berkowitz, L. (1962). *Aggression: A social-psychological analysis*. New York: McGraw-Hill.

Berman, P. (1994). Introduction: The other and the almost the same. In P. Berman (Ed.), *Blacks and Jews: Alliances and arguments*. New York: Dell Publishers.

Bieber, I., Dain, H. J., Dince, P. R., Drellich, M. G., Grand, H. G., Gundlach, R. R., ... Bieber, T. B. (1962). *Homosexuality: A psychoanalytic study of male homosexuals*. New York, NY: Basic Books.

Bigsby, M. (2002). Seeing eye to eye? Comparing students' and parents' perceptions of bullying behavior. *School Social Work Journal, 27*(1), 37–57.

BloomBecker, B. (1990). *Spectacular computer crimes*. Homewood, IL: Dow Jones-Irwin.

Blumenfeld, W. J. (Ed.). (1992). *Homophobia: How we all pay the price*. Boston, MA: Beacon Press.

Blumenfeld, W. J. (2001). *Black and off-white: An investigation of African American and Jewish conflict from Ashkenazi Jewish American perspectives* (Doctoral dissertation). Social Justice Education Program, University of Massachusetts, Amherst, MA.

Blumenfeld, W. J. (2006). Making schools safe for lesbian, gay, bisexual, transgender, and questioning students and staff. An original resource handout for workshops on increasing LGBTQ visibility and reducing heterosexism in schools. Unpublished.

Blumenfeld, W. J. (2013). Heterosexism: Chapter introduction. In M. Adams, W. J. Blumenfeld, R. Castañeda, H. Hackman, M. Peters, & X. Zúñniga (Eds.), *Readings for diversity and social*

justice: An anthology on racism, antisemitism, sexism, heterosexism, ableism, and classism. New York, NY: Routledge.
Blumenfeld, W. J., & Cooper, R. M. (2010). LGBT and allied youth responses to cyberbullying: Policy implications. *International Journal of Critical Pedagogy*, 3(1), 114–133.
Blumenfeld, W. J., & Raymond, D. (1993). *Looking at gay and lesbian life*. Boston, MA: Beacon Press.
Bochner, S. (1982). The social psychology of cross-cultural relations. In S. Bochner (Ed.), *Cultures in contact* (pp. 5–44). New York, NY: Pergamon.
Bond, L., Carlin, J. B., Thomas, L., Rubin, K., & Patton, G. (2001). Does bullying cause emotional problems? A prospective study of young teenagers. *British Medical Journal*, 323, 480–484.
Bonvillain, N. (2003). *Language, culture, and communication: The meaning of messages* (4th ed.). Upper Saddle River, NJ: Pearson Education.
Borich, G. D. & Tombari, M. L. (1997). *Educational psychology: A contemporary approach*. New York: Pearson.
Borton, T. (1970), *Reach, touch, & teach*. New York: McGraw-Hill.
Boswell, J. (1980). *Christianity, social tolerance, and homosexuality: Gay people in western Europe from the beginning of the Christian era to the fourteenth century*. Chicago, IL: University of Chicago Press.
Bosworth, D. A. (2011). *American Indian boarding schools: An exploration of global ethnic & cultural cleansing*, Mount Pleasant MI: Ziibiwing Center of Anishinabe Culture & Lifeways.
Boulding, K. E. (1962). *Conflict and defense: A general theory*. New York, NY: Harper.
Bourdieu, P. (1986). The forms of capital. In J. Richardson (Ed.), *Handbook of theory and research for the sociology of education* (pp. 241–258). New York, NY: Greenwood.
Brain, M., & Fenlon, W. (n.d.). How computer viruses work. Howstuffworks. Retrieved June 6, 2018 from http://www.howstuffworks.com/virus.htm/printable.
Branco, K. J., & Williamson, J. B. (1982). Stereotyping and the life cycle: Views of aging and the aged. In A. G. Miller (Ed.), *In the eye of the beholder: Contemporary issues in stereotyping* (pp. 364–410). New York, NY: Praeger.
Breen, M. S., & Blumenfeld, W. J. (Eds.). (2005). *Butler matters: Judith Butler's impact on feminist and queer studies*. London: Ashgate.
Britt, L. (2003). 14 tenets of fascism. *Free Inquiry*, n.p.
Brodkin, K. (1998). *How Jews became white folks & what that says about race in America*. New Brunswick, NJ: Rutgers University Press.
Bronfenbrenner, U. (1981). *The ecology of human development: Experiments by nature and design*. Cambridge, MA: Harvard University Press.
Brookfield, S. (1995). *Becoming a critically reflective teacher*. San Francisco, CA: Jossey-Bass.
Brown, M. K., Carnoy, M., Currie, E., Duster, T., Oppenheimer, D. B., Schultz, M. M., & Wellman, D. (2003). *Whitewashing race: The myth of a color-blind society*. Berkeley, CA: University of California Press.
Bruner, E. M. (1956). Primary group experiences and the process of acculturation. *American Anthropologist*, 58, 605–623.

Burke, D. (2018, June 26). Does the Supreme Court have a double standard on religion. CNN Politics, Retrieved from https://www.cnn.com/2018/06/26/politics/does-the-supreme-court-have-a-double-standard-on-religion/index.html.

Burke, T. P. (2010). The origins of social justice. *Modern Age, 52*(2), 97–106.

Burley-Allen, M. (1995). *Listening: The forgotten skill*. Hoboken, NJ: John Wiley & Sons.

Butler, J. (1990). *Gender trouble: Feminist and the subversion of identity*. New York, NY: Routledge.

Butler, J. (1993). *Bodies that matter: On the discursive limits of "sex."* New York, NY: Routledge.

Butler, J. (1997). *Excitable speech: A politics of the performative*. New York, NY: Routledge.

Butler, J. (2000). Critically queer. In P. du Gay, J. Evans, & P. Redman (Eds.), *Identity: A reader* (pp. 108–118). London: Sage Publications.

Butler, J. (2010). Performative agency. *Journal of Cultural Economy, 3*(2), 147–161.

Butler, R. N. (1975). *Why survive? Being old in America*. New York, NY: Harper and Row.

Butte Bystander. (1873, February 11). n.p.

BuzzFeed News. (2018, February 20). Donald Trump Jr. liked tweets promoting a conspiracy theory about a Florida shooting survivor. Retrieved from https://www.buzzfeed.com/tasneemnashrulla/donald-trump-jr-conspiracy-theory-florida-shooting-survivor?utm_term=.rvGvZjd7J#.bp84ml1e9

Byrnes, D. A. (1995). *Teacher they called me a ____: Confronting prejudice and discrimination in the classroom*. New York, NY: Anti-Defamation League of B'nai Brith.

Cameron, S. C., & Wycoff, S. M. (1998). The destructive nature of the term race : Growing beyond a false paradigm. Journal of Counseling & Development, 76, 277–285.

Carr, P. R., Pluim, G., & Thésée, G. (2017). The dimensions of, and connections between, multicultural social justice education and education for democracy: What are the roles and perspectives of future educators? *Citizenship Education Research Journal, 6*(1).

Castañeda, C., Hopkins, L. E., & Peters, M. L. (2013). Introduction: Ableism. In M. Adams, W. J. Blumenfeld, R. Castañeda, H. Hackman, M. Peters, & X. Zúñiga (Eds.), *Readings for diversity and social justice* (3rd ed.). New York, NY: Routledge.

Castañeda, C., & Zúñiga, X. (2013). Introduction: Racism. In M. Adams, W. J. Blumenfeld, R. Castañeda, H. Hackman, M. Peters, & X. Zúñiga (Eds.), *Readings for diversity and social justice* (3rd ed.). New York, NY: Routledge.

Catalano, C. (2018). Introduction to sexism, heterosexism, and transgender oppression. In M. Adams, W. J. Blumenfeld, R. Castañeda, H. Hackman, M. Peters, & X. Zúñiga (Eds.), *Readings for diversity and social justice* (4th ed.). New York, NY: Routledge.

CBS News. (2014). Bergeron's restaurant: Home of God, guns, and gumbo. November 12. CBS Interactive Inc.

Chauncey, G. (1993). The postwar sex crime panic. In W. Graebner (Ed.), *True stories from the American past*. New York, NY: McGraw-Hill.

Chavez, N. (2018, February 21). School shooting survivor knocks down 'crisis actor' claim. Retrieved from https://www.cnn.com/2018/02/21/us/david-hogg-conspiracy-theories-response/index.html

Clifton, J. & Van De Mieroop, D. (2016). *Master narratives, identities, and the stories of former slaves*. Amsterdam: John Benjamins Publishing Company.

Cohen, J. (2006). Social, emotional, ethical, and academic education: Creating a climate for learning, participation in democracy, and well-being. *Harvard Educational Review*, 76(2), 201–237.

Collins, P. H. (1998). It's all in the family: Intersections of race, gender, and nation. *Hypatia*, 13(3), 62–82.

Collins, S. (2008–2010). *The hunger games* (Series). New York: Scholastic Inc.

Cook, J., Nuccitelli, D., Green, S. A., Richardson, M., Winkler, B., Painting, R., ... Skuce, A. (2013). Quantifying the consensus on anthropogenic global warming in the scientific literature. *Environmental Research Letters*, 8(2).

Cooley, C. H. (1918). *Social process*. New York, NY: Schribner's Sons.

Cordileone, S. (2015). Statement to the *Sacra Liturgia* conference, New York City, June 3.

Corrigall-Brown, C. (2005, August 12). *Social movement participation among youth: An examination of social-psychological correlates*. Paper presented at the annual meeting of the American Sociological Association, Marriott Hotel, Loews Philadelphia Hotel, Philadelphia, PA.

Coser, L. A. (1956). *The functions of social conflict*. New York: The Free Press.

Coser, R. L. (1974). *The family: Its structures & functions*. New York, NY: St. Martin's Press.

Cremin, L. A. (1970). *American education: The colonial experience, 1607–1783*. New York, NY: Harper & Row.

Crenshaw, K. (1995). Race, reform, and retrenchment. In K. Crenshaw, N. Gotanda, G. Peller, & K. Thomas (Eds.), *Critical race theory: The key writings that formed a movement*. New York, NY: The New Press.

Curtis, H. P. (2015). Assault rifle with Bible verse to repel Muslim terrorists reveiled in Apopka. *Orlando Sentinel*, September 2, n.p.

Dabney, R. L. (1871). Women's rights women. *The Southern Magazine*, n.p.

Darwin, C. (1859). *The origin of species*. London: John Murray.

Darwin, C. (1871/2009). *The descent of man*. Digireads.com Books.

de Gobineau, J.-A. (1853/1967). *Essays on the inequality of the human races*. New York, NY: Howard Fertig.

de Tocqueville, A. (1835/2000). *Democracy in America*. Chicago, IL: University of Chicago Press.

D'Emilio, J. (1993). Capitalism and gay identity. In H. Abelove, M. A. Barale, & D. M. Halperin (Eds.), *The lesbian and gay studies reader* (pp. 467–476). New York, NY: Routledge.

The Denver Post. (2010, August 28). Focus on family says anti-bullying efforts in schools push gay agenda. Retrieved from http://www.denverpost.com/news/ci_15928224

DeVoe, J., Kaffenberger, S., & Chandler, K. (2005). *Student reports of bullying. School crime supplement to the National Crime Victimization Survey*. Education Statistics Services Institute.

Dewey, J. (1900/1965). *The school and society and the child and the curriculum*. Chicago, IL: The University of Chicago Press.

Dunbar, C. N. (2008). *One nation under God: How the left is trying to erase what made us great*. Oviedo, FL: Onward.

Eco, U. (1995, June 22). Er-fascism. *New York Times Review of Books*. Retrieved from http://www.nybooks.com/articles/1995/06/22/ur-fascism/

Engels, F. (1884). *The origin of the family, private property, and the state*. Zurich: Hollingen-Zurich.

Erikson, E. (1950/1963). *Childhood and society*. New York, NY: Norton.

Erikson, E. (1968). *Identity, youth, and crisis*. New York, NY: Norton.

Evens, N. J., & Washington, J. (2013). Becoming an ally: A new examination. In M. Adams, W. J. Blumenfeld, R. Castañeda, H. Hackman, M. Peters, & X. Zúñiga (Eds.), *Readings for diversity and social justice* (3rd ed., pp. 411–420). New York, NY: Routledge.

Everytown for Gun Safety. Retrieved from https://everytownresearch.org/school-shootings/

Fabiano, P. (1999, July 29). *Learning lessons and asking questions about college social norms campaigns*. Presentation given at the Second National Conference on the Social Norms Model: Science Based Prevention, Big Sky, MT.

Faludi, S. (1991). *Backlash: The undeclared war against American women*. New York, NY: Crown Publishing Group.

Feagin, J., & Feagin, C. (1993). *Racial and ethnic relations*. New York, NY: Prentice Hall.

Festinger, L. (1954). A theory of social comparison process. *Human Relations, 7*, 117–140.

"Firing Line" with William F. Bucklley Jr. (1974). Shockley's thesis, recorded June 10.

Forel, A. (1907). *Hypnotism; or, suggestion and psychotherapy: A study of the psychological, psychophysiological and therapeutic aspects of hypnotism*. New York, NY: Rebman Company.

Fortna, V. P. (2015). Do terrorists win? Rebels' use of terrorism and civil war outcomes. *International Organization, 69*(3), 519–556.

Foucault, M. (1975). *Discipline and punish: The birth of the prison*. New York, NY: Vintage Books.

Foucault, M. (1980). *The history of sexuality, Part 1*. New York, NY: Vintage Books.

Freire, P. R. N. (1970). *Pedagogy of the oppressed*. Harrisburg, PA: Continuum Publishing.

Freire, P. R. N. (1985). *The politics of education: Culture, power, and liberation*. Westport, CT: Bergin & Garvey.

Gallop. (1939). Survey on U.S. allowing European children to enter the country. The Gallop Organization.

Freud, S. (1930). *Civilization and its discontents*. London: Hogarth Press.

Freud, S. (1914). On Narcissism. The Standard Edition of the Complete Psychological Works of Sigmund Freud, Volume XIV (1914–1916): On the History of the Psycho-Analytic Movement,

Papers on Metapsychology and Other Works, 67–102, London: Hogarth Press.

Freud, S. (1912). The dynamics of transference. The Standard Edition of the Complete Psychological Works of Sigmund Freud, Volume XII (1911–1913): The Case of Schreber, Papers on Technique and Other Works, 97–108.

Garrett, A. G. (2003). *Bullying in American schools. Causes, preventions, interventions*. Jefferson, NC: Mcfarland & Company, Inc., Publishers.

The Gazette. (2012). Weddings and guns? North Liberty jeweler offering unique promotion. October 16, n.p.

Gilman, S. L. (1991). *The Jew's body*. New York, NY: Routledge.

Gilman, S. L. (1993). *The case for Sigmund Freud: Medicine and identity at the fin de siècle*. Baltimore, MD: The Johns Hopkins University Press.

Glazer, N., & Moynihan, D. P. (1963). *Beyond the melting pot: The Negroes, Puerto Ricans, Jews, Italians, and Irish of New York City* (2nd ed.). Cambridge, MA: MIT Press.
GLSEN. (2005). *National School Climate Survey*. New York, NY: Gay, Lesbian, and Straight Education Network.
Gramsci, A. (1971). *Selections from the prison notebooks* (Q. Hoare & G. N. Smith, Trans.). New York, NY: International.
Grant, C. A., & Sleeter, C. E. (2007). *Doing multicultural education for achievement and equity*. New York, NY: Routledge.
Grant, M. (1916). *The passing of the great race*. New York, NY: C. Scribner's Sons.
Greenberg, D. F. (1988). *The construction of homosexuality*. Chicago, IL: University of Chicago.
Griffin, P. (1998). *Strong women, deep closets: Lesbians and homophobia in sport*. Human Kinetics.
Griffin, P., & Harro, B. (2016). Action continuum. In M. Adams & L. A. Bell (Eds.), *Teaching for diversity and social justice* (3rd ed.). New York, NY: Routledge.
Gudykunst, W. B. (1994). *Building bridges: Interpersonal skills for a changing world*. Thousand Oaks, CA: Sage Publishing.
Gullette, M. M. (2017). *Ending ageism or how not to shoot old people*. New Brunswick, NJ: Rutgers University Press.
Halperin, D. M. (1997). *Saint Foucault: Toward a gay hagiography*. Oxford: Oxford University Press.
Hamadi, L. (2007). The concept of ideology in Marxist literary criticism. *European Scientific Journal, 13*(20), 154–168.
Hamer, F. L. (1971). Nobody's free until everybody's free. Speech at the National Women's Political Caucus, Washington, DC.
Hamilton, A. M. (1896). The civil responsibility of sexual perverts. *American Journal of Insanity, 52*, 503–509.
Hardiman, R., & Jackson, B. (1997). Conceptual foundations for social justice courses. In M. Adams, L. A. Bell, & P. Griffin (Eds.), *Teaching for diversity and social justice* (pp. 16–29). New York, NY: Routledge.
Hardiman, R., Jackson, B., & Griffin, P. (2013). Conceptual foundations. In Adams, M., Blumenfeld, W. J., Castañeda, R., Hackman, H., Peters, M., and Zúñiga, X. (Eds.). *Readings for diversity and social justice* (3th edition), New York: Routledge, pp. 26–35.
Harmon, A. (2004, August 26). Internet gives teenage bullies weapons to abuse from afar. America Online. The New York Times Company.
Harrington, S. J. (1995). The anomaly of other directedness when normally ethical I.S. personnel are unethical. *Special interest group on computer personnel research annual conference proceedings of the 1994 computer personnel research conference on reinventing I.S.: Managing information technology in changing organizations*, Alexandria, VA. pp. 35–43.
Harris, M. L., & Bringhurst, N. G. (Eds.). (2015). *The Mormon Church and blacks: A documentary history*. Chicago, IL: University of Illinois Press.
Harro, B. (2013a). Cycle of socialization. In M. Adams, W. J. Blumenfeld, R. Castañeda, H. Hackman, M. Peters, & X. Zúñiga (Eds.), *Readings for diversity and social justice* (3rd ed., pp. 45–52). New York, NY: Routledge.

Harro, B. (2013b). Cycle of liberation. In M. Adams, W. J. Blumenfeld, R. Castañeda, H. Hackman, M. Peters, & X. Zúñiga (Eds.), *Readings for diversity and social justice* (3rd ed., pp. 618–625). New York, NY: Routledge.

Helmreich, A. and Marcus, P. (1998). Black-Jewish conflict and the regions of the mind. A. Helmreich and P. Marcus. (Eds.), *Blacks and Jews on the couch: Psychoanalytic reflections on black-Jewish conflict*. Westport, CT: Praeger.

Hawker, D. S. J., & Boulton, M. J. (2001). Subtypes of peer harassment and their correlates: A social dominance perspective. In J. Juvonen & S. Graham (Eds.), *Peer harassment in school: The plight of the vulnerable and victimized* (pp. 378–397). New York, NY: Guilford Press.

Hawthorn, N. (1850). *The scarlet letter.* Boston, MA: Ticknor and Fields.

Herskovits, M. (1955). *Cultural anthropology*. New York, NY: Knopf.

Hewstone, M., and Giles, H. (1986). Stereotypes and intergroup communication. In W. Gudykunst (Ed.), *Intergroup communication*. London: Edward Arnold.

Hinckley, T. C. (1967). *The Americanization of Alaska, 1867–1897*. Palo Alto, CA: Pacific Books.

Holborn, M., & Steel, L. (2012). Marxism and "the" family. *Earlham Sociology Pages*. Retrieved from http://www.earlhamsociologypages.co.uk/marxismfamily.html, n.p.

hooks, b. (1994). *Teaching to transgress. Education as the practice of freedom*. New York, NY: Routledge.

Hurtado, A., Gurin, P., & Peng, T. (1994, February). Social identities—A framework for studying the adaptation of immigrants and ethnics: The adaptations of Mexicans in the United States. *Social Problems*, 4(1).

Ingold, S. (2012). At life's end, a final home on the (shooting) range. National Public Radio, November 13, n.p.

Irizarry, J. G., & Antrop-González, R. (2007). RicanStructing the discourse and promoting school success: Extending a theory of culturally responsive pedagogy to DiaspoRicans. *Centro Journal of the Center for Puerto Rican Studies*, 20(2), 3–25.

Jacob Wetterling Resource Center, Sexuality of Offenders. Retrieved from http://www.gundersenhealth.org/ncptc/jacob-wetterling-resource-center/keep-kids-safe/sexual-offenders-101/sexuality-of-offenders/

JAMA: Journal of the American Medical Association. (2001). 285(16). April 25.

Jefferson, T. (1782). Notes on Virginia. viii. In J. P. Foley (Ed.), *The Jefferson Cyclopedia: A comprehensive collection of the views of Thomas Jefferson (1900)*. New York, NY: Funk and Wagnalls Company.

Jenny, C., Roesler, T. A., & Poyer, K. I. (1994, July). Are children at risk for sexual abuse by homosexuals? *Pediatrics*, 94, 41–46.

Johnson, A. G. (1997). *The gender knot: Unraveling our patriarchal legacy*. Philadelphia, PA: Temple University Press.

Johnson, A. G. (2006). *Power, privilege, and difference* (2nd ed.). Mountain View, CA: Mayfield Publishing Company.

Jones, R. G., & Calafell, B. M. (2012). Contesting neoliberalism through critical pedagogy, intersectional reflexivity, and personal narrative: Queer tales of academia. *Journal of Homosexuality*, 59(7), 957–981.

Kaiser Family Foundation. (2005). *Generation M: Media in the lives of 8–18 years-olds*. Retrieved from http://www.kff.org/entmedia/7251.cfm

Kallen, H. (1915). Democracy versus the melting pot. *The Nation, 100*(2590), 190–194, 217–230.

Kapelovitz, L. H. (1987). *To love and to work/A demonstration and discussion of psychotherapy*. Lanham, MD: Jason Aronson Inc.

Kaplan, D. (2000). The definition of disability: Perspective of the disability community. *Journal of Health Care Law and Policy, 3,* 352–364.

Kegan, R. (1982). *Theory of human development: The evolving self*. Cambridge, MA: Harvard University Press.

Kens, K. (2017, December 6). 11 little-known facts about left-handers. *Huffington Post*.

Ketner, L. (2007). Heterosexual privilege. Retrieved from http://members.aol.com/ahotcupofjava/hetero.html

Keynes, J. M. (1936). *The general theory of employment, interest, and money*. London: Palgrave Macmillan.

Kick, R. (Ed.). (2003). *Abuse your illusions: The disinformation guide to media mirages and established lies*. New York, NY: The Disinformation Company Ltd.

Keirsey, D., and Bates, M. (1978). *Please understand me: Character and temperament types*. Del Mar, CA: Prometheus Nemesis.

Kim, S. (2010, November 19). Buy a truck, get an AK-47 assault rifle. *ABC News*.

Kim, Y.-S., Koh, Y.-J., & Leventhal, B. L. (2005). School bullying and suicidal risk in Korean middle school students. *Pediatrics, 115,* 357–363.

Kincheloe, J. L., & Steinberg, S. R. (1997). *Changing multiculturalism*. Buckingham: Open University Press.

King, C. S. (2000). Plenary address. National Gay and Lesbian Task Force, Creating Change Conference, Atlanta, GA.

King, M. L. Jr. (2001). *A call to conscience: The landmark speeches of Dr. Martin Luther King, Jr.* (C. Carson & K. Shepard, Eds.). New York, NY: Warner Books.

Kirk, G., & Okazawa-Rey, M. (2013). *Women's lives: Multicultural perspectives* (6th ed.). New York, NY: McGraw-Hill Education.

Kolb, D. A. (1981). Learning styles and disciplinary differences. In A. W. Chickering & Associates (Eds.), *The modern American college: Responding to the new realities of diverse students and a changing society*. San Francisco, CA: Jossey-Bass.

Kottke, J. (2016). The 14 features of eternal fascism. Retrieved from https://kottke.org/16/11/the-14-features-of-eternal-fascism

La Greca, A. M., & Harrison, H. W. (2005). Adolescent peer relations, friendships, and romantic relationships: Do they predict social anxiety and depression. *Journal of Clinical Child and Adolescent Psychology, 34,* 49–61.

Laughlin, H. H. (1914). *Report of the committee to study and to report on the best practical means of cutting off the defective germ-plasma in the American population*. Legal Information Institute. Loving v. Virginia. Retrieved from https://www.law.cornell.edu/supremecourt/text/388/1. Eugenics Record Office, bulletin 10. Cold Spring Harbor, NY.

Lenhart, A., Madden, M., & Hitlin, P. (2005). *Teens and technology: Youth are leading the transition to a fully wired and mobile nation*. Washington, DC: Pew Internet & American Life Project.

Leondar-Wright, B., & Yeskel, F. (2007). Classroom curriculum design. In M. Adams, L. A. Bell, & P. Griffin (Eds.), *Teaching for diversity and social justice* (2nd ed., pp. 309–333). New York, NY: Routledge.

LeVine, R. A., and Campbell, D. T. (1972). *Ethnocentrism: Theories of conflict, ethnic attitudes, and group behavior*. New York: John Wiley.

LeVine, R. A., and Campbell, D. T. (1972). *Ethnocentrism: Theories of conflict, ethnic attitudes, and group behavior*. New York: John Wiley.

Lewin, K. (1948). *Resolving social conflict: Selected papers on group dynamics*. New York, NY: Harper and Brothers.

Lewis, E. and Ardizzone, H. (2001). *Love on trial: An American scandal in black and white*, New York: W. W. Norton.

Lichtenstein, P. M. (1921). The "fairy" and the lady lover. *Medical Review of Reviews*, 27.

Lichtenstein, P. M., Small, M. D., & Small, S. M. (1943). *A handbook of psychiatry*. New York, NY: W. W. Norton.

Linnaeus, C. (1735/1758), *Systema naturae per regna tria naturae: secundum classes, ordines, genera, species, cum characteribus, differentiis, synonymis, locis* (10th ed.), Stockholm: Laurentius Salvius.

Lippy, C. H. (2004). Christian national or pluralistic culture: Religion in American life. In J. A. Banks & C. A. McGee Banks (Eds.), *Multicultural education* (5th ed., pp. 110–131). Hoboken, NJ: Wiley.

Lipsky, S. (1977). Internalized racism. *Black Re-Emergence*, 2, 5–10.

Lorde, A. (1997). *The cancer journals*. San Francisco, CA: Aunt Lute Books.

Lorde, A. (1984). Age, race, class, and sex: Women redefining difference. *Sister outsider*. CA : Crossing Press.

Lorde, A. (1983). There is no hierarchy of oppression. In *Homophobia and education: Interracial books for children*, 3/4: 9. New York, NY: Council on Interracial Books for Children.

Lorde, A. (1984). Age, race, class, and sex: Women redefine difference. In *Sister outsider: Essays and speeches* (pp. 114–123). Freedom, CA: Crossing Press.

Love, B. J. (2013). Developing a liberatory consciousness. In M. Adams, W. J. Blumenfeld, R. Castañeda, H. Hackman, M. Peters, & X. Zúñiga (Eds.), *Readings for diversity and social justice* (3rd ed., pp. 601–605). New York, NY: Routledge.

Love, B. J., & Phillips, K. J. (2007). Ageism and adultism curriculum design. In M. Adams, L. A. Bell, & P. Griffin (Eds.), *Teaching for diversity and social justice* (2nd ed.). New York, NY: Routledge.

Lund, J. L. (1967), *The Church and the Negro: A discussion of Mormons, Negroes, and the priesthood*, Salt Lake City: Paramount Publishers.

MacKeller, C., & Bechtel, C. (Eds.). (2015). *The ethics of the new eugenics*. New York, NY: Berghahn.

Mackey, N. (1992). From noun to verb. *Representations*, 39(Summer), 51–70.

Maluso, D. (2007). Retrieved from http://www.dianemaluso.org/prejudice/prej-frameset.html

Marcuse, H. (1961). *Eros and civilization*. Boston: Beacon Press.
Marks, J. (2002). *What it means to be 99% chimpanzee: Apes, people, and their genes*. Berkeley, CA: University of California Press.
Marx, K. (1867). *Das Kapital. Kritik der politischen Ökonomie (Capital: Critique of political economy)*. Germany: Verlag von Otto Meisner.
McClure, M., & Shirataki, S. (1989). Child psychiatry in Japan. *Journal of the American Academy of Child Adolescent Psychiatry, 28*, 488–492.
McIntosh, P. (1988). *White privilege and male privilege: A personal account of coming to see correspondences through work in women's studies*. Wellesley, MA: Wellesley College Center for Research on Women.
McNamee, S., & Miller, R. (2009). *The meritocracy myth*. New York, NY: Rowman & Littlefield Publishers.
Medoff, R. (2003). Kristallnacht and the world's response. Retrieved from http://www.aish.com/ho/i/48957091.html.
Mehren, E. (1999, December 7). A new drama begins after play is canceled. *New York Times*, n.p.
Memmi, A. (1957). *The colonizer and the colonized*. Boston, MA: Beacon Press.
Merriam-Webster. (1983). *New collegiate dictionary*.
Merriam-Webster. Retrieved from http://m-w.com/dictionary/sexist
Merriam-Webster. (2018a). Culture. Retrieved from https://www.merriam-webster.com/dictionary/culture
Merriam-Webster. Sexism. Retrieved from https://www.merriam-webster.com/dictionary/sexism
Merriam-Webster. (2018b). Oppression. Retrieved from https://www.merriam-webster.com/dictionary/oppression
Merton, R. K. (1949). *Social theory and social structure*. Glencoe, IL: The Free Press.
Michigan Department of Education. (2018, May). Michigan K-12 Standards: Social Studies (Draft). Retrieved from https://www.michigan.gov/documents/mde/SS_May_2018_Public_Final_622357_7.pdf
MTV. (2008, February 21). Lawrence King—Student who was murdered for being gay—To be honored during National Day of Silence. Retrieved from http://www.mtv.com/news/articles/1582039/20080221/id_0.jhtml
Myrdal, G. (1944). *An American dilemma: The Negro problem and modern democracy*. New York: Harper & Row.
Nansel, T. R., Overpeck, M., Pilla, R. S., Ruan, W. J., Simons-Morton, B., & Scheidt, P. (2001). Bullying behaviors among U.S. youth: Prevalence and association with psychosocial adjustment. *Journal of the American Medical Association, 285*(16), 2094–2100.
The National Academies Press. (2013). Priorities for research to reduce the threat of firearm-related violence. Retrieved National Institute of Justice, (2013). Racial profiling. Retrieved from https://www.nij.gov/topics/law-enforcement/legitimacy/pages/racial-profiling.aspx.
National i-SAFE Survey. (2004, June 28). National I-SAFE survey finds over half of students are being harassed online. Retrieved from www.isafe.org.
Nellis, A. (2016). The color of justice: Racial and ethnic disparity in state prisons. The Sentencing Project, June 14.

Nelson, T. D. (2005). Ageism: Prejudice against our feared future self. *Journal of Social Issues*, 61(2), 207–221.

The New England Primer. (1687). Boston: Benjamin Harris.

New York Times. (1973, December 23). The APA ruling on homosexuality: The issue is subtle, the debate still on.

Nieto, S. (2002). Affirmation, solidarity, and critique: Moving beyond tolerance in education. In E. Lee, D. Menkart, & M. Okazawa-Ray (Eds.), *Beyond heroes and holidays: A practical guide for K-12 anti-racist, multicultural education, and staff development* (pp. 7–18). Washington, DC: Network of Educators on the Americas.

Nieto, S. (2010). *The light in their eyes: Creating multicultural learning communities*. New York, NY: Teachers College Press.

Nieto, S., & Bode, P. (2012). *Affirming diversity: The sociopolitical context of multicultural education* (6th ed.). New York, NY: Pearson.

Okun, T. (2010). *The emperor has no clothes: Teaching about race and racism to people who don't want to know*. Charlotte, NC: Information Age Publishing.

Olweus, D. (1993). *Bullying at school: What we know and what we can do*. Cambridge: Blackwell.

Orpinas, P., & Horne, A. M. (2006). *Bullying prevention: Creating a positive school climate and developing school competence*. Washington, DC: American Psychological Association.

Owens, L., Shute, R., & Slee, P. (2000). "Guess what I just heard!" Indirect aggression among teenage girls in Australia. *Aggressive Behavior*, 26(67), 67–83.

Perkins, H., & Berkowitz, A. (1986). Perceiving the community norms of alcohol use among students: Some research implication for campus alcohol education programming. *International Journal of the Addictions*, 21(9/10), 961–976.

Perlmutter, P. (1992). *Divided we fall: A history of ethnic, religious, and racial prejudice in America*. Ames, IA: Iowa State University Press.

Perry, W. G. (1981). Cognitive and ethnical growth: The making of meaning. In A. Chickering (Ed.), *The modern American college*. San Francisco, CA: Jossey-Bass.

Pescara-Kovach, L. (2006). Using multimedia to reduce bullying and victimization in third-grade urban schools. *Professional School Counseling*. Retrieved from http://www.thefreelibrary.com/Using+multimedia+to+reduce+bullying+and+victimization+in+th ird-grade...-a0157032927

Pharr, S. (1988). *Homophobia: A weapon of sexism*. Inverness, CA: Chardon Press.

Pharr, S. (1996). *In the time of the right: Reflections on liberation*. Inverness, CA: Chardon Press.

Phillips, K. (2010, January 28). MSNBC's Matthews: "I forgot he was black." *The New York Times*, n.p.

Pliner, S. M. (1996). Learning disabilities as a positive social identity: The connections between racial identity development models, minority identity development models, and learning disabilities. Comprehensive Examination for the Doctorate of Education. Social Justice Education Program, University of Massachusetts Amherst.

Pollock, M. (2004). *Racemute: Race talk dilemmas in an American school*. Princeton, NJ: Princeton University Press.

Pope Francis. (2013). Apostolic Exhortation, *Evangelii Gaudium of the holy father Francis*, to the bishop, clergy, consecrated persons and the lay faitful on the proclamation of the

Gospel in today's world. Rome: The Vatican. Pratt, R. H. (1892). In *Official Report of the Nineteenth Annual Conference of Charities and Correction*, 46–59. Reprinted in R. H. Pratt, The advantages of mingling Indians with whites, *Amicanizing the American Indians: Writing by the "Friends of the Indian" 1880–1900* (pp. 260–271). Cambridge, MA: Harvard University Press.

Prinstein, M. J., Boergers, J., & Vernberg, E. M. (2001). Overt and relational aggression in adolescents: Social-psychological functioning of aggressors and victims. *Journal of Clinical Child Psychology, 30*, 477–489.

Quattrone, G. A. (1986). On the perception of a group's variability. In S. Worchel & W. G. Austin (Eds.), *Psychology of intergroup relations*. Chicago, IL: Nelson-Hall.

Rand, A. (1957). *Atlas shrugged*. New York, NY: Random House.

Random House Webster's College Dictionary. (1999). New York: Random House.

Renan, E. (1882/1996). Qu'est-ce qu'une nation? (What is a Nation?). In G. Eley & R. G. Suny (Eds.), *Becoming national: A reader* (pp. 41–55). New York, NY: Oxford University Press.

Reuters. (2012, March 14). Santorum to Puerto Rico: Speak English if you want statehood. Retrieved from https://www.reuters.com/article/us-usa-campaign-puertorico/santorum-to-puerto-rico-speak-english-if-you-want-statehood-idUSBRE82D16Z20120314

Rich, A. (1983). Resisting amnesia: History and personal life. In *Blood, bread, and poetry: Selected prose, 1979–1985*.

Rich, A. (1994a). Compulsory heterosexuality and lesbian existence. In *Blood, bread, and poetry*. New York, NY: Norton.

Rich, A. (1994b). Invisibility in academe. In L. Buzzard, J. Gaunge, D. LePan, M. Moser, & T. Roberts (Eds.), *The Broadview anthology of expository prose* (2nd ed., pp. 217–218). Toronto: Broadview.

Rigby, K. (2002). *New perspectives on bullying*. London: Jessica Kingsley.

Rigby, K., & Slee, P. T. (1999). Australia. In P. K. Smith (Ed.), *The nature of school bullying* (pp. 324–339). London: Routledge.

Rochlin, M. (1971). The heterosexual questionnaire. Unpublished by author.

Rogers, R., & Hammerstein, O. (1949). You've got to be carefully taught. *South Pacific*.

Rolfe, G., Freshwater, D., & Jasper, M. (2001). *Critical reflection in nursing and the helping professions: A user's guide*. Basingstoke: Palgrave Macmillan.

Roosevelt, T. (1907). Teddy Roosevelt on immigrants in America. Retrieved from https://rense.com/general77/ted.htm

Ross, D. M. (2002). Bullying. In J. Sandoval (Ed.), *Handbook of crisis counselling, intervention, and prevention in the schools* (electronic version) (2nd ed., pp. 105–135). Mahwah, NJ: Lawrence Erlbaum Associates.

Rothenberg, P. S. (2008). *White privilege: The other side of racism* (3rd ed.). New York, NY: Worth Publishers.

Rutherford, A. (2017). *A brief history of everyone who ever lived: The human story told through our genes*. London: Weidenfeld & Nicolson.

Saenger (1953). *The social psychology of prejudice*. New York: Harper.

Salaman, R. N. (1912). Heredity and the Jew. *Eugenics Review, 3*, 187–200.

Salancik, G. & Pfeffer, J. (1978). A social information processing approach to job attitudes and task design. *Administrative Science Quarterly*, 23, 224–253.

Salmivalli, C., Lagerspetz, K., Björkqvist, K., Österman, K., & Kaukiainen, A. (1996). Bullying as a group process: Participant roles and their relations to social status within the group. *Aggressive Behavior*, 22, 1–5.

Schirch, L. (2005). *Ritual and symbol in peacebuilding*. Bloomfield, CT: Kumarian Press.

Schlossberg, L. (2001). Introduction: Rites of passing. In M. C. Sánchez & L. Schlossberg (Eds.), *Passing: Identity and interpretation in sexuality, race, and religion* (pp. 1–12). New York, NY: New York University Press.

Scott, C. (1997, June 18). Suspect's friend to sell story. *Las Vegas Sun*, n.p.

Schribner's Magazine. Retrieved from https://www.quora.com/Why-was-Theodore-Roosevelt-a-progressive#

Sefa Dei, G. J. (2000). Towards an anti-racism discursive framework. In G. J. Sefa Dei, A. Calliste (Eds.). *Power, knowledge, and anti-racism education: A critical reader* (pp. 34–40). Halifax, Canada: Fernwood Publishing, pp. 34–40.

Sharron-del Rio, M. (2018). Intersectionality is not a choice: Reflections of a queer scholar of color on teaching, writing, and belonging in LGBTQ studies and academia. *Journal of Homosexuality*.

Shibutani, T. (1955). Reference groups as perspectives. *American Journal of Sociology*, 60, 562–570.

Shufeldt, R. W. (1902). Dr. Havelock Ellis on sexual inversion. *Pacific Medical Journal*, 65, 199–207.

Shurkin, J. (2006). *Broken genius: The rise and fall of William Shockley, creator of the electronic age*. London: Macmillan.

Simmel, G. (1955). *Conflict*. Clencoe, IL: The Free Press.

Skutnabb-Kangas, T. (1984). *Bilingualism or not – the education of minorities*. Clevedon: Multilingual Matters.

Smedley, A., & Smedley, B. D. (2005, January). Race as biology is fiction, racism as a social problem is real: Anthropological and historical perspectives on the social construction of race. *American Psychologist*, 60(1), 16–26.

Smith, J. E. (2015). *Nature, human nature, and human difference: Race in early modern philosophy*. Princeton, NJ: Princeton University Press.

Smith, P. K., Morita, Y., Junger-Tas, J., Olweus, D., Catalano, R., & Slee, P. (Eds.). (1999). *The nature of school bullying: A cross-national perspective*. London: Routledge.

Smithsonian Institution Center for Cultural and Folklife Heritage. (2009). What does borders and identity mean? Retrieved from https://folklife-media.si.edu/docs/folklife/education_exhibits/resources/borders-identity-english-02.pdf

Snyder, M. (1979). Self-monitoring processes. *Advances in Experimental Social Psychology*, 12, 85–128.

Spero News. (2006, August 17). 1 of 3 teens are victims of cyber bullying. Retrieved from http://www.speroforum.com/site/article.asp?idCategory=31&idsub=129&id=4494&t=1

Spring, J. (2004). *Deculturalization and the struggle for equality: A brief history of the education of dominated cultures in the United States* (4th ed.). New York, NY: McGraw-Hill.

Steele, C. M. (1997). A threat in the air: How stereotypes shape intellectual identity and performance. *American Psychologist, 52*(6), 613–629.

Stephan, W. G., & Stephan, C. W. (1996). *Intergroup relations.* Boulder, CO: Westview Press.

Stearns, P. N. & Tassel, D. V. (1986). Introduction: Themes and prospects in old age history. In *Old age in a bureaucratic society,* ed. D. V. Tassel and P. N. Stearns, ix–xx. New York: Greenwood Press.

Stryker, S., & Whittle, S. (2013). *The transgender studies reader.* New York, NY: Taylor and Francis.

Style, E. (1988). *Listening for all voices.* Summit, NJ: Oak Knoll School Monograph.

Suler, J. (2001). Psychology of cyberspace—The online disinhibition effect. Retrieved from http://www.rider.edu/~suler/psycyber/disinhibit.html

Suler, J. (2005 revised). The basic psychological features of cyberspace: Elements of a cyberpsychology model. Retrieved from http://users.rider.edu/~suler/psycyber/basicfeat.html

Sumner, W. G. (1906). *Folkways.* Boston, MA: Ginn.

Sutton, J., & Smith, P. K. (1999). Bullying as a group process: An adaptation of the participant role approach. *Aggressive Behavior, 25,* 97–111.

Sutton, M. A., & Dochuk, D. (Eds.). (2016). *Faith in the new millennium: The future of religion and American politics.* New York, NY: Oxford University Press.

Swearer, S. M., Grills, A. E., Haye, K. M., & Cary, P. T. (2004). Internalizing problems in students involved in bullying and victimization: Implications for intervention. In D. L. Espelage & S. M. Swearer (Eds.), *Bullying in American schools: A social-ecological perspective on prevention and intervention* (pp. 63–83). Mahwah, NJ: Lawrence Erlbaum Associates.

Tajfel, H. (1978). *Social psychology of minorities.* Cambridge: Cambridge University Press.

Tajfel, H. (1981). *Human groups and social categories.* Cambridge: Cambridge University Press.

Tajfel, H. (1982). *Social identity and intergroup relations.* Cambridge: Cambridge University Press.

Tajfel, H., Billig, M. G., Bundy, R. F., & Flament, C. (1971). Social categorization and intergroup behavior. *European Journal of Social Psychology, 1,* 149–177.

Tajfel, H., & Turner, J. C. (1986). The social identity theory of intergroup behavior. In S. Worchel & W. G. Austin (Eds.), *Psychology of intergroup relations* (Second Edition). Chicago: Nelson-Hall.

Tajfel, H., & Turner, J. C. (1979). An integrative theory of intergroup conflict. In S. Worchel & W. G. Austin (Eds.), *Psychology of intergroup relations.* Monterey, CA: Brooks-Cole.

Takaki, R. (1993). *A different mirror: A history of multicultural America.* Boston, MA: Little Brown.

Tallmer, A. (n.d.). Anti-lesbian violence. National Gay and Lesbian Task Force Monograph Series, Violence Project, Washington, DC.

Tardieu, A. (1857). *Etude medico-légale sur les attentats aux moeurs.* Paris: J.-B. Baillière.

Tatum, B. D. (1999). *Why are all the black kids sitting together in the cafeteria, and other conversations about race.* New York, NY: Basic Books.

Taylor, D. M., & Doria, J. R. (1981). Self-serving and group-serving bias in attribution. *Journal of Social Psychology, 113,* 201–211.

Teräshjo, T., & Salmivalli, C. (2003). "She is not actually bullied." The discourse of harassment in student groups. *Aggressive Behavior, 29*, 134–154.

Thandeka. (1999). The cost of whiteness. In *Tikkun*, May/June.

Tietje, L., & Cresap, S. (2005). Is lookism unjust?: The ethics of aesthetics and public policy implications. *Journal of Libertarian Studies, 19*(2), 31–50.

Tinney, J. S. (1983). Interconnections. In *Interracial books for children bulletin 14* (pp. 3–4). New York, NY: Council on Interracial Books for Children.

Tong, R. (1989). *Feminist thought: A comprehensive introduction.* Boulder, CO: Westview Press.

Townsend, B. K. (2009). Community college organizational climate for minorities and women. *Community College Journal of Research and Practice, 33*, 731–744.

Transyouth.net. (2002, October 19). In memory of Gwen Araujo. Retrieved from http://www.transyouth.net/stories/gwen-araujo.html

Turkle, S. (1995). *Life on the screen: Identity in the age of the internet.* New York, NY: Simon & Schuster.

Tyack, D. B. (1974). *The one best system: A history of American urban education.* Cambridge, MA: Harvard University Press

Union of the Physically Impaired Against Segregation. (1975). *Fundamental principles of disability.* Retrieved from http://www.leeds.ac.uk/disability-studies/archiveuk/UPIAS/fundamental%20principles.pdf

United States Government. (2018). *National climate assessment.* Washington, DC: U.S. Government Printing Office.

United States Holocaust Memorial Museum. The Voyage of the St. Louis. Retrieved from https://encyclopedia.ushmm.org/content/en/article/voyage-of-the-st-louis

U. S. Department of Justice, Federal Bureau of Investigation. (2006). *Hate crimes statistics, 2006.* Washington, DC: Criminal Justice Information Services Division.

Visions, Inc. (1994). *From lecture on Afrocentrism. Workshop: Changing racism: A personal approach to multiculturalism.* Cambridge, MA.

Vygotsky, L. S. (1962). *Thought and language.* Cambridge, MA: MIT University Press.

Vygotsky, L. S. (1978). *Mind in society: The development of higher mental process.* Cambridge, MA: Harvard University Press.

Vygotsky, L. S. (1988). *The collected works of Lev Vygotsky.* New York, NY: Plenum Press.

Walmsley, R. (2013, November 21). *World prison population list* (10th ed.). International Centre for Prison Studies Publications.

Warner, M. (1991). Introduction: Fear of a queer planet. *Social Text, 29*, 3–17.

Washington Post. (2011, December 1). Michelle Bachmann gets things straight on gay marriage, n.p.

Watt, S. (2007). The privileged identity exploration model. *The College Student Affairs Journal, 26*(2), 114–126.

Webster's Ninth New Collegiate Dictionary. (1983). Springfield, MA: Merriam-Webster, Inc.

Weinberg, G. (1972). *Society and the healthy homosexual.* New York, NY: St. Martin's Press.

Wikipedia. (2018). Estimated number of guns per capita per country. Retrieved from https://en.wikipedia.org/wiki/Estimated_number_of_guns_per_capita_by_country

Wistrich, R. S. (1991). *Antisemitism: The longest hatred.* New York, NY: Pantheon.

Wittig, M. (1992). *The straight mind and other essays*. Boston: Beacon Press.
Wolak, J., Mitchell, K., & Finkelhor, D. (2006). *Online victimization of youth: Five years later*. National Center for Missing and Exploited Children.
Wood, I. M., & Associates (Producer). (1998). *A little history worth knowing: Disability down through the ages*. Brooklyn, NY: Program Development Associates.
Woolfolk, A. (2004). *Educational psychology* (9th ed.). Boston, MA: Pearson.
World Health Organization. (2013). *Violence report*. Retrieved from http://www.emro.who.int/health-topics/violence/index.html
Wurzel, J. (1986). The functions and forms of prejudice. In *A world of difference: Resource guide for reduction of prejudice*. Boston, MA: Anti-Defamation League of B'nai B'rith and Facing History and Ourselves National Foundation.
Ybarra, M., & Mitchell, K. (2004). Youth engaging in online harassment: Associations with caregiver-child relationships, internet use, and personal characteristics. *Journal of Adolescence, 27*(3), 319–336.
Young, D. (1932). *American minority peoples: A study in racial and cultural conflicts in the United States*, New York: Harper.
Young, I. M. (1990). Five faces of oppression. In *Justice and the politics of difference*. Princeton, NJ: Princeton University Press.
Zinn, H. (1980). *A people's history of the United States*. New York, NY: Harper.
Zúñiga, X. (2013). Introduction: Working for social justice. In M. Adams, W. J. Blumenfeld, R. Castañeda, H. Hackman, M. Peters, & X. Zúñiga (Eds.), *Readings for diversity and social justice* (3rd ed.). New York, NY: Routledge.
Zúñiga, X., Naagda, B. A., & Sevig, T. D. (2010). Intergroup dialogues: An educational model for cultivating engagement across differences. *Equity & Excellence in Education, 35*(1), 7–77.

INDEX

A

abject bodies, 17, 140
Abington School District v. Schempp, 138, 231
ableism, 108–111
Act Concerning Servants and Slaves, 244
action continuum, 204–205
Adams, Maurianne, 164
Additive Approach, 173
Adorno, Theodor W., 71, 87
adultism, 111–113
affirmative action, 73, 214
ageism, 113–114
agender, 6
AIDS Coalition to Unleash Power (ACT UP), 9
Alger, Horatio, 78
  Horatio Alger Myth, 78
allocation theory, 116
Allport, Gordon, 65, 75, 97
  Allport Scale of Prejudice and Discrimination, 75

ally, 146, 193
American dilemma, the, 72, 254
American Library Association, 73
American Party, the, 245–246
American Psychiatric Association, 29, 37–38
American Psychological Association, 38, 55
Americans with Disabilities Act, 109
Amherst Regional High School, 173
Amin Dada, Idi, 69
Amnesty International, 254–255
antioppression education, 168
antisemitism, 6, 71, 75, 87, 214
Anzaldúa, Gloria, 19–20
apartheid, 69, 75, 149
Army Corps of Engineers, U.S., 132
asexual, 235–242
assimilation, 100, 253
Auschwitz Concentration Camp, 5
authoritarian
  defined, 69
  personality, 71

B

Bachmann, Michelle, 12
backlash, 147–151
Bandura, Albert, 82–85
banking system of education, 161
Banks, James, 167, 173–174
banned books, 157
basic education, 168
Bazile, Leon, 13, 252
Belgium
    Antwerp, 7
    Resistance Movement, 7
Bell, Lee Ann, 8, 63, 89–90, 97, 111
Bell, Derrick, 130
Belzec Concentration Camp, 5
Benkert, Karoly Maria, 37
Bentham, Jeremy, 47
Berkowitz, Alan D., 211
Bernstein, Leonard, 173
Bieber, Irving, 37
Bigsby, M. J., 212
binarism, 114
binary, 28, 30, 34, 49–61, 114, 139–140, 142
    defined, 49
bioecological model, 41–42
biphobia, 125–126
Black Codes, 67
Black Is Beautiful, 131
Black Lives Matter, 131, 186
Black Power Movement, 131
blaming the victim, 95
Blitzer, Wolf, 117
blood libel, 33–34
BloomBecker, Buck, 60
Blumenfeld, Abraham, 6
Blumenfeld, Blanche, 5
Blumenfeld, Howard, 6
Blumenfeld, Warren, 4–7
Bobo Doll experiments, 82–85
Bochner, Stephen, 124
Bode, Patty, 168–169
Borich, G. D., 174
Boswell, John, 72–73
Bourdieu, Pierre, 117–118, 168

Branstad, Terry, 129
Brewer, Jan, 154, 251
    SB 1070, 251
Britt, Lawrence, 71
Brodkin, Karen, 73
Bronfenbrenner, Urie, 41–42
Brookfield, Stephen, 220, 223
Brown, Justice Henry, 66
Brown v. Board of Education, 66–68, 130, 247
Brownwell, Herbert Jr., 251
Bruner, Jerome, 121, 124,
bullying, 55–60, 95–96, 112–113, 210–213
    defined, 55
Bulwer-Lytton, Edward, 157
Burley-Allen, Madelyn,196
Butler, Judith, 17, 28–31
Butler, Robert N., 114
bystander, 7, 195–196, 212

C

Caetano v. Massachusetts, 264
capitalism, 115, 142–143, 155
Carlisle Indian School, 246
Carrey, Jim, 141
Cash, David, 194
Castañeda, Carmelita Rosie, 34, 109, 130
Catalano, Chase, 19
chauvinism, 124, 126–127
Chavis, Benjamin Jr. 132
Chinese Exclusion Act of 1882, 247
Christian, resisters, 7
cisfemale, 114
cisgender, 114
cismale, 114
cissexism, 114–115
civil disobedience, 187–190
Civil Rights Act of 1964, 67–68
Civil War, U.S., 155
class, socioeconomic, 115
classism, 115–118
coalition, 9, 99, 113, 171–172, 181–182, 193–194, 200–205, 210, 214
Coercive Power, 175

cognitive dissonance, 199
Cohen, Jonathan, 213
Colbeck, Patrick, 153–154
Collins, Suzanne, 112–113
Collins, Patricia Hill, 43–44, 142
colonialism, 51, 64–65, 165, 191
    psychological colonization, 97
colorblindness of race, 133–134, 170
colormuteness of race, 134
coming out, 6
common schools, 156
communism, 6
compulsory heterosexuality, 125
Confederacy, the, 155
conscientized, 162, 191
Conservative approach, 165
Constitution, South Africa, 164
Constitution, U.S., 164
    First amendment, 190, 231
    Second amendment, 148, 263–266
    Thirteenth amendment, 66–68, 131
    Fourteenth amendment, 66–68, 190
    Three-Fifths Clause, 131
constructivism, 163
Content Integration, 167
Contributions Approach, 173
Cooley, Charles Horton, 39
Cooper, Anderson, 148
Core Standards, 116–117
Corrigall-Brown, Catherine, 183
Coser, Lewis A., 42
Council on American-Islamic Relations, 137–139
Crenshaw, Kimberlé, 17
critical consciousness, 223–225
Critical Multicultural Education, 172
Critical Multiculturalism Approach, 172
critical pedagogy, 168
Critical Teaching Approach, 172
critical thinking, 153–154
Critical Transgender Politics (CTP), 18–19
cultural capital, 117–118, 168
    embodied, 117
    institutionalized, 118
    objectified, 117–118

cultural deficiency model, 169
cultural deficit model, 169
cultural enrichment, 170
cultural genocide, 102–104
cultural homogeneity, 172
cultural imperialism, 102–105, 135–136
cultural pluralism, 164, 171, 254
cultural pluralism approach, 172
cultural tourism, 170
culturally competent pedagogy, 162
culture
    components, 14
    cultural pluralism, 14
    defined, 14
    subcultures, 14
culture of poverty, 169
cyberbullying, 55–60, 210
    defined, 55–56
Cycle of Liberation, 197–201
Cycle of Socialization, 43–46, 197

D

Dabney, Robert Lewis, 93
Dakota Access Pipeline, 132
Darwin, Charles, 31–32, 246
    social Darwinists, 31–32
Davis, Jefferson, 155, 245
Declaration of Independence, the, 164
deculturalization, 102–104
defined norm, 90–91
democracy, 63–64, 72, 155, 158, 164–165, 172, 248, 255
Dickey Amendment, 265
disability
    social construction, 34–35
discourses, 64, 131, 135
discrimination, defined, 65, 81–87
    de facto, 65–68, 75, 111
    de jure, 65–68, 75, 111
displacement, 86–87
    displacement mechanism, 86
    socially institutionalized displacement target mechanism, 86

distortion, 94
District of Columbia v. Heller, 263
dominant group, 18, 44–47
    privilege defined, 76
Douglass, Frederick, 144
Dred Scott v. Sandford, 245
dualism, 49–50
Dunbar, Cynthia, 154
Dykes on Bikes, 181
Dylan, Bob, 187
Dynamic Education, 168

E

Eckhardt, Christopher, 189
Eco, Umberto, 69–70
ecoism, 118–120, 132–133
economic power, 91
education defined, 161
Education for All Handicapped Children Act, 109
Education for Social Justice, 168
Education Statistics Services Institute, 59
educational psychology, 161
educator and leadership power, 174–175
Eisenhower, Dwight David, 67, 251
Ellis, Haverlock, 37
emancipatory pedagogy, 172–173
emotional intelligence, 213
empathy, 57, 170, 194–196, 224
    empathetic listening, 196
Empowering School Culture and Social Structure, 167–168
enemy memory, 96
enfranchisement, 93, 143, 149
Engel v. Vitale, 138, 231
Engles, Friedrich, 46, 142
English-Only Movement, 128
environmental oppression, 118–120
environmental racism, 132–133
equality defined, 12
equity defined, 12
Equity Pedagogy, 167
Erikson, Erik, 15, 17

erotophobia, 145
ethnic cleansing, 76, 149
ethnocentrism, 87, 120–124
eugenics, 33–34, 36, 246
Eugenics Record Office, 246
Evans, Nancy, 193–194
Executive Order 9066, U.S., 251
exoticism, 170
Expert Power, 174
exploitation, 101, 123

F

Fabiano, Patricia, 212
Faludi, Susan, 149
fascism, 69–71
    eternal fascism, 69–71
    Ur-fascism, 69–71
Federalism, 263–264
Feminism, 140–142
Festinger, Leon, 120–121
firearms and masculinity, 144
Florey v. Sioux Falls School District, 231
Focus on the Family, 37
Ford, Gerald, 22
Forel, August, 36
Fortes, Abe, 190
Foucault, Michel, 47, 64
Freedom Trail Marching Band, 181
Freire, Paolo Reglus Neves, 101, 158, 161–162, 192
Freud, Sigmund, 58, 87, 112, 120
Frustration-Aggression-Displacement Theory, 86
functionalism, 42–44

G

Galton, Francis, 25–26, 32–34, 246
Galton Society for the Study of the Origin and Evolution of Man, 247
Garrett, Anne G., 60
Gays for Patsy Klein, 181

Gay/Straight Alliance (GSA), 12, 182
gender, 28
gender dysphoria, 29
gender identity disorder, 29
gender normative, 114
gender role, 39, 52–53, 114, 139–141
genderism, 114
General Electric, 148–149
genocide, 7, 76, 133–134, 185, 195
    African, 76
    Armenian, 76
    Bosnian, 76
    Cambodian, 76
    cultural genocide, 102, 133
    First Nations, 76
    Jewish, 76
    Hellenes, 76
    Rwandan, 76
    Ukrainian, 76
Gentlemen's Agreement of 1907, 247
German Student Association, 158
Gershwin, George, 173
Gershwin, Ira, 173
Gestapo, German, 7
G. I. Bill of Rights, 73
Gilman, Sander, 32–33, 249
globalization, 116
Gobineau, Arthur de, 31
Goebbels, Joseph, 158
Gonzalez, Emma, 185–186
Gramsci, Antonio, 64
Grant, Carl A., 169–173
Grant, Madison, 247–248
Griffin, Pat, 68, 204–205
group
    dominant, 18, 44–47
    subordinate, 18, 44–47
Gullette, Margaret Morganroth, 114
Gun control, 147, 185–190
Gun Safety Movement, 265

H

Halperin, David, 27

Hamer, Fannie Lou, 107–108
Hamilton, Allan McLane, 36
Hardiman, Rita, 16, 68, 72
Harro, Bobbie, 40–41, 43–46, 196–201, 204–205, 214
Hawthorn, Nathanial, 53
hegemony, 19, 45, 64, 102, 105, 135–137, 142–143
    Christian, 135–137, 143, 153–158
    patriarchal, 143,
Heritage Foundation, 155
heroes and holidays approach, 170–171, 173
heteronormativity, 125
heterosexual questionnaire, 90–91
Hirschfeld, Magnus, 157–158
hijab, 27
Hitler, Adolph, 7, 69, 193, 247–248
Hogg, David, 148,
homophobia, 125
Hopkins, Larissa, 34, 109
Holocaust, 7, 71, 195
    Holocaust Memorial Museum, U.S., 7, 250
    Yad Vashem, 7
Hoover, Herbert, 249
horizontal hostility, 99–100
horizontal oppression, 99
horizontal violence, 99
Horne, Tom, 158
hooks, bell, 162
Houghteling, James L., 250
Houghteling, Laura Delano, 250
Human Relations Approach, 170
Hunger Games, The, 112–113
Huppenthal, John, 158
Hussein, Saddam, 69
hypermasculinity, 144

I

identity, 120–124, 183
    achieved, 15
    ascribed, 15, 41, 44
    assignment, classroom, 219–21

border, 19–20
conscious, 15
defined, 15
identity crisis, 15
innate drive, 15
interpersonal-intergroup continuum, 16
intersectional, 17
macro level, 18
meso level
micro level, 18
mixed, 16
permanent, 15
personal, 16
politics, 171
social, 14, 16, 123
socially constructed, 15, 21–38
temporary, 15
unconscious, 15
ideology politics, 171
Immigration Act of 1917, 247
Immigration and Nationality Act of 1965, 251
immigration as racial policy, 243–255
imperialism,
 religious, 257–258
in loco parentis, 175
Independent Living Movement, 109
Indian boarding schools, 103–104, 156, 246
Indian Citizenship Act of 1924, 104, 244
Indian Removal Act of 1830, 104
Individualized Education Plan, 110–111
Individualized Family Services Plan, 111
individualized solutions, 100
Individuals with Disabilities in Education Act, 110
indoctrination, 46–47
Institute for Sexual Sciences, 157–158
institutional power, 91
interest convergence, 130, 257
intergroup dialogue, 209–210
internalized dominance, 77, 96–101
internalized oppression, 46, 96–101
International Labor Organization, 8
intersectional politics, 171

intersectionality (intersectionalism), 17–19, 34, 78, 90, 107, 130, 162, 171, 235, 238
intersex, 28, 50–51, 94, 139, 149, 235–242
invisibility, 94
Iowa State University, 210, 214
Islam, 27, 65, 170
 Five Pillars, 138
Islamophobia, 137–139, 170, 252
isolation, 99–100
isolationism, 126
Israel, 7
Iverson, Sherrice, 194

J

Jackson, Andrew, 104
Jackson, Bailey, 16, 68, 72
Jefferson, Thomas, 104, 156
Jewish
 Ashkenazi, 4
 community, 4–7
 racialized, 31–34
Jim Crow, 33, 67, 131, 247
Jingoism, 124, 126–127
Joan of Arc, 51
Johnson, Allan, 142
Johnson-Reed Immigration Act of 1924, 245–251

K

Kaepernick, Colin, 186
Kallen, Horace M. 171–172, 254
Kegan, Robert, 163
Kennedy, John Fitzgerald, 127
Kertbeny, Karl Maria, 37
Keynes, John Maynard, 116
Keynesian economics, 116
Kimball, Spencer W., 74–75
Kincheloe, Joe L., 165–173
King, Coretta Scott, 17

King, Martin Luther Jr., 11, 107, 155
Kinsey Institute, 158
Kirk, Gwyn, 17–18
Know Nothings, the, 245–246
knowledge,
    defining, 153
    production of, 153–158
    construction process, 167, 259
Korematsu v. United States, 251

L

labor activism, 186
lack of prior claim, 93–94
Ladson-Billings, Gloria, 244
Laughlin, Harry Hamilton, 246–247
Law, Bernard, 93
learning edges, 162
Left-Essentialist Approach, 171
left-handedness social construction, 21–24, 51, 192
Legitimate Power, 174–175
Leondar-Wright, Betsy, 115
leveling effect, 56–57
Lewin, Kurt, 122
Liberal Approach, 170
liberation, 144, 179–266
liberatory consciousness, 201–202
Lichtenstein, Perry M., 36
Limbaugh, Rush, 148
Lincoln, Abraham, 155
linguicism, 103, 127–129
Linnaeus, Carl, 25, 131, 244
Lipsky, Suzanne, 97–98
Little Rock, Arkansas, 67
lookism, 129–130
Lorde, Audre, 18, 107–108, 192
Love, Barbara, 201–202
Loving v. Virginia, 13, 252
    Loving, Mildred, 13, 252
    Loving, Richard Perry, 13, 252
Luther, Martin, 157
Lydston, G. Frank, 36

M

machismo, 70
Mackey, 92
Madison, James, 155
Mafia, 6
Mahler, Anja, 7
Mahler, Bascha, 4, 7
Mahler, Charles, 7, 127
Mahler, Eva, 4
Mahler, Georg, 7
Mahler, Jacque, 7
Mahler, Nanette, 7
Mahler, Selma, 7
Mahler, Simon, 4, 7
Mahler, Wolf, 4, 7
Maluso, Diane, 82
Manifest Destiny, 103–104, 165, 245
Mann, Horace, 156
Marcus, Herbert, 112
marginalization, 101, 123
Marjorie Stoneham Douglass High School, 147–148, 185, 187
marriage
    different-sex couples, 13
    interracial, 13
    marriage equality, 13
    polygamous, 75
    same-sex couples, 13, 93
Marxism, 43–44, 69, 131, 142
Matthews, Chris, 133
McCarthy, Joseph, 6
    McCarthyism, 6, 155
McCarran-Walters Act of 1952, 251
McGuffey Reader, 157
McGuffey, William Holmes, 157
McIntosh, Peggy, 76
McVeigh, Timothy, 137
Media Awareness Network, 57
Mein Kampf, 248–249
melting pot, 100, 172, 253
meritocracy, 76–79, 95, 100, 117, 227–230
Merton, Robert K., 169–170
#MeToo movement, 186

Mexican Repatriation, 249
Michelangelo, 24, 73
microaggression, 7
Milk, Harvey, 105
minoritize, defined, 94
miscegenation, 13
misogyny, 139–146
modeling
  abstract, 82
  response mimicry, 82
monoculturalism, 165, 172, 253–254
monotheism, 51–53
Moral Majority, 155
Mormons, 74–75
Multicultural Curricular Content Integration Scale, 173–174
multicultural education 161–164
Multicultural Education Approach, 171
Multicultural and Social Reconstructionist Approach, 172
multiculturalism, 161–164
Mussolini, Benito, 69
Myrdal, Gunnar, 72, 254
Myers-Briggs Personality Profile, 219–220
myth of scarcity, 91

N

National Association for the Advancement of Colored People (NAACP), 132
National Association for Multicultural Education, 164
National Collegiate Athletic Association, 236
National Football League, 186
National Rifle Association, 155, 186, 265
nationalism, 126–127
nativism, 124, 126–127, 246
National Climate Assessment, 118
National Origins Act, 33
Naturalization Act of 1790, 104, 244
Nazis, 4, 7, 26, 70, 157–158
neoliberalism, 116–117
#NeverAgain movement, 185, 265

New England Primer, The, 156
Nieto, Sonia, 14, 168–169, 176
Nietzsche, Friedrich, 29
No Child Left Behind, 116
Noriega, Manuel, 69
Nuremberg laws, 75

O

Obama, Barack, 133
objectivism, 49–50
Obuchenie, 162
Official English, 128
Okazawa-Rey, Margo, 17–18
Okun, Tema, 150
Olweus, Dan, 196
one drop blood rule, 32, 66, 74, 247
Ongoing Education, 168
online disinhibition effect, 56–57
oppression,
  defined, 63
  dimensions, 68–69
  elements, 90–100
  faces, 101–105
  internalized, 46
  levels, 68–76
  mentality, 96
  oppressor, 7
othering, 17, 91–92
outgroup homogeneity effect, 123
Ozawa, Takao, 249

P

Pace v. Alabama, 13, 252
Pace University, 257
pacifism, 70
panopticon, 47
pansexual, 140, 235–242
Parents, Families, and Friends of Gays and Lesbians, 181
Paris Climate Accord, 118–119
parochial schools, 156

Parsons, Talcott, 43
passing, 122
patriarchy, 17, 46–47, 119, 139–146, 165, 176
   defined, 142
patriotism, 126–127
Patterson, Levi, 148
Paul, Ron, 117
performativity, 28–30
Perkins, H. Wesley, 211
Perkins, Richard, 195
Perón, Juan, 69
persecution-produced traits, 97
Pervasive Education, 168
Peters, Madeline, 34, 109
Pharr, Suzanne, 90–100, 105, 141, 203
phrenology, 33
Plessy v. Ferguson, 66–68, 247, 247
pluralism, 164, 254
   religious, 231–233
Pluralist Approach, 170
Poland
   Krosno, 4, 7
   Welcoming Jews Document, 7
Pollock, Mica, 134
polytheism, 51–53
Pope Francis, 115, 117
Pope Gregory IX, 157
Pope John XXI, 157
populism, 70
post-racial, 133
Postal Service, U.S., 6
power, 54–55
   power with v. power over, 203
powerlessness, 101–102
Pratt, Richard, 103, 246
praxis, 162, 191
prejudice defined, 65, 81–87, 95
Prejudice Reduction, 167
Principles of Community, 214
Prinz, Joachim, 193
privilege (dominant group), 17–18, 24
   defined, 76
Privilege Identity Exploration Model, 150
prison industrial complex, 131–132

profiling, 255
   racial, 255
Protestant Tutor, The, 156
Public Law of 1986, 110
Public Safety and Recreational Firearms Use Protection Act, the, 264–265
Putin, Vladimir, 69

Q

Quattrone, Georgia A., 123
queer theory, 28
Quran, 258

R

race
   social construction, 24–31
   critical race theory, 27
   passing, 30–31
Racial Integrity Act, 13
racialization, 26–28
racism, 73–74, 130–134
   environmental, 132–133
Rand, Ayn, 49–50
Reagan, Ronald, 251
Realistic-Group-Conflict Theory, 123
reconstruction, 131
Reference Group Theory, 122
Referent Power, 174
regimes of truth, 64
Rehabilitation Act, 109
religious oppression, 134–139
Renan, Ernest, 31
repression, 112
Revolutionary War, U.S., 156
Reward Power, 175
Rich, Adrienne, 96, 125, 161
Riggs, Steven, 103
Robinson, Lisa D., 209
Rochlin, Martin, 90–91
Rogers, Edith, 249
role model, 82

Roosevelt, Eleanor, 249
Roosevelt, Franklin Delano, 137, 249
Roosevelt, Theodore, 127, 248, 254
Rosewood, Florida, 26
Rothenberg, Paula, 68
ruthless Americanization, 253

S

Saint Basil the Great, 115
Saint Pius X High School, 187
San José State University, 161, 188
Santorum, Rick, 127
scapegoat,
  defined, 61
Schaffley, Phyllis, 155
Scharron-del Rio, Maria, 191
Schlossberg, Linda, 30–31
Schmidt, Jane, 12
Schorr, Daniel, 133
Schroeder, Gustav, 250
Sefa Dei, George, 244
segregation, 66–68
self-fulfilling prophecy, 169–170
separate but equal, 66–68
Separate Car Act, 66–68
Sessions, Jefferson Beauregard, 253
sexism, 28, 70–71, 139–146
sexphobia, 145
sexual identities
  social construction, 35–38
sexual orientation disorder, 37
Shepard, Judy, 54
Shepard, Matthew, 54
Shockley, William, 26
Silence = Death, 9
Single-Group Studies Approach, 171
Skutnabb-Kangas, Tove, 129
slavery, 130, 144, 149, 151, 155–156, 244–245
Sleeter, Christine E., 169–173
Smith, Joseph Fielding, 74
Socarides, Charles, 38

Socarides, Richard, 38
Social Action Approach, 174
social capital, 117–118, 168
Social Cognitive Theory, 82–85
Social Identity Theory, 120–122
  social categorization, 121
  social comparison, 121–122
  social identification, 122
Social Learning Theory, 82–85
social justice
  defined, 8
social justice education, 161–164
Social Model of Disability, 111
Social Modeling Theory, 82–85
Social Norms Theory, 211–213
  actual norm, 212
  misperception, 212
  perceived norm, 212
social production of knowledges, 153–158
Social Rank Theory, 85
Social Reconstructionist Approach, 172
Social Reproduction Theory, 131, 153, 176
social power, 68
social role, 39
socialization, 39–47, 192, 196
  ruthless, 96
sociopathic personality disorder, 37
Sola, Camille, 173
Sondheim, Stephen, 173
Sotomayor, Sonia, 253
spheres of influence, 210
Spring, Joel, 102, 104
Stakely, Rheua, 207
Stalin, Joseph, 69
Standing Rock Sioux, 132
Statute of Kilkenny, 75
Steinberg, Shirley, 165–173
Steele, Claude, 96
Steele, Shelby, 96
stereotype, 94–95, 121–123
sterilization laws, 246–247
  Law for the Prevention of Hereditarily Diseased Offspring, 247
stigma, 53–54

stimulus generalization, 86
St. Louis, MS, 250
Strohmeyer, Jeremy, 194
strongman, 69
Style, Emily, 163
subordinate group, 44–47
Suler, John, 56–60
Sumner, William Graham, 120, 123
Supreme Court, U.S., 13
surplus repression, 112
surveillance, 46–47

T

Tafjel, Henri, 16, 120–124
Takaki, Ronald, 102–105
Takao Ozawa v. United States, 249
Taliban, the, 176
Talmud, the, 157
Taney, Roger B., 245
Tardieu, Ambrose, 36
Taparelli, Luigi, 8
Tatum, Beverly Daniel, 17–18, 39, 130
Teaching the Exceptional and the Culturally Different, 169
Tennyson, Lord Alfred, 139
terrorism defined, 54
Texas School Board, 154–155
Texas Standards of Knowledge and Skills, 154
Thandeka, 32
thick education, 164
Three-Fifths Clause, U.S. Constitution, 131
Till, Emmett, 26
#TimesUp movement, 186
Tinker, John, 189
Tinker, Mary Beth, 189
Tinker v. Des Moines Independent Community School District, 189
Tinney, James S., 72
Title VI, 68
Tocqueville, Alexis de, 63–64
tokenism, 100

Tombari, M. L., 174
Townsend, Barbara K., 213–214
trafficking, 149
Trail of Tears, 104
traits due to victimization, 97
transference defined, 58
    erotic transference, 58
Transformation Approach, 174
transgender policy, 235–242
transgender oppression (cissexism), 13, 28, 114–115
transgenderphobia, 114
Treaty of Fort Laramie, 133
True Pundit, 148
Truman Show, the, 141
Trump, Donald, 148, 252–253
Trump, Donald Jr., 148
Trump, President of the United States, et al. v. Hawaii et al., 253
Truth, Sojourner, 51
Turner, John, 120–124
Twitter, 182
tyranny of the majority, 64

U

Union of Physically Impaired Against Segregation, 111
United Nations, 8, 155, 164
    Universal Declaration of Human Rights, 164
universal design, 109
University of Heidelberg, 247
University of Massachusetts-Amherst, 8, 209, 236
upstander, 193, 212

V

Vienna Declaration and Programme of Action, 8
Vietnam War, 11

violence, 54–55, 91, 105
    defined, 54
Voltaire, 25
Vygotsky, Lev, 82–83, 162

W

Wagner, Robert F., 249
Wagner-Rogers Act, 249
Wall, Vernon, 12
Warner, Michael, 125
Warren, Earl, 67
Washington, George, 104
Washington, Jaime, 193–194
Watt, Sherry, 149–150
Weinberg, George, 125
white supremacy, 130–134
Wistrich, Robert S., 87
Wittig, Monique, 28
Workers rights, 149
World Congress of Human Rights, 8
World Health Organization, 54
Wurzel, Jaime, 87
    utilitarian function 87
    value-expressive function, 87

X

xenophobia, 54, 70, 105, 123–124

Y

Yeskel, Felice, 115
Young, Brigham, 74
Young, Iris Marion, 63, 72, 89, 101–105,
    108–109
Yousafzai, Malala, 176

Z

Zarathustra, 49
Zoroastrianism, 49
Zúníga, Ximena, 130

A BOOK SERIES FOR EQUITY SCHOLARS & ACTIVISTS

Virginia Stead, H.B.A., B.Ed., M.Ed., Ed.D., *General Editor*

Globalization increasingly challenges higher education researchers, administrators, faculty members, and graduate students to address urgent and complex issues of equitable policy design and implementation. This book series provides an inclusive platform for discourse about—though not limited to—diversity, social justice, administrative accountability, faculty accreditation, student recruitment, admissions, curriculum, pedagogy, online teaching and learning, completion rates, program evaluation, cross-cultural relationship-building, and community leadership at all levels of society. Ten broad themes lay the foundation for this series but potential editors and authors are invited to develop proposals that will broaden and deepen its power to transform higher education:

(1) Theoretical books that examine higher education policy implementation,
(2) Activist books that explore equity, diversity, and indigenous initiatives,
(3) Community-focused books that explore partnerships in higher education,
(4) Technological books that examine online programs in higher education,
(5) Financial books that focus on the economic challenges of higher education,
(6) Comparative books that contrast national perspectives on a common theme,
(7) Sector-specific books that examine higher education in the professions,
(8) Educator books that explore higher education curriculum and pedagogy,
(9) Implementation books for front line higher education administrators, and
(10) Historical books that trace changes in higher education theory, policy, and praxis.

Expressions of interest for authored or edited books will be considered on a first come basis. A Book Proposal Guideline is available on request. For individual or group inquiries please contact:

Dr. Virginia Stead, General Editor | *virginia.stead@alum.utoronto.ca*

To order other books in this series, please contact our Customer Service Department at:

(800) 770-LANG (within the U.S.)
(212) 647-7706 (outside the U.S.)
(212) 647-7707 FAX

Or browse online by series at www.peterlang.com